"In Andrew Root's debut, he has produced a book that every youth worker (and every sponsor, volunteer, parent and pastor) should read. With incisive thinking and articulate writing, Root argues that relationships are not a means to a goal—they are the goal. He treats history fairly, develops a compelling Christology and compellingly shows how Christ is present within human relationships. Without hyperbole, I predict this book will change the face of Christian youth ministry."

TONY JONES, *national coordinator of Emergent Village (www.emergentvillage.org) and author of* The New Christians: Dispatches from the Emergent Frontier

"Andy Root has unveiled the most significant challenge in youth ministry today—unconditional relationships. Too often we use relationships to achieve our goals and in the process abandon teenagers when those goals are not achieved. Andy has brilliantly laid before us an essential course correction for relational youth ministry that is faithful to the incarnation of Jesus."

MARK W. CANNISTER, *professor of youth ministries, Gordon College, and editor of* Journal of Youth Ministry

"Andrew Root combines biblical studies, history, sociology and theology in a well-researched mix that, I hope, will drive our youth ministry thought and practice. In a day and age when every youth ministry practitioner owes it to the One who first modeled incarnational ministry and to the kids we serve to be thoughtful about what we do, this is a book that will get you thinking about what you're doing."

WALT MUELLER, *president, Center for Parent/Youth Understanding, and author of* Engaging the Soul of Youth Culture

"In this groundbreaking book, Andrew Root explodes the myth that those involved with youth ministry can be excused from being theologians and that theologians can be exempted from writing a theology for youth ministry. Drawing upon the incarnational and transformational theology of Dietrich Bonhoeffer, among others, Root argues for a relational ministry that is incarnational rather than merely instrumental. He presents Jesus as a living person rather than merely providing a pattern for incarnational ministry, and shows us how a relational ministry can go beyond merely connecting with others to create and inhabit a transforming space. Andy knows how to enter and interpret the culture of adolescence and youth, and shares this wisdom with us. His case studies and creative scenarios put faces on his facts and lend dramatic life to his theories. The book provides the course on theology of ministry that most youth leaders and pastors never got in Bible school or seminary, and the one indispensable text that professors of youth ministry have been longing for."

RAY S. ANDERSON, *senior professor of theology and ministry, Fuller Theological Seminary, and author of* An Emergent Theology for Emerging Churches

"*Revisiting Relational Youth Ministry* establishes Andrew Root as a seminal voice in a new generation of youth ministry scholars. Fresh, wise and disciplined, Root exposes the sand on which much 'relational youth ministry' of the late twentieth century has been based, and recasts the church's ministry with young people in the Christology of Dietrich Bonhoeffer. In so doing, Root injects youth ministry with both a needed missional direction and a welcome theological humility. Drawing on 'real life' relational ministries, Root offers concrete practices that reestablish youth ministry's footing in the suffering love of God in Jesus Christ. Andrew Root is poised to lead the field in rethinking youth ministry as a practical theological discipline, and this book is a breathtaking step in the right direction."

KENDA CREASY DEAN, *associate professor of youth, church and culture, Princeton Theological Seminary, coauthor of* The Godbearing Life *and author of* Practicing Passion

Revisiting Relational Youth Ministry

FROM A STRATEGY OF INFLUENCE

TO A THEOLOGY OF INCARNATION

ANDREW ROOT

IVP Books

An imprint of InterVarsity Press
Downers Grove, Illinois

InterVarsity Press
P.O. Box 1400, Downers Grove, IL 60515-1426
World Wide Web: www.ivpress.com
E-mail: email@ivpress.com

InterVarsity Press® is the book-publishing division of InterVarsity Christian Fellowship/USA®, a movement of students and faculty active on campus at hundreds of universities, colleges and schools of nursing in the United States of America, and a member movement of the International Fellowship of Evangelical Students. For information about local and regional activities, write Public Relations Dept., InterVarsity Christian Fellowship/USA, 6400 Schroeder Rd., P.O. Box 7895, Madison, WI 53707-7895, or visit the IVCF website at <www.intervarsity.org>.

Scripture quotations, unless otherwise noted, are from the New Revised Standard Version of the Bible, *copyright 1989 by the Division of Christian Education of the National Council of Churches of Christ in the USA. Used by permission. All rights reserved.*

Design: Cindy Kiple
Images: cross: Andy Roberts/Getty Images
girl sitting: Clarissa Leahy/Getty Images

ISBN 978-0-8308-3488-4

Printed in the United States of America ∞

Library of Congress Cataloging-in-Publication Data

Root, Andrew, 1974-
Revisiting relational youth ministry / Andrew Root.
p. cm.
Includes bibliographical references and index.
ISBN 978-0-8308-3488-4 (pbk.: alk. paper)
1. Church work with youth. I. Title.
BV4447.R655 2007
259'.23—dc22

2007026761

P	22	21	20	19	18	17	16	15	14	13	12	11	10	9	8	7
Y	26	25	24	23	22	21	20	19	18	17	16	15	14	13			

To Kara

Contents

Preface

For my high school graduation I was given a guitar. I was thinking about being a religion major in college, and maybe someday being in youth ministry. Therefore, a guitar made sense. I learned the basic chords and soon was able to switch between them, playing what I thought sounded like worship songs and melodies from pop hits. But soon my friends were telling me that although I thought I was playing a particular song, it just didn't sound right. It was too fast or simply weird. I was shocked; it sounded good to me but unfortunately not to anybody else.

I still own that guitar; it sits dusty in the back of a closet. I never thought I would be a rock star, nor even a modest songwriter, but I was drawn to the guitar for its ability to serve as a portal into a world where feeling and thinking combine. I was drawn to how musicians can express themselves in such a way that an inner reality is opened up and those listening see the world in which they live differently (and sometimes, with the best musicians, more truthfully).

Because of my musical insufficiencies, my iPod now serves as this portal. Listening to certain musicians I am taken deep into the big questions of human existence: What is life about? What is love? Why do we suffer? Who am I? How do we deal with disappointment? (To name a few.) Sitting in an uncomfortable airplane seat, with my knees pressed up against the seat in front of me, I am taken by my iPod to another world, or better, taken under the routine social crust of this world, forcing me to think and feel at the same time, forcing me to confront big questions.

Art has a way of doing this, but so should theology. I am not arrogant enough to believe that reading this book will be like listening to The Shins or GreenDay (I'm not even arrogant enough to suggest it is like listening to Jessica Simpson). But theology, like good music, should invite us into an inner reality to ask big questions and should provide us with thoughts that touch something deep within us and our world. It is my hope that this book will in some way do this for you.

The inner reality that relationships in ministry possess offers us more than we see at first glance; in their inner reality relationships are the concrete location of God's presence in our midst. Therefore, I argue in this project that relationships are not only significant for youth ministry but are transformative to people. Yet unfortunately relationships and youth ministry have been so linked that the profound inner reality of them has become mere background noise, elevator music. Relationships have become so normal and regular that we have stopped noticing them, stopped wondering about the power of relationships in themselves. Instead of seeking to touch the mysterious inner reality of relationships we have too often settled for using relationships as a means to influence kids toward certain ends.

Therefore, in this project I seek to revisit relational youth ministry, calling us beyond seeing relationships as tools for influence and into seeing the beautiful inner reality of relationships as the invitation to share each other's place, to be with each other in both joy and suffering, and in so doing to witness to Christ among us.

Just as no song is written in a vacuum, so too is no theological piece. Therefore, I owe deep thanks to many individuals who have allowed me to "jam" with them, working out these ideas as they critiqued and supported the thoughts that now make up the following pages.

I am most indebted to Kenda Creasy Dean and Richard Osmer. Both allowed me to think deeply and freely when I was under their care as a Ph.D. student at Princeton. Dr. Dean assured me through her own work that rigorous reflection could be done on the practice of youth ministry and that such work should never be divorced from the passion of helping the church be faithful to its children. Dr. Osmer more than anyone else has shown me what it means to be a scholar, and I desire to emulate his model in my own career. I would also like to thank Gordon Mikoski from Princeton for his thoughtful feedback and encouragement as this project took form.

Dear friends have also made this project possible with both direct insight and helpful encouragement. Thanks to Theresa Latini, Matt Skinner, Rolf Jacobson and David Lose. I would most especially like to thank my friend Tony Jones for advocating for the publication of this project. His counsel on publishing has been invaluable. Tony, whether in affirmation or opposition, always pushes me to think; it has been a pleasure to know him.

I also would like to thank my revered colleague Roland Martinson not only for his support in seeing this project to publication but for his affirmation and encouragement of my vocation as teacher and scholar. He is a treasure to the church, and in my short time as a colleague at Luther Seminary, he has been a treasure to me. Thirty plus years of work by Dr. Martinson can be seen in the wonderful Children, Youth and Family team that he has built at Luther; it has been my pleasure to work with them. His work can also be seen in the exceedingly gifted and engaged students that have made and are making their way to Luther. It is a joy and a blessing to work in a world that he has created, I only hope I can add something to it.

I am also indebted to two theologians, now at the end of their careers, that have so generously reached out to me, affirming and supporting a young scholar less than half their age. To me, as well as to many others, these men are giants. Their erudition, and more directly their passion and compassion, will live on in my own scholarship. Great thanks for support and inspiration go to Ray Anderson and Douglas John Hall.

Yet my greatest debts are owed to my family: to my son Owen who was born just days before I read the first page in research or typed the first letters of the dissertation that would become this project. And to my daughter Maisy, who as I write this preface is literally on her way into this world. With the birth of Owen this project began and with the birth of Maisy it will end. I only hope it will make them proud!

And finally to my wife, Kara (to whom this project is dedicated), for being my sounding board, proofreader and fellow thinker, but most important, for being my friend. I am reminded daily of the blessing you are to me. Most literally this project could not have been completed without your support, help and skill.

All glory to the incarnate, crucified and resurrected Person, Jesus the Christ!

Introduction

During seminary, I was invited to join a youth ministry that found itself in a precarious position. To the surprise of the youth pastor, a group of teenagers from the lower-income, ethnically diverse part of Los Angeles had decided to use the church's steps as its new skateboard park and hangout spot. Recognizing the opportunity for ministry, the church agreed to hire someone to be a "bridge" from the church youth ministry to these "neighborhood kids" (for lack of a better term). Because of my Young Life experience, I was invited to be this bridge person. The ministry team (comprising well-educated, well-read and experienced youth workers) decided that our best strategy for reaching these neighborhood kids (and assimilating them into the program) was through relational or incarnational ministry. The idea was that we would seek to form relationships with them in their own world, believing our relationship of care would give us a platform to speak into their lives. The congregation's leadership stood behind this new ministry initiative, insisting that through our incarnational connection we would influence these unchurched youth.

Soon it was apparent that the incarnational model of ministry was not working. As our team slowly formed relationships with these adolescents, it became clear that they were not only unchurched but at-risk. While spending time with them in their own milieu, we found that each connection we made called us into a depth of suffering we were not trained for. Much of our anguish came from witnessing the adolescents' own severity of suffering—broken families, a violent neighborhood and failing schools. But the suffering we experienced was also the suffering they purposely inflicted on us. With deep emotional wounds just under their baggy jeans and T-shirts, our offerings of friendship and care were answered with abuse and ridicule. These wounded children had never learned how to allow themselves to be cared for, and we had no idea how to care for those who, on the one hand, refused our care, but on the other, continued to ask for it.

Many of the adults from the congregation who accompanied us in this venture simply could not take it. The kind of youth ministry they were taught had nothing to do with suffering abuse and ridicule; rather it was about mentoring friendships wrapped in fun and games. They had expected the kind of ministry that I had been taught in my Young Life training and from popular youth ministry books, the kind that was easy, that was simply about relationships. We couldn't blame these adults for refusing to participate in the ministry. We too were emotionally ravaged, saddened and hurt by the adolescents' insults, and yet perplexed by their consistent participation. But, as good evangelicals (as I then saw myself to be) we were even more frustrated by the kids' lack of change, by their inability to behave "better" and to understand and accept Jesus. We all felt like failures. Our relationships with and incarnational witness to them, we were taught, would be a means to a greater end, changed lives. Through our relationships with these adolescents we believed we would lead them to the "third thing," that is, we could usher them beyond our relationship and into a relationship with Jesus. It was clear to us that we were not only suffering but also failing.

The leaders in the congregation eventually changed their tune as well. After encountering stolen money, spray-painted walls, sexual harassment and drug dealing, they had had enough. This once-open congregation that freely reached out in ministry had turned into a place where troubled youth had to *earn* the right to participate. Overall, the congregation was not prepared for the suffering that this ministry demanded.

I hit rock bottom; my relational ministry was not working and could not work as it was presented to me by my Young Life mentors. It was during this time, through reading the theological writings of Dietrich Bonhoeffer, the great German twentieth-century theologian and martyr, that I discovered the incarnation was not a model or example, but was the very power of

God present in human form among us today. I discovered that Jesus Christ is concretely present to us in our relational lives, in our person-to-person encounters, in the *I* and *you*. Thus there is no "third thing," no "end" to which the relationship should lead. Bonhoeffer's theology alerted me to the possibility that the relationship is the "end." It is the place where Christ is present, the place where the adolescent (and I, for that matter) encounter Christ. What mattered was not the adolescents' ability to accept and conform to the "third thing," to become spiritual or Christian, but to be human alongside others, alongside me. And this is only possible, Bonhoeffer stated, through Jesus Christ who died and rose again as our human brother.

Ministry, then, is not about "using" relationships to get individuals to accept a "third thing," whether that be conservative politics, moral behaviors or even the gospel message. Rather, ministry is about connection, one to another, about sharing in suffering and joy, about persons meeting persons with no pretense or secret motives. It is about shared life, confessing Christ not outside the relationship but within it. This, I learned, was living the gospel.

I realized then that there is no such thing as success or failure with these adolescents. There is only faithfulness, faithfulness to Christ, which calls me to be faithful to these adolescents' very humanity. Ministry is not about helping these kids be better Christians; it is about helping them be what God created them to be—human. And it is the degradation of their humanity, brought about by broken and abusive families, violent neighborhoods, failing schools and poverty, that caused them to lash out so forcefully. Ministry is about suffering with them in their dehumanization, celebrating their human endeavors and in all things pointing to the true human, Jesus Christ our Lord.

Having reflected on my early ministry experience, I chose to put it into action by taking a job at a nonprofit organization in Los Angeles County where I was responsible for visiting four public schools each week and counseling (one on one) current or potential gang members. Students were referred to me by the school administration because they were in a gang, had a family member in a gang or were manifesting gang-like behavior in the classroom (e.g., violent outbursts, physical threats, etc.). To the disappointment of the administration, I could see only five students per day;

they often remarked that they could give me a hundred names if I wanted them. I had only one hour, once a week, to help each adolescent. Each referral was given to me with a short and traumatic back story. His mother is in jail. We think she is using crystal meth. His brother is a major banger in the neighborhood. She lives with her family in a two-bedroom house with three other large families. He is overweight, has never seen his dad, and his mom is an illegal alien who drives an ice-cream truck. Her father beats her and her mother. He was arrested for prostitution. She cuts herself. He watched his father beat his mother within an inch of death. She's pregnant. He's being investigated for a shooting. And this back story was only the tip of iceberg. Underneath the frigid waters of these adolescents' lives was incident after incident of neglect and abuse. I had one hour each week! I realized that there was nothing I could do: I couldn't change their situation, I couldn't erase the past, and I had no words to awaken them from the perpetual nightmare that was their life. I decided that all I could do for one hour, once a week is share in their nightmare with them. I could be present with them in their personal hell. I couldn't change their situation but I could assure them, through my friendship, that they were not suffering alone; I could in my open friendship witness to God on a cross.

Over checkers, Connect Four, Sorry and other board games I invited them to tell me their stories, and I told them mine. I had no agenda other than to be with them. Slowly we became friends, and I was given permission to be their advocate, to confront negative behavior, asserting, "You can't do that. Listen to me, I am your friend. That is going to hurt you, and as your friend that would hurt me." I was allowed to celebrate their successes: "You did it! See, I told you that you would pass! I know you're smart, you beat me at checkers all the time." In our time together I watched them change. I did not bring answers or change their circumstances. But as I was with and for them, our relationship served as a new perspective from which to see themselves and the world around them.

As I walked into or out of each school, my eyes were drawn to the masses of adolescents huddled in their groups talking and laughing, and I knew that underneath their "throwback" sports jerseys and low-cut jeans was an ocean of pain that they carried alone. I often wondered, *Where is the church?* I wondered if we had forgotten how to be friends to those who are so painfully isolated. I wondered why every member of every congregation couldn't be an adult friend to an adolescent in his or her community. I wondered if the church realized the power and possibility of relationships for transformation, and the theological mandate for action that is demanded of us by the incarnation.

Evangelical youth ministry has historically discussed relationships as if it had the corner on the market. Yet if we are honest, many would admit that we do not understand what we mean by relational or incarnational ministry, and few of us understand how such ministry is connected to the theological reality of the incarnation. Many of us have become frustrated with relational ministry, intuitively recognizing that what we have been taught to see as easy is in fact very complicated and multidimensional, far from simple, straightforward or flat.

In this book I hope to cut through the thin crust of the popular evangelical presentations of relational ministry and into the reservoirs of beauty and possibility that a theological understanding of relationships opens up to us and our ministries. This book promises to provide a rigorous examination of relational/incarnational ministry. It will critically examine how relational forms of ministry have been embedded within evangelicalism's subcultural identity as a strategy of engagement within a pluralistic culture. I will show that incarnational ministry has been formed from the material of cultural engagement rather than from the theological pillars of the work of the incarnate Christ in the world. This, I believe, ultimately has hampered our ministries, leading some within youth ministry to call for a "postrelational youth ministry."[1] I believe that youth ministry has not yet constructed a relational ministry that takes into account the full profundity of human social relations opened up to us by the incarnation. In this work, then, I will *not* issue a call for postrelational ministry, but by turning to the theology of Dietrich Bonhoeffer I hope to develop a truly *relational* relational ministry.

---

[1]In 2004 *Youthworker Journal* published an article titled "Post-Relational Youth Ministry." The article, though filled with philosophical and theoretical inconsistencies, made some provocative points. Yet I believe, in the end, what the authors meant to call for through their inconsistent cultural philosophy was not a postrelational ministry but a truly relational ministry. See Dave Wright and Dixon Kinser, "Post-Relational Youth Ministry: Beyond Youthwork as We Know it" *Youthworker Journal* (September-October 2004).

It should not be presumed by the critical cadence of the first half of this work that I assume that no one is doing proper or good relational ministry. Rather, I believe that there are many youth workers doing precisely what I will present in this project. I believe that it is my responsibility to articulate and explain what they intuitively know and are already doing. By explaining the depth of relationships, it is my hope that those already drawing from this depth will recognize themselves and be encouraged and sharpened, and others will be enlivened to reassess and reorient their ministries in this direction.

Some might assume from reading the first chapters of this work that I am anti-evangelical or postevangelical. This is not the case. Rather, my history is heavily indebted to evangelicalism, which was an important part of shaping me. This book's critiques, and at times critical observations, come from a supportive but questioning individual who desires only the best for evangelicalism. Evangelicalism is discussed here because it was within evangelicalism that relational ministry was developed. Understanding it helps direct us as we explore relational/incarnational ministry past and present.

I have already asserted that I hope to drive readers deep into the beauty and possibilities of relationships and their potential for ministry. But this is not my only hope for this book. I also hope that this work can move youth ministry further along in its quest to become a respected field of study. For the last two decades youth ministry has taken leaps and bounds in this direction. But much of the work done in furthering this field (with notable exceptions) has occurred in one of two ways: a stance of *autism* (focused only on youth workers and having little concern for mutual cross-fertilization between disciplines), which is an inevitable response to the second, a stance of *justification* (vigorously asserting why youth ministry matters and is important from a biblical and cultural perspective).

It is time for youth ministry studies to move beyond autism and justification into *construction*, the kind of construction that is helpful to those in other fields (e.g., pastoral care, congregational ministries, Bible, theology and history). For this to happen, those in the field of youth ministry not only need to construct creative and rigorous projects, but they also must locate these projects within the larger field of practical theology. Without locating ourselves within practical theology we are locked away from further discussion that would allow us to learn from others and vice versa. By locating ourselves within the larger discipline of practical theology, we are forced into cross-disciplinary discussions and moved forward into rigorous construction. Thus this book is a practical theology of youth ministry.

You may be wondering, *What is practical theology?* The unique nature of the discipline of practical theology is seen in the compound that makes up its name. The term *practical* refers in one way or another to human action. Practical theology directs itself toward the experiences of the human agent as he or she is found in many contexts (family, congregation, community, culture, society, etc.). This concentration on human action opens up practical theology to necessary interdisciplinary discussions. Practical theologians are often in dialogue with sociology, psychology, anthropology and their subdisciplines. Systematic theology, biblical studies and historical theology lack this cross-disciplinary necessity. That is not to say that these disciplines are not in dialogue across distinct fields, but that this dialogue is not as essential for the integrity of these disciplines as it is for practical theology. Without concentration on human action, practical theology is no longer practical and thus no different than the other theological disciplines.

However, without its essential grounding in theology practical theology is only an eclectic social science. Practical theology may be reflection on human action within the church and society, but it is also, in the same breath, theological refection on God's distinct and unique act of revelation within history and for humanity. Practical theology then is essentially reflection on both divine and human action, discerning and articulating ways that they find association and ways that human communities (and individuals) should respond to God's action in the world.[2]

My own personal narrative of how I became involved in thinking and writing about relational ministry is an example of practical theological reflection. While in ministry with adolescents in Los Angeles, I was brought up short, confronted with new perplexities that challenged my early un-

---

[2]This is what James Loder has called the core problematic of the field of practical theology (James Loder, "Normativity and Context in Practical Theology: 'The Interdisciplinary Issue,' " in *Practical Theology: International Perspectives*, ed. Friedrich Schweitzer and Johannes A. van der Ven [Berlin: Peter Lang, 1999], pp. 359-62).

derstanding of both adolescents (human action) and God's movement in their lives (divine action). These new experiences forced me to begin reflecting on what I was doing. I turned to social-scientific literature to help me better understand the adolescents I was ministering to and the contexts they lived in. But, more importantly, I also reexamined my theological understandings, placing myself in dialogue with Bonhoeffer and others. In the midst of my reflection, I moved back into ministry, now as a gang-prevention counselor, with a refined understanding of how to minister to the adolescents I encountered and how God was concretely present and active in their lives. This three-step move from experience to reflection to new action is a continual process; my new action becomes new experience that pushes me into further reflection, and so the cycle continues. This three-step process is what practical theologians have called the praxis-theory-praxis loop.[3]

Practical theologian Richard Osmer has explained that there are four questions that help us to get inside this three-step process.[4] Osmer explains that almost all practical theologians ask an empirical descriptive question ("What is happening?"), an interpretive question ("Why is this happening?"), an explicitly theological or normative question ("What ought to be happening?") and finally a pragmatic question ("How should we act or what should we do in light of what is happening?").

This book, which is broken into two major parts, will follow this practical theological perspective. Part one focuses on the interpretative and empirical tasks, setting up the potential problems of an influence-based relational/incarnational youth ministry. Part two focuses on the normative and pragmatic tasks, directly conversing with Bonhoeffer's theology to rethink and reimagine the practice in the direction of what I will call "place-sharing."

My hope is that this book will contribute to the field of youth ministry a critical examination of relational ministry and a reimagining of the practice from a more rigorous theological perspective.

---

[3]By *praxis* I mean simply theory-laden reflection on practice. For further discussion about the praxis-theory-praxis loop, see Don Browning, *A Fundamental Practical Theology* (Minneapolis: Fortress, 1991), pp. 1-13.

[4]See Richard Osmer, "Johannes van der Ven's Contribution to the New Consensus in Practical Theology," in *Hermeneutics and Empirical Research in Practical Theology: The Contribution of Empirical Theology by Johannes A. van der Ven*, ed. Chris A. M. Hermans and Mary E. Moore (Boston: Brill, 2004).

PART ONE

It was in a large ballroom in Hartford that I realized that we youth workers have a problem with our language (and therefore understanding) of relationships. We had all gathered to hear the data results of a national survey on effective youth ministries. The research project was expansive and the conference was unique. Sitting in the room were professors, publishers and youth ministry organizational leaders, but also pastors, youth directors and laypeople. We were all invited to dialogue about the findings.

On this morning the researchers unpacked their finding that relationships were an essential component to young people discovering and maintaining faith. Most people nodded their heads. *Of course,* many thought. The importance of relationships has been understood as a necessary part of youth ministry lore since at least the 1950s.

Yet as the question-and-answer period was coming to an end a young man in his early thirties raised his hand, stood and said, "I get that relationships are important, but relationships are also hurtful. Growing up, I had a strong relationship with my youth director, but in eleventh grade I started to think about other faiths and became interested in Buddhism. At first my youth director tried to convince me that Buddhism was bankrupt and reminded me I was abandoning my faith. Once it was clear that he couldn't influence me he stopped calling me and soon I never saw him. That experience really hurt me!"

As the young man finished, a professor stood and asked the researcher, "What do you mean by relationships? I think we would all agree that the Hitler Youth did a great job of relational ministry, as we talk about it in youth ministry, but I know none of us would assert that it was the ministry of God."

So what then do we mean by relational youth ministry? To answer this question, part one of this book will be a critical examination of relational ministry. Like a physician giving a physical exam to a patient it will begin by seeking a historical understanding in chapters one and two. While a physician may ask, is there heart disease or breast cancer common in your family? we will ask, How did relational ministry come to be? What force caused its birth? And how have its youth ministry creators understood incarnational ministry?

Just as a physician asks background questions from within a framework of genetic biology, we will ask our questions in light of modernization/ globalization theory and its impact on America's religious consciousness throughout the late ninetieth and twentieth century. History will reveal that evangelicalism deserves a patent for this ministry form in youth ministry. We will see how evangelicalism has been in a constant state of conflict with the forces of modernity (modernization/globalization) and how relational youth ministry was used as a strategy in this battle.

Often after jotting down some history, the physician will ask the patient to hop on the examining table, so that his or her vital signs and a sample of blood can be taken and examined. Chapter three will do much the same; we will take our understanding of the history of relational ministry and put it under the microscope of sociological inspection, seeking to discover if there are hidden problems and deficiencies in our understanding of the practice. To keep us from sliding too deeply into sociological theory I have supplemented this chapter with examples and cases from research I did on five evangelical youth ministries in Southern California.[1] These youth ministries were nominated to be studied because they were known for doing excellent relational youth ministry. While affirming the passionate commitment in their ministry, this chapter will reveal that these ministries' knowingly or unknowingly practiced incarnational ministry for more cultural than theological reasons.

In the end this examination will reveal that relational youth ministry does *not* have a clean bill of health but has a dangerously high reading of

---

[1]This research was done as a research fellow for Princeton Theological Seminary's Lilly-funded "Faithful Practices Project." For further information about the project or my research methodology visit www.faithfulpractices.org or www.AndrewRoot.net.

cultural influence in its blood stream. I will argue that relational ministry is engendered almost solely from cultural changes rather than theological commitments. The practice has been untethered to rigorous theological contemplation. Therefore, relational ministry has had more to do will cultural conflict and fear of adolescent moral decay than sharing in the deep suffering and joy of the adolescent's humanity as the place of God's action in the world. This deficiency has caused youth ministry to see relationships in a goal-oriented rather than a companionship-oriented fashion that is more faithful to a theology of the incarnation.[2]

Yet, if we are willing to see it, there is good in the examination's findings! Though the diagnosis is bleak, it need not be fatal; relational youth ministry can and should survive. But if it is to be healthy it must lower its intake of influence and seek a new course of theological depth (this will be the objective of part two). Because the practice of incarnational ministry has been so dominant within youth ministry, both within and outside of evangelicalism, it is important that critical theological reflection takes place. Otherwise the practice will continue to pass on its limitations and its problematic use of goal-oriented relationships.

---

[2]This is what sociologist Murray Milner calls "instrumental associations" versus "expressive associations." For further discussion of these, see his *Freaks, Geeks and Cool Kids* (New York: Routledge, 2004), pp. 31, 63-64.

1

The Historical Ascent of Relational Ministry

I was just told last year that Santa Claus was an invention of the Coca-Cola Company in the 1930s. It's true, the 1930s (I'm still shocked)! Of course Saint Nick has been with us for a long time, but his depiction as a fat, jolly man in a red-and-white suit was a marketing ploy (maybe the best ever) that has become entrenched in our Western consciousness. If asked, I would have guessed that the jolly red-and-white-dressed fat man had been with us from at least the seventeenth century.

Many of my students react the same way when I inform them that adolescence, evangelicalism and youth ministry are themselves distinctly *new* cultural realities. Many of them imagine, as I had with Santa Claus, that these significant cultural realities stretch back hundreds of years. Of course, as with Santa Claus, they have their antecedents, but their present forms are not old at all.

Surprising to many of my students, the developmental "stage" of adolescence only burst on the scene of the American consciousness in 1904 with the publication of Stanley Hall's *Adolescence*. In the years following this work "adolescence" became a common way to define young people between the ages of thirteen and twenty-one.

American evangelicalism can trace its history back to the nineteenth century in America and to the sixteenth century in Europe. But the evangelical phenomenon that is now present and powerful within the American cultural landscape began in the 1940s and can be traced back to the so-called fundamentalist-modernist schism within the Protestant church in the early twentieth century.

Of course, children have always played meaningful roles within societies, and the church has always worked to pass on its faith to its young people. But age-specific ministry to young people—youth ministry—is no older than the late nineteenth century.

To understand how relational ministry has become the prominent practice of age-specific ministry in our time, we will observe the inception of age-specific ministry to youth and watch it develop through a century in which it intertwined with the cultural forces of adolescence and American evangelicalism.

As we journey through four time periods—pre-1900, 1900 to 1940 (in this chapter), 1940 to 1960, and 1960 to 2000 (in the next)—we will unpack how the two forces of adolescence and American evangelicalism have molded the approach taken toward youth ministry in each era, eventually leading to what we have come to recognize as relational youth ministry.

PRE-TWENTIETH CENTURY

My wife and I have recently gotten hooked on the HBO show *Deadwood*. It is a graphic picture of life in a South Dakota prospecting camp in the nineteenth century. The show is no documentary, but the creators have tried to be as historically honest as possible. What stuck out to me, besides the graphic portrayal, was that there were no adolescents in the camp. Surely there were young people, but there were no adolescent hangouts, no differences in clothes or musical tastes. Young people found themselves on the same hills or in the kitchens doing the same work as their fathers, mothers, aunts and uncles. As a matter of fact, many of these young people (as young as fourteen) left their families, not to discover themselves but to make their own fortunes as adults.

Throughout the eighteenth and nineteenth centuries young people in America were considered just that, "young" people. The limbo between childhood and adulthood, known since the twentieth century as "adolescence" (which can last over a decade), was not a category that pre-twentieth century people used to understand their children.[1] In the eighteenth and early nineteenth centuries the transition from childhood to adulthood was most often based not on age but on size. "If a fourteen-year-old looked big and strong enough to do a man's work on a farm or in a factory or mine, most people viewed him as a man."[2] Due to the need for "people power" in both the agricultural economy of the pre-nineteenth century and the early industrial economy of the pre-twentieth century, boys as young as thirteen or fourteen worked hand in hand with their fathers and uncles on the farm, and their neighbors and fellow townsmen in mills.

This meant that what we think of as adolescence was not a distinct stage of life with its own task and purpose in society (e.g., forming an identity and becoming educated). Harvey Graff explains, "There was relatively little of what has come to be called age synchronization, a standardized march through childhood, adolescence, and youth on the road to adulthood."[3] Of course, there were distinct activities that young people participated in, for example, grammar school and apprenticeships. These tasks were nevertheless governed by their benefit to the familial structure rather than being culturally age-specific assignments. "Age norms of all kinds were rather loosely maintained. The pattern—or, rather, the absence of pattern—can . . . be seen in the records of school attendance. In virtually all the schools of the period students of widely differing ages were mixed up together, often in a single classroom."[4]

---

[1]Joseph Kett alerts us to the fact that before the twentieth century there was no such thing as adolescence, therefore we can say that adolescence is an invention of modernity. "If adolescence is defined as the period after puberty during which a young person is institutionally segregated from casual contacts with a broad range of adults, then it can scarcely be said to have existed at all, even for those young people who attended school beyond age 14" (*Rites of Passage* [New York: Basic Books, 1977], p. 36).

[2]Thomas Hine, *The Rise and Fall of the American Teenager* (New York: Avon Books, 1999), p. 16. Clearly the physical ability to fulfill the adult workload depended on the biological arrival of puberty, but as Kett explains, puberty itself was the doorway to adulthood. " 'Full' incorporation [into adulthood] probably occurred around the time of puberty—that is, at 15 a boy was judged physically able to carry a man's work load. Prior to the middle of the 19th century, contemporaries associated puberty with rising power and energy rather than with the onset of an awkward and vulnerable stage of life which would later become known as adolescence" (Kett, *Rites of Passage*, p. 17).

[3]Harvey Graff, *Conflicting Paths: Growing Up in America* (Cambridge, Mass.: Harvard University Press, 1995), p. 66.

[4]John Demos, *Past, Present, and Personal* (New York: Oxford University Press, 1986), p. 101.

This occurred because education was often offered only in the winter months so it would not interfere with farm work, and it was only permitted at all if circumstances allowed for it. School was not the child's task or job, as we sometimes think of it today. Rather, school was an (nonessential) opportunity for personal betterment most often sought when one was young. Apprenticeship also was a common activity for young people. It was an adult task, which allowed young people to leave home and learn a skill. Yet the apprentice nevertheless remained connected and accountable to his or her family of origin.

However, by the late nineteenth and early twentieth century, both schooling and the apprenticeship were undermined by cultural transition. With the acceleration of industrialization and the concomitant mechanization the apprenticeship received a deathblow.[5] The staggering effect of its demise was exacerbated by the influx of immigrants from Europe willing to take unskilled labor for a fraction of what former apprentices demanded. Modern mechanization and the influx of immigration drove young apprentices back home, as skilled labor was no longer needed. A machine could now make shoes or copy a document much more effectively and cheaply than a person could. This same modern mechanization pushed families from farms to cities to find opportunity in the large factories and the burgeoning construction projects located in urban centers.

With the apprenticeship dead, the family farm gone and the machine producing more with fewer workers, young people found themselves with little to do. The rapid passage from childhood to adulthood had ceased, making way for a new understanding of the young as a cohort needing specialization through a liminal stage of education, thereby making a way for the arrival of the "adolescent," and church and parachurch ministries began to give specific attention to them.

American evangelicalism. European Protestantism's flavor did not taste right in America. European Protestantism had "stressed faith as a lifelong struggle with sin and temptation, for which the teaching of and worship in the church provided assistance and encouragement. This . . . version of

---

[5]See William J. Reese, *The Origins of the American High School* (New Haven, Conn.: Yale University Press, 1995), p. 18.

Protestantism was objective (rather than personal) in the sense that to be a church member involved being conformed to the doctrines and liturgy of the church."[6] But the first great American theologian, Jonathan Edwards, and one of America's infamous preachers, George Whitefield, seasoned Protestantism with a uniquely American theology constructed from the particular experience of colonial life. Edwards and Whitfield looked beyond European Protestantism's impersonal ecclesial-centric faith and saw instead the importance of personal conversion. This shifted pastoral concern from facilitating the liturgical and sacramental needs of a particular community to mediating new and dynamic religious experiences brought forth by feelings of crisis and despair. The pastor was "to preach in ways designed to bring hearers to a point of crisis, at which they despaired over their sinfulness and experienced the love of God in an immediate way."[7]

In this new American recipe of faith, what became essential was not communal commitment but personal acceptance of God's love and mercy. The convert was expected to personally exhibit his or her conversion by devotion and righteous acts as well as avoidance and disdain for worldly activities.

By the mid-nineteenth century, evangelical Protestantism had become what D. G. Hart calls "the functional equivalent of an established church [in America]."[8] Building on the momentum of the Second Great Awakening during the 1820s and 1830s, early evangelicalism worked fervently to bring about personal and social unity and reform in American society. Early evangelicals created groups and associations that sought to overcome evils in society and the world. "In the North this involved opposition to slavery, Sabbath-breaking, and alcohol, and an effort to provide care and education for those in need."[9] These initiatives were launched from the belief that personal conversion led to righteous living and holy societies.

In the late nineteenth and early twentieth century, however, evangelical Protestantism was knocked off balance by the changing currents of cultural thought, leaving it exposed to the crashing wave of modernization. This wave was encompassed in skepticism of traditional authorities brought

---

[6]D. G. Hart, *That Old-Time Religion in Modern America* (Chicago: Ivan R. Dee, 2002), p. 7.
[7]Ibid.
[8]Ibid., p. 12.
[9]Ibid.

forth by immigration and, most boldly, scientific advance.

> Darwinism offered accounts of the origins of life. . . . Freudianism added
> naturalistic explanations for the human sense of meaning, of love and
> beauty, and of religion itself. Marxism . . . claimed to explain the meaning
> and . . . direction of history. . . . Biblical criticism turned the fire power of
> such scientific-historical explanation point-blank on . . . the Bible itself."[10]

As this wave crashed, the biblical foundation that evangelicals stood upon, that just decades before was trusted without question, seemed to be washed from under their feet. Consequently evangelicalism entered the first decades of the twentieth century as a movement fighting frantically for its life and authoritative foundation.

Fearful that their children would be swept away by the currents of modernization, conservative Protestants gave direct ministerial attention to the emerging cohort called adolescence. Thus youth ministry can be understood as a creation of evangelical Protestantism in reaction to modernization.

Age-specific ministry to youth. To trace the historical line of relational ministry as the dominant form of youth ministry in America, we must start in the busy streets of London at the height of industrialization. Newspaper man Robert Raikes became disturbed by the situation of children working in industrial factories. Concerned for the overworked and undereducated children as well as the great cities of England soiled by their unsupervised delinquency, Raikes developed what he called the "Sunday school." Sunday school met on the one day of the week when young people were not laboring in factories, and its leaders taught children skills in reading and writing as well as basic manners and morals.

Facing the similar problems of industrialization and the arrival of modernization, America's churches adopted Raikes's program. The Sunday school became the first distinct ministry to youth in America, arriving from England in the middle of the nineteenth century. The uniquely evangelical flavor of American religious life following the two Great Awakenings eventually modified the Sunday school, discarding

---

[10]George Marsden, "The Collapse of American Evangelical Academia," in *Reckoning with the Past: Historical Essays on American Evangelicalism from the Institute for the Study of American Evangelicals,* ed. D. G. Hart (Grand Rapids: Baker, 1995), p. 226.

its educational emphasis and replacing it with an objective of converting young people to Christ. The Sunday school became a program for youth evangelism.[11] "No longer a philanthropic expedient for conveying the rudiments of morality and literacy to street waifs, Sunday schools were now portrayed as divinely appointed instruments for the regeneration of the nation."[12]

Yet as the population became more urbanized, it became clear that the Sunday school was not enough. In cities throughout the country large populations of young people were freed from the covering of village life and a single family focus. To provide protective outlets of activity for these youth, the Young Men's Christian Association and Young Women's Christian Association were formed. "The purpose of [these] . . . agencies was to help Christian young people retain their Christian commitments after they had moved into the urban jungles."[13] The YMCA recognized the nascent arrival of a distinct youth cohort made possible by the pluralization of modernization as well as the threats that this pluralization inflicted on an individual's Christian commitment to live a holy life. At its beginnings, then, the intent of these early youth ministries was twofold: to reinforce Christian commitments and to protect young people from the perceived threats of menacing city life.

THE EARLY TWENTIETH CENTURY

The early decades of the twentieth century saw the dominant agrarian culture in America finally overthrown. Modernization had arrived and with it came sweeping changes within society, culture and education. The arrival of modern society meant the construction of new institutions like the school, the corporation and the nuclear family, which were distinct worlds isolated from each other. With the demise of the apprenticeship and the arrival of a machine-centered economy, human muscle was needed much less and human organization much more. This meant that

---

[11]Joseph Kett says, "The first of several changes which were to affect Sunday schools came in the 1820s when, under the impulse of evangelical revivals, Sunday school promoters began to emphasize the possibility of converting children *en masse*" (*Rites of Passage*, p. 117).

[12]Ibid.

[13]Mark Senter, *The Coming Revolution in Youth Ministry* (Wheaton, Ill.: Victor, 1992), p. 90.

middle-class jobs shifted from blue collar to white. With this shift came a need for new types of training which would give individuals the specialization needed in a modern society. Where just decades earlier reading and arithmetic were nonessential opportunities for personal betterment, in the modernized twentieth century they became essential for participation in society.[14]

The high school became the place where individuals could receive the training and education needed to thrive in a modernized world. William Reese states, "Young people faced a world where machines had transformed the nature of work, where science and technology helped conquer the natural environment. Educators argued that high schools prepared boys especially for the world of business and the professions."[15]

The rise of the high school as the location for young people to receive their needed training meant two things. First, young people remained in their parents' homes much longer than in the past. Second, young people, though remaining in their parents' homes, spent fewer meaningful hours with their parents. Whereas in the decades of agrarianism and apprenticeships, young and old worked side by side and skills were passed on through working together, in the high school young people spent most meaningful hours with their peers, away from the work of parents and other adults. Reed Ueda explains, "The high school institutionalized the peer society. . . . The high school also insulated the peer society, thereby strengthening its ability to discipline its members. Away from parents, away from the church, and away from the workplace, high school students felt pressure to conform to the standards of the group."[16]

In the cities and suburbs adults may have had fewer hours of contact with their older children, but these hours were more intense. The intensity built as young and old tried to transverse a widening gap in shared experiences and perspectives. The young person may have also felt rising pressure as he or she anticipated operating in a complicated modernized world,

---

[14]Kett explains further how education served modern industries: "Schools served the needs of business in a variety of ways. As the informal machine shop with a dozen journeymen and apprentices gave way to the modern business corporation, education provided a form of certification for young people. A diploma could act as a kind of letter of introduction" (*Rites of Passage,* p. 153).

[15]Reese, *Origins of the American High School,* p. 96.

[16]Reed Ueda, *Avenues to Adulthood* (Cambridge: Cambridge University Press, 1987), p. 120.

having had little direct contact with it.[17] "To be a high school student at the turn of the century was to be acutely conscious that the era ahead was to be radically different from the one their parents knew."[18] And parents too may have felt frustrated, interpreting their children's ambivalence as an inability to comprehend the difficulty of living in a modernized world. They began to wonder if their children were crazy. At times young people were preoccupied with their own peer world and seemed completely uninterested in the "real world," but then at other times, they seemed overwhelmed by the fear and stress of being held out of and then entering into a complex society.

Reflection on these experiences led psychologist G. Stanley Hall to assert that those in high school were not children and not yet adults, but adolescents.[19] The period of adolescence, in which persons are caught between one time and another, Hall explained, was biologically determined as a period of stress and anxiety (storm).[20] Therefore, Hall affirmed (quite differently from the common thought of the nineteenth century) that adolescents were ontologically distinct and this distinction included a penchant for trepidation revealed in odd behaviors.[21]

While in the first two decades of the twentieth century the high school was gaining importance in American society, it wasn't until the

---

[17]"The high school students of the turn of the century believed they were growing up in a more brutally competitive world. They assumed it was their duty to equip themselves to rise in this setting. The social competition in the peer-group societies of the high school and the interscholastic competition with other high schools stimulated at an early age a keen sense of rivalry and emulation" (ibid., p. 139).

[18]Ibid., p. 143.

[19]"The belief that a normal adolescence is 'abnormal' can be traced as far back as G. Stanley Hall's *Adolescence* (1904). Yet the most important current expression stems from psychoanalysis, initially in the work of Anna Freud, later taken up and elaborated. This view of adolescence initially focused upon a revitalized conflict between the drives, and the defensive and superego forces" (Joseph Adelson, *Inventing Adolescence: The Political Psychology of Everyday Schooling* [New Brunswick: Transaction Books, 1986], p. 127).

[20]Hall traced this biological distinction to the awakening of sexuality in the period of adolescence. Hall claimed "the rise of sexual potency convulsed the whole system and threw the adolescent into storm and stress" (Kett, *Rights of Passage*, p. 206).

[21]Anthropologist Margaret Mead opposed Hall's thesis from the start. In traveling to Samoa she showed that young people in that social context were not in a stage of stress and storm. Her research indicated that such an understanding of adolescence as Hall's must be seen in light of modern society and not as an ontological universal. See Margaret Mead, *Coming of Age in Samoa* (New York: William Morrow, 1928).

1920s that high school became the norm for all young people (whether middle, upper or lower class).[22] With the popular embrace of Hall's work as well as the arrival of a worldwide economic depression, the high school became both scientifically endorsed and culturally necessary. While young people had found fewer and fewer employment opportunities stretching back to the last decades of the nineteenth century, with the arrival of the Great Depression all remaining work evaporated. With nothing else to do, the majority of young people, now known as adolescents, entered high school. Being an adolescent meant being a high school student, and schooling became the developmental task of the teen years.

To build loyalty and camaraderie, high schools introduced extracurricular clubs and activities—a trend seized and built on by youth ministry and denominational bodies. As a uniquely modern institution the high school opened itself to pluralism, whether by class, ethnicity or gender. It was naively believed that by placing young girls, middle-class white boys and new immigrants in the same classrooms the high school could serve society by molding individuals from distinct backgrounds into good democratic Americans.

In the 1930s the high school became "the" experience of American adolescents.[23] But the universalization of the high school did not bring uniformity as hoped; rather it brought the pluralizing forces of modernization into the world of the adolescent. As in the offices and factories of their parents, adolescents were confronted with numerous voices and perspectives. Through both education and peer culture, adolescents were becoming aware of the multiple life options available to citizens of a modernized

---

[22]See Thomas Hine, *The Rise and Fall of the American Teenager* (New York: Avon, 1999), p. 204.

[23]It must be recognized that without the high school, the concept of adolescence as a distinct stage of life would never have come to be. Friedrich Schweitzer helpfully explains, "One of the most important factors responsible for the historically late emergence of adolescence as a distinct stage within the life cycle is the scarcity of educational institutions in earlier history and cultures. Only with the introduction of mandatory schooling beyond the age of ten was there a social and institutional basis for adolescence to become a general experience in today's sense, and this kind of schooling is largely a twentieth-century innovation" (*The Postmodern Lifecycle* [St. Louis: Chalice Press, 2004], p. 43). This is not to assume that biology has nothing to do with adolescence. Rather, it must be seen, as Schweitzer argues, that space is given for biological and psychological maturation by social forces.

world.[24] The hoped-for monolithic high school experience fragmented into a diversified youth culture in the 1940s and beyond, and the denominational youth societies likewise lost their dominance.

American evangelicalism. Modern society meant the construction of new institutions isolated from each other (such as schools, corporations and the nuclear family). Through these institutions individuals were exposed to a plethora of distinct human experiences and perspectives. As Peter Berger asserts, "Modern society . . . confronts the individual with an ever-changing kaleidoscope of social experiences and meanings. It forces him *[sic]* to make decisions and plans. . . . It forces him into reflection. . . . Not only the world but the self becomes an object of deliberate attention and . . . scrutiny."[25]

This need for deliberate reflection is what social theorists call reflexivity. "The more societies are modernized, the more agents (subjects) acquire the ability to reflect on the social conditions of their existence and to change [them]."[26] Due to the exposure to multiple life worlds and new scientific knowledge made possible by modernization, individuals in the early decades of the twentieth century were forced to rethink and revise their social practices.[27] The need for reflexivity and reenvisioned social practices became so strong that it led individuals and society as a whole to reconsider their understandings of their children (as we just saw) and their religion.

At the end of the nineteenth century, religious reflexivity had cracked the evangelical Protestant shell. In the early decades of the twentieth century the escalation of new scientific theories and progress, coupled with the cultural pluralization of urban centers due to immigration, shattered the

---

[24]"The peer-group culture of the high school supervened the family to introduce students at an impressionable age to new values and habits that affected their aspirations in adulthood. The conformist pressures of high school youth culture catalyzed the sense of unique generational identity among turn-of-the-century adolescents" (Ueda, *Avenues to Adulthood*, p. 2).

[25]Peter Berger, *The Homeless Mind: Modernization and Consciousness* (New York: Vintage Books, 1973), p. 79.

[26]Ulrich Beck, Anthony Giddens and Scott Lash, *Reflexive Modernization: Politics, Tradition and Aesthetics in the Modern Social Order* (Stanford, Calif.: Stanford University Press, 1994), p. 174.

[27]"The reflexivity of modern social life consists in the fact that social practices are constantly examined and reformed in the light of incoming information about those very practices, thus constitutively altering their character" (Anthony Giddens, *The Consequences of Modernity* [Stanford, Calif.: Stanford University Press, 1990], p. 38).

once dominant evangelical Protestant hold on American culture.[28] Two Protestant responses emerged from the rubble of evangelical hegemony. One was to accept the scientific methods and pluralizing forces that threatened certain Protestant commitments. Those who accepted the new scientific methods (soon to be called "the modernists") would reappropriate them for their distinctly religious pursuits. The modernists looked to forms of psychology, evolutionary theory and literary criticism to show the relevance of Protestantism to a pluralistic modern society with the hope that in so doing they could reshape and revive Protestant Christianity in the twentieth century.[29]

The second group responded much differently. They interpreted the turn toward modern scientific methods and the escalation of pluralism as threatening and potentially deadly to Christianity. From their perspective what was needed was not an appropriation of modern scientific methods but a return to Protestantism's core tradition, biblical authority. This group came to be known as the fundamentalists.[30] The fundamentalists saw themselves cornered by both a culture opposed to their worldview and a modernist (heretical, from their perspective) Protestantism that had traded its birthright for a bowl of stew. Now cornered, the fundamentalists decided to come out swinging. Holding to an inerrant view of the Bible, the

---

[28]Mark Noll drives this point deeper: "Those who would become fundamentalists feared what the massive immigration of Roman Catholics, Jews, and the unchurched was doing to a United States they considered a Protestant country; they were bewildered by the burgeoning cities that were rapidly displacing small towns and the countryside (where Protestantism had thrived) as the centers of American civilization; and they were appalled by the vogue for naturalist philosophy, and with it the dismissal of the Bible, that extended far beyond the universities" (*The Scandal of the Evangelical Mind* [Grand Rapids: Eerdmans, 1994], p. 114). The authors of *Global Dreams* continue, "The 35 million people who made up the great European migration that occurred between 1800 and 1914 constituted a fourth stream. These immigrants, who willingly braved long, harsh voyages for a chance to make a new life in the New World, eventually succeeded in turning the former English colonies into a multiethnic nation. Poles, Irish, Germans, Jews, and Slavs were joined by Asians, most of whom entered the work force at the very bottom in dangerous, exhausting, and pitifully paid jobs" (Richard Barnet and John Cavanagh, *Global Dreams: Imperial Corporations and the New World Order* [New York: Touchstone, 1994], p. 298).

[29]An example of this way of thinking can be seen in the work of religious educator George Albert Coe.

[30]George Marsden provides a succinct and helpful definition: " 'fundamentalism' refers to a twentieth-century movement closely tied to the revivalist tradition of mainstream evangelical Protestantism that militantly opposed modernist theology and the cultural change associated with it" ("Evangelicals, History, and Modernity," in *Evangelicalism and Modern America*, ed. George Marsden [Grand Rapids: Eerdmans, 1984], p. 303).

fundamentalists worked to expose and devalue any group or individual that opposed or worked outside this commitment.

The modernist-fundamentalist battle came to a head in 1925, when Tennessee high school teacher John T. Scopes taught evolutionary theory in direct opposition to state law. The fundamentalists won the battle— Scopes was found guilty—but they lost the war. The case had become a national media phenomenon and in the court of popular opinion the fundamentalists had lost badly. In newspapers throughout the country fundamentalists were portrayed as rigid, hateful, backward and ignorant.

Shocked by this negative reaction and by the loss of the northeastern denominations to the modernists, and now bolstered by the arrival of a new theological perspective, the fundamentalists departed from the public square and took refuge in exclusive communities. Dispensationalist theology, which spoke of an evil world and a holy remnant within it that would soon be plucked from the world before its tribulation, gave the fundamentalists justification to lock themselves away from the world.[31] Individuals were taught to see their time "in the world" as an opportunity to convert others and lead them into the holy remnant through their personal evangelism.

Personal contact was essential because society's institutions could not be trusted, due to the pluralism of modernization. "Having lost two of the most important cultural institutions for a good society, namely, the churches and the schools, many [fundamentalists] looked to create an alternative world that would preserve stability and virtue, if not within the nation, at least among the faithful."[32] Thus fundamentalists between 1920 and 1940 created a number of Bible colleges and seminaries free from the propaganda of modernist science.

In response to the modernizing move toward a pluralistic, open, cosmopolitan society, fundamentalists sought to protect the very sacred tradition which they felt was under attack. Anthony Giddens explains that modern-

---

[31]"Dispensationalism was a version of premillennialism, the doctrine that Christ will return personally to found a kingdom in Jerusalem where he will reign for one thousand years" (ibid., p. 5). D. G. Hart notes that events of the 1920s through the 1940s, among them the Great Depression and another world war, served Dispensationalists as evidence that their interpretation of history was correct. The rise of radio extended their influence as messages of the end of days and Christ's imminent return went over the airwaves (Hart, *That Old-Time Religion*, p. 39).

[32]Ibid., p. 57.

ization places tradition in doubt by challenging it to defend its legitimacy in confrontation with other traditions and perspectives.[33] This very need would motivate evangelicals to focus more attention on the education and protection of their children.

Age-specific ministry to youth. The dominant form of age-specific youth ministry between 1900 and 1940 actually had its start on February 2, 1881, when young pastor Francis Clark from Maine inaugurated the first "Young People's Society for Christian Endeavor." The idea came about after Clark's frustration that in his growing church young people were not going on to become vital members of the congregational life after initial conversion experiences. He and his wife searched for a way to engender commitment and continued involvement among the congregation's young. Building on the conversion emphasis of the Sunday school, Clark drew upon the YMCA's focus on the social gathering of young people and the example of other extracurricular activities that had become popular among middle-class high school students to shape an age-specific ministry to youth in his church. Demanding a depth of accountability and responsibility, Clark received positive responses from his young people. Each member of the society had to pledge to attend each meeting and to share with the group his or her progress in the Christian life. What resulted were meetings numbering close to a hundred participants.

Through the writings of Clark, the idea of a pledging youth society spread like wildfire as local churches across denominations recognized the same issues that Clark had been addressing. By the 1920s most denominations had constructed their own youth societies, complete with curriculum and summer camps. Thus the youth society became a denomination-wide activity, as denominational officials took responsibility for youth ministry.

The Christian youth society served adolescents well in the early twentieth century. Pledging provided a distinct commitment, a choice among a growing buffet of possible lifestyles. In committing to Christian progress through Bible study and witness, adolescents were able to grab hold of a distinct tradition and claim it for themselves. Youth societies, while pro-

---

[33]Anthony Giddens, *Runaway World* (New York: Routledge, 2003), p. 48.

viding an opportunity to claim a tradition, also appeared relevant by grounding themselves in the larger bureaucratic denominations. Adolescents could feel like they were part of something significant and modern, something in step with large, bureaucratic modernized society.

The 1930s, however, foreshadowed the end of youth societies. Reeling from the backlash of the Scopes trial, fundamentalists developed an ambivalent attitude toward both traditional denominations and the public high school. Many denominations were divided between modernists and fundamentalists, often leading to a modernist victory. Fundamentalists criticized public schools (though their children continued to attend) for their adoption of modernist science and willingness to replace the church as the center of local community life.

The denominational youth societies mistakenly anticipated that with the expansion of the high school population in 1930s adolescents would be drawn in larger numbers to denominationally supported societies. But with the growth of school populations and the expansion of a distinct youth culture in the 1940s, adolescents demanded new entertainment sophistication as well as more possibilities for personal intimacy than the denominational societies could provide.

With the continued rise of modernization and the invention of adolescence as a distinct stage of life, the high school became the institutional locus of American youth. Moving through the world apart from their families, adolescents began to increasingly operate outside of the influence of the youth societies. Conservative Protestants by the 1930s felt Christian tradition was coming under deadly attack from science and culture, and recognized that a new strategy beyond the now flagging youth societies was needed to save their children.

2

The Historical Ascent of Relational Ministry

If the middle of the twentieth century had a mascot, it may be Theodore Cleaver or, as most people know him, the Beaver. The TV show *Leave It to Beaver* revealed the cultural transitions that had occurred within our conception of childhood, family and school after 1940. There is, no doubt, an idyllic nature to these cultural realities of Beaver's world. He seemed to exist in a kind of childhood paradise, the whole world seemed constructed for him to walk around looking for four-leaf clovers, talking to fireman and watching men dig holes. The trouble Beaver always found himself in was due to the adventure of his childhood paradise. And the paradise wasn't just for Beaver; rather Beaver represented a belief (which I doubt was ever true) that the late forties, fifties and early sixties were indeed paradise for us all!

Yet underneath this idyllic crust were new realities created by modernization and globalization that reshaped our conception of ourselves, each other and world. The technical operations of the economy were filtering into human relationships as individuals were becoming more and more cut free from traditional units and groupings. The world was changing, but in the midst of the change we tried to hold on to the values of family, religion and childhood.

World War II finally ended with the dropping of atom bombs on two Japanese cities. Thus our mid-century paradise began with the instigation of a literal hell a world away. Yet sitting in our newfound utopia we sensed that it had been won at a hidden cost. The technology that had won us paradise promised to make life better, but we could not shake the deadly shadow side of technological advancement from the corners of our consciousness. With further progress by scientists around the world, the A-bomb became the hydrogen bomb. With the cooling of American and Soviet relations, it became conceivable that a nuclear Armageddon could wipe out life on the planet. This led to an all-out cultural war against the risks of communism.[1]

In addition to the threatening Cold War, the very technological advances that were making life better came with potentially greater and greater risks. Highways brought deadly car accidents, high-tech power plants polluted communities and threatened local residents, and airplanes crashed. With advancing progress, modernization and globalization also brought new dangers.[2] Technological advances not only interjected risk into the consciousness of Americans, they also initiated new patterns of interconnection between individuals, and between people and institutions. Throughout the twentieth century modernization had been indoctrinating individuals into the rationalization of technology. But "because technology operates according to its own logic and its own rules, it is increasingly autonomous from human values and, therefore, increasingly unharnessable by those who have created it."[3]

Technological rationale demanded that people be seen as numbers,

---

[1]It is not as though risk never occurred within human history before modernity; risk of famine, drought or flood was always a threat to premodern peoples. Yet Anthony Giddens wants to draw a distinction between natural risk and what he calls "manufactured risk." Manufactured risk is the result of modernity. He explains that manufactured is "created by the very impact of our developing knowledge upon the world. Manufactured risk refers to risk situations which we have very little historical experience of confronting. . . . At a certain point, however—very recently in historical terms—we started worrying less about what nature can do to us, and more about what we have done to nature. This marks the transition from the predominance of external risk to that of manufactured risk" (Anthony Giddens, *Runaway World* [New York: Routledge, 2003], p. 26).

[2]For a more in-depth discussion of risk and the risk society see Ulrich Beck, *Risk Society: Towards a New Modernity* (London: Sage, 1992).

[3]James Davison Hunter, *Evangelicalism: The Coming Generation* (Chicago: University of Chicago Press, 1987), p. 197.

cogs or parts in a corporate machine. The bottom line determined how employees would be treated. This rationality moved outside the business world and was used by individuals in their day-to-day lives. Personal connections and responsibilities would ultimately be judged by their contribution to individual personal happiness. And personal happiness was supposedly available through the material comforts made possible by the growing technological economy. This meant that instead of "seek[ing] meaning and personal fulfillment in deep interpersonal bonds . . . [these] things are sought in an obsessive and competitive materialism."[4]

The common use of technical rationality and the slow decay of community and kinship structures of the family led to a new emphasis on the self-chosen relationship to provide individual feelings of intimacy.[5] In a modernized world that undercuts tradition by allowing individuals to choose their own destinies, preexisting social units (like families, communities, tribes, ethnic groups, etc.) no longer have the power to determine social interactions and therefore provide intimacy. Rather, in a modernized world the individual must negotiate all meaningful relationships on his or her own terms. Where in the past people could not escape such social units, in a modernized world mobility and diversification allow people the freedom to individually choose friends and lovers.

Giddens explains that the self-chosen relationship is a relatively recent development that allows individuals to enter into contractual connections with others.[6] Due to the multitude of life worlds and the penchant toward technical rationale within modern society, relationships are individually negotiated zones of shared intimacy. In a modern world, who to relate with and what this relationship means is personally determined and chosen. In a modernized world, then, the self-chosen relationship,

---

[4]Ibid., p. 197.

[5]Giddens has called this the "pure" relationship, and I will lean heavily on his theory and definitions. However, for clarity's sake, in this book I will use the term "self-chosen relationship" rather than his "pure relationship."

[6]Giddens explains further that the self-chosen (pure) relationship is "for its own sake, for what can be derived by each person from a sustained association with another; and which is continued only in so far as it is thought by both parties to deliver enough satisfactions for each individual to stay within it" (Anthony Giddens, *The Transformation of Intimacy: Sexuality, Love and Eroticism in Modern Societies* [Stanford, Calif.: Stanford University Press, 1992], p. 58).

as cool, the possibilities of intimacy through self-chosen relationships were endless, but if the teenager failed and was seen as uncool, he or she was imprisoned in a world of loneliness and isolation. It was in this culture that Young Life's focus on intimacy through the self-chosen relationship thrived, as we will see.

Modernization always brings diversification. This means that soon that which was cool became subjectively located as more and more options in music, fashion and entertainment confronted the adolescent. By the 1960s cool was coming in more flavors; the monolithic youth culture was fragmenting, and those excluded from the self-chosen relationship due to lack of popularity were beginning to huddle together to redefine cool for themselves (with the help of a diversified popular culture).

1940 TO 1960

Along with the exhilarating victory in WWII, the country's newfound international leadership and the middle-class ethos came a heightened nationalism. This nationalism bred a dominant spirit of conservatism, which became paradigmatic of the 1950s. But in the late 1940s fundamentalism was confronted with a crisis from within the center of its ranks. Because of the battles lost, post-1925 fundamentalists had worked hard to create safe colleges and seminaries for their children. But having been educated, many of these children became discontent with their parents' stance toward society. Following the Allies' victory, and benefiting from the national opposition to atheistic communism and the new conservative middle-class ethos, young fundamentalists worked to reform their image by engaging American society with a biblical but friendly faith and resurrecting the nineteenth-century nomenclature *evangelical*.[11]

Yet the evangelical movement, though intellectually secured by a group of young scholars, was in need of more direct contact with the American

---

[11]Jon R. Stone draws out nicely the differences between evangelicals and fundamentalists concerning their stance toward culture and society. "Evangelical and fundamentalist responses to modern culture differed in that evangelicals have traditionally sought to engage the world and transform it from within, while fundamentalists have more typically resisted contact with secular culture, seeking not to transform secular society but to rescue individuals from its damning influence" (*On the Boundaries of American Evangelicalism* [New York: St. Martin's, 1997], p. 12).

public.[12] A young, tall, handsome Wheaton College graduate provided just the appeal the new movement needed. To the surprise of many, starting in the late 1940s America began a love affair with Billy Graham. Graham's clear, energetic and patriotic preaching had been heard at the rallies of the growing Youth for Christ movement, and he debuted in his own crusade in 1949 in Los Angeles. Billy Graham was received not as a backward, hateful fundamentalist but as compassionate, principled American.[13]

Graham's message struck two chords with the American public. First, in his early years Graham preached a nationalist message of American domination over the risk of atheistic communism.[14] "Aside from his own rhetorical skills, good looks, and accompanying musicians, he gained a national audience beyond the evangelical rank and file through the political themes of his message."[15] He strongly supported a conservative republicanism which rang with popular appeal in the post-WWII, Truman-Eisenhower America now awakening to the risks of modernization. Politically conservative media moguls loved Graham's politics and presented him as the ideal American patriot in their newspapers, speaking highly of his crusades.

Whereas the fundamentalists had lost their battle over modern science, the new evangelicals regained a public voice through a message of nation-

---

[12]The momentum for these reforms came from a group of highly talented scholars who received undergraduate degrees from fundamentalist institutions before entering the nation's top research universities to complete their education. Individuals like Carl F. H. Henry, E. J. Carnell, George Eldon Ladd and Paul King Jewett graduated from either Harvard or Boston University prepared to defend biblical Christianity in a nonseparatist fashion. Directed by the leadership of Harold John Ockenga they called themselves neo-evangelicals. Following the funding streams of fundamentalist radio personality Charles Fuller, this young and talented group created the first evangelical institution of higher learning that did not desire separatist education but engaged discourse—Fuller Theological Seminary.

[13]Mark Noll says, "For nearly thirty years, from the end of the war into the 1970s, the great visibility of Billy Graham and the heightened influence of institutions that he favored gave the impression that a unified, culture-shaping evangelicalism had returned to America. If the impression was false, it still testified powerfully to the charismatic impact of Graham" (*American Evangelical Christianity* [Malden, Mass.: Blackwell, 2001], p. 18).

[14]Joel Carpenter explains, "As the threat of confrontation with the Soviet Union intensified, national leaders such as President Harry S. Truman and General Dwight D. Eisenhower called for national spiritual renewal to meet the challenge. The new evangelists eagerly picked up and quoted such jeremiads, and when they were praised for their efforts by public officials, a new civic and religious alliance began to take shape" ("From Fundamentalism to the New Evangelical Coalition," in *Evangelicalism and Modern America*, ed. George Marsden [Grand Rapids: Eerdmans, 1995], p. 15).

[15]D. G. Hart, *That Old-Time Religion in Modern America* (Chicago: Ivan R. Dee, 2002), p. 111.

alism and anticommunism. Following the American "can do" confidence, evangelicals supported an antistructuralist cultural position, similar to the middle-class republican spirit, which believed individuals could choose their own destiny free from the meddling of the government.[16] D. G. Hart explains evangelicals held that conversion empowered people to take responsibility for themselves:

> Conversion leads to a highly disciplined and moral life where born-again believers stand more or less on their own two feet, without depending on others for help. This outlook may not automatically commit an evangelical to the principles of free enterprise and unregulated markets; but it certainly gives plausibility to the kinds of political arrangements that have benefited middle-class entrepreneurs who own or work in a family business.[17]

The second chord that Graham's message struck with the American public was his simple, straightforward theology of the need for a personal (individual) relationship and intimacy with Jesus Christ. In a culture dominated by technical rationality and the arrival of the self-chosen relationship, Graham's message of a Jesus who can be trusted as an intimate friend was strikingly relevant. Choosing with whom to be in intimate relationship had become the task of living in a modernized and globalized world, so choosing a friendship with Jesus made perfect sense. Graham steered clear of speaking of hell and damnation; instead he focused on calling individuals into intimate friendship with a trusted Savior.

This relational message did not, however, lead to evangelical cultural assimilation. Rather, in tune with the effects of the self-chosen relationship as illustrated in the social dynamics of the high school, it provided a more entrenched identity. The self-chosen relationship demands that a person

---

[16]George Marsden explains the background of the new leaders of the evangelical movement: "All the men who . . . shared [a] classic American, rugged individualist outlook. All, for instance, were conservative Republicans. They represented a mostly upper lower-class or lower middle-class aspiring white constituency: those who characteristically had struggled through the depression but who had maintained their pride and firm attachments to the traditional Protestant American values of hard work and self-help. They believed that freedom from external control was a chief social virtue and that rugged individualism was the key to success" (*Reforming Fundamentalism* [Grand Rapids: Eerdmans, 1995], p. 29).

[17]Hart, *That Old-Time Religion in Modern America*, p. 107.

choose one friendship, thus denying another. In the modern world no one can be in intimate relationship with everyone. For evangelicals, choosing to be in relationship with Jesus provided a distinct boundary which marked the separation between true and false believers. Evangelicals then strategically began engaging culture through the use of the self-chosen relationship, believing that if they could be trusted as intimate friends, they could share the source of their own personal intimacy, their relationship with Jesus. The focus on the self-chosen relationship as well as on political conservatism was particularly successful in the free marketplace of American religion between 1940 and 1960. The strength and vitality of this emerging subculture of evangelicals was based on the energy of the teenagers and the young adults working with them, finding its catalyst in emerging youth ministries of the 1940s and 1950s.[18]

In the 1920s and 1930s youth ministry was governed by large denominational bodies that provided youth societies to train young people and hold them accountable to the Bible. But in the 1940s and 1950s what became important was evangelistic engagement through nationalistic and relational strategies. The leadership of this new evangelistic engagement was not coming from denominational bureaucrats but from grassroots entrepreneurs, such as the founders of Young Life and Youth for Christ. Nathan Hatch and Michael Hamilton explain, "Para-church groups [had] picked the denominations' pockets, taking over denominational functions, inventing wholly new categories of religious activity to take into the marketplace, and then transmitting back into the denominations an explicitly nondenominational version of evangelical Christianity."[19]

The nationalist-relational perspective demanded a significant amount of autonomy from large bureaucratic denominations and smaller congregations. If someone could invent a successful approach to ministry and or-

---

[18]"They created a spiritual subculture geared toward families, teens, and young adults. In many respects evangelical piety demanded an emphasis on young people because of its conviction that entrance into the faith required the fully free decision of the sovereign individual" (ibid., p. 81).

[19]Nathan Hatch and Michael Hamilton, "Epilogue: Taking the Measure of the Evangelical Resurgence, 1942-1992," in *Reckoning with the Past: Historical Essays on American Evangelicalism from the Institute for the Study of American Evangelicals*, ed. D. G. Hart (Grand Rapids: Baker, 1995), p. 398.

ganize its replication, he or she could create a parachurch organization.[20] The new and vital movement—evangelicalism—thrived on the free-flowing and creative impulses of parachurch innovation.

Thus relational ministry to adolescents was officially born in the post-WWII era. Up until this time, age-specific ministry to youth reacted in response to the changes of culture and the need to hold onto a faith commitment. Within these ministries the traces of incarnational ministry were present and building. But from 1940 to 1960 the parachurch movement swept the nation and the primary model of relational ministry was unleashed. Jim Rayburn and his organization, Young Life, invented this form of age-specific youth ministry, but Young Life did not arrive on the scene alone. It was joined by Youth for Christ. Both organizations in their own ways confronted the two major shifts occurring within the broader American culture: the arrival of a distinct youth culture was most prominently addressed by Youth for Christ, and Young Life focused on the new attitude toward relationships within society that was allowing for greater choice in the realms of friendship, sexuality and intimacy.

"Ten years of depression followed by six years of wartime austerity left the nation in a mood starved for an opportunity for public gatherings."[21] Youth for Christ offered adolescents this opportunity. Youth for Christ was born from the leadership of Jack Wyrtzen, a dynamic preacher and organizer. Wyrtzen had the vision of organizing Saturday night rallies in New York's Times Square and broadcasting them across the country on "WHN, one of America's most powerful independent radio stations."[22] Within five years Wyrtzen was packing the largest venues in New York (20,000 in Madison Square Garden) and calling them "Youth for Christ Rallies." From the success of the Saturday night rallies in New York similar Youth for Christ rallies sprung up across the nation, building to their climax with 1944's "Victory Rally" at Soldiers Field in Chicago, where thirty thousand adolescents came to celebrate the American war effort and hear the gospel presented.

---

[20]"Liberated from denominational constraints, evangelicalism has turned loose its women and men of entrepreneurial bent upon America's spiritual problems. The movement's decentralized arrangement has encouraged people with a unique vision to tailor innovative outreach methods to specific groups of people in specific circumstances" (ibid.).

[21]Mark Senter, *The Coming Revolution in Youth Ministry* (Wheaton, Ill.: Victor, 1992), p. 42.

[22]Ibid., p. 114.

The youth rally fused together exactly what was most desired by the new evangelicals, who had resurrected themselves from the ashes of fundamentalism: a biblical faith that was fully engaged in American life. These rallies in many ways were the birth of the new evangelical movement; they not only produced and popularized Billy Graham and others but also poignantly presented evangelicalism's new mission of engaged orthodoxy.[23] As Joel Carpenter says, "Youth for Christ thus became the spearhead of a postwar evangelistic thrust and the first dramatic sign that American evangelicals were 'coming in from the cold.' "[24]

The success of these rallies, however, must be seen in light of the new power of the youth subculture brought on by modernization. The rallies' young organizers presented the gospel in the language and style of cool as determined by the youth subculture familiar to themselves.[25] Carpenter explains, "They emulated the entertainment world's stars and restyled gospel music to the 'swing' and 'sweet' sounds then popular. And like the radio newsmen, their messages were fast-paced, filled with late-breaking bulletins, and breathlessly urgent."[26] The rally, then, was not only about listening to the preacher but also swaying to the popular (sounding) music and hearing from contemporary sports and war celebrities. The success of Youth for Christ can be seen in its ability to capitalize on late 40s, early 50s unified youth culture. By presenting cool youth-centered events, the organizers of the rallies could be confident that most adolescents in a particular high school would want to participate and therefore be accessible to hear the gospel.

---

[23]"Youth for Christ was one of the most striking early signs of a rising new evangelical movement, which has remained a prominent factor in American life since then. By the late 1940s, rallies had grown to over one thousand in number, with an estimated weekly attendance of one million people: Youth for Christ evangelists had preached by then in forty-six countries" (Joel Carpenter, "Youth for Christ and the New Evangelicals," in *Reckoning with the Past: Historical Essays on American Evangelicalism from the Institute for the Study of American Evangelicals,* ed. D. G. Hart [Grand Rapids: Baker, 1995], p. 356).

[24]Ibid.

[25]Evangelicals at the local level had already been involved in reaching out to and providing shelter for teenagers, D. G. Hart notes. In major cities (e.g., New York, Boston, Philadelphia, Detroit, Chicago) leaders of evangelical churches actively pursued teenagers, packaging their brand of Protestantism "in the idiom of popular culture." The long-ranging impact of these men is evident in the staying power of the evangelical subculture throughout their era. They made it, as Hart puts it, "fun to be an evangelical" (Hart, *That Old-Time Religion,* p. 78).

[26]Carpenter, "Youth for Christ and the New Evangelicals," p. 363.

Yet while the youth rallies could provide cool events in a popular nationalistic flavor, they could not provide the one thing adolescents desired most: intimacy through self-chosen relationships. This inability soon deflated the Saturday night rally, leading to its cultural insignificance by the late 1950s. But another organization was ready to step in and provide what the Youth for Christ rally could not. This organization is Young Life.

The creation and implementation of the Young Life Campaign actually preceded the formation of Youth for Christ.[27] But the organization's early days, though important, were unknown to most Americans. Young Life's origins in southwestern suburban life, away from the big cities of New York and Chicago, as well as its focus on one-on-one contact, kept it out of the national limelight, which city-to-city, thousand-person rallies tended to attract. Yet by the 1950s the growth of Young Life could not be ignored. Not only were Young Life clubs popping up in high schools across the country, but the organization was also investing in large and expensive real-estate ventures that would become high-end youth resorts for its camping ministry.[28]

Young Life was created from the vision and energy of Jim Rayburn. Rayburn was the son of a fundamentalist evangelist who traveled from town to town in the Southwest, preaching. Rayburn would reluctantly follow his father into the family business. Yet, frustrated in his own evangelistic mission in New Mexico and Arizona, Rayburn decided to rectify things by attending seminary. While at Dallas Theological Seminary Rayburn began working at a local Presbyterian church. He was told by the pastor that his responsibility would be youth, but not the youth of the church. "The minister explained, 'I'm not particularly worried about the kids who are in. They're safe, and as far as they're concerned I don't need your services. To you I entrust the crowd of teen-agers who stay away from church.

---

[27]Youth for Christ was created officially in 1945 by Torrey Johnson; Young Life's creation was in 1941.

[28]Char Meredith explains the justification for the high quality of the camp experience: "In a day when lean-tos, tent houses, and meager surroundings were synonymous with most Christian conference grounds, Jim believed in excellence. Anyone who was part of the early work remembers the sound of Jim's concern, 'Who started the idea that Christians ought to have camp in tents? We talk about the King of kings; let's act like He's in charge! We're going to have the classiest camps in the country' " (*It's a Sin to Bore a Kid: The Story of Young Life* [Waco, Tex.: Word, 1978], p. 46).

The center of your widespread parish will be the local high school.'"[29] With those words, in 1938 the evangelistic mission of Young Life was born. Young Life was the first ministry to turn its energies directly to the educational institution born from modernization, the high school.

Rayburn soon discovered that getting modern teenagers to participate in his planned programs was easier said than done. Following the school-club movement of late 1940s and 1950s, where students participated in particular interest groups (e.g., sports, math, science, etc.), Rayburn organized his own Bible club after school hours. But to his disappointment only a few students participated. Clearly, in the eyes of adolescent ringleaders his event was not cool. Rayburn decided that the only way to get students to come to his event was to invite them personally.[30] After striking up a conversation about sports, music or fashion (about the distinct youth culture) in the adolescent's own environment, Rayburn would invite the student to participate in his event.[31] To Rayburn's surprise they often came and brought their friends. He discovered that by his relational contact with adolescents he could "win the right" of their participation in his event. In the same vein, the better he connected with them, the more receptive they were to his evangelistic message. By being in relationship with adolescents, Rayburn formed a strategy for helping them come into personal relationship with Jesus Christ. Mark Senter notes, "Rayburn's approach to youth ministry was essentially a missionary effort by Christian adults to win uncommitted high school students to a personal relationship with God through Jesus Christ."[32]

Rayburn also discovered that by becoming friends with adolescents who held the greatest cool currency in the school (the football captain, cheer-

---

[29]Émile Cailliet, *Young Life* (New York: Harper & Row, 1963), p. 11.

[30]Calliet explains, "In order to establish useful communication with these teens, therefore, Jim resolved to accept their language, preferences, peculiarities, ways of thinking, and so on; to familiarize himself with their tradition, share their values, learn to speak their vernacular, and somehow move into their understanding. A new world of possibilities opened up to him as he reassessed the task before him" (ibid., p. 13).

[31]"Perhaps the best-known contribution of Rayburn's Young Life Campaign was its emphasis on 'winning the right to be heard' by secular high school students. By this slogan Young Lifers meant they needed to gain the friendship and respect of students before expecting them to listen to the claims of Christ. This had to be done on the young person's own turf—football games and practices, high schooler's hangouts such as soda fountains, school events and, when permitted by school authorities, the high school cafeteria" (Senter, *Coming Revolution in Youth Ministry*, p. 126).

[32]Ibid., p. 125.

leaders, etc.), adolescents with less cool currency would follow them to Rayburn's events. Unbeknownst to himself, Rayburn had discovered the power of the self-chosen relationship in a modernized world. By using the adolescent's search for intimacy in relationships of their own design, Rayburn could lead them through a relationship with himself into a relationship with Jesus Christ. But to do this Rayburn himself had to accrue a currency of cool by incarnating himself within the distinct youth culture and receiving cool capital from the most popular students. Émile Cailliet explains Rayburn's and Young Life's philosophy: "Once the leaders that students look up to for orientation have been won over, there is no limit to the Young Life worker's outreach. The most hardened youngsters are drawn in and are sooner or later bound to come face to face with the Christ and his claims on their life."[33]

Rayburn's theological justification for this approach to ministry is the incarnation of Jesus Christ. Because God, in the person of Jesus Christ, had entered a foreign cosmos to save it from destruction, so Rayburn (and Young Life leaders after him) entered a foreign world of youth culture to save it for Christ.[34] Using the incarnation as a pattern, an example of how ministry could be done, Rayburn positioned the incarnation as ministerial justification (rather than theological explication) of ministry.[35] Because of this perspective, relational ministry to this day is infused with this understanding of the incarnation as solely a pattern for ministry.[36]

The genius of Young Life is its ability to connect with the adolescent at his or her place of most vulnerable need in a modernized world, the self-chosen relationship. Cailliet shows the organization's commitment to and use of the self-chosen relationship: "We come to the basic appeal of Young

---

[33]Cailliet, *Young Life*, p. 63. Merideth states, "If you can interest the leaders in the school, other kids will follow" (*It's a Sin to Bore a Kid*, p. 21).

[34]Cailliet places the theology of Young Life within the discussion of a seeking God, which he believes is biblical motif of the New Testament. This seeking God becomes incarnate to reach people according Cailliet's articulation of Rayburn's theological position (see Cailliet, "A New Testament Pattern," *Young Life*).

[35]The word *pattern* is problematic as I will elicit in the following chapters.

[36]This is not to say that some have not done deep theological reflection on the practice of relational/incarnational ministry. Darrell Guder, now at Princeton Theological Seminary, and Jack Fortin, now at Luther Seminary, both while working for Young Life developed an in-depth theology of relational/incarnational ministry. While their perspective influenced many individual youth workers, it unfortunately did not permeate the larger currents of the practice.

Life: the opportunity of genuine friendship implied in 'friendship evangelism.' Like all great achievements, friendship is an incarnation. It is noteworthy that the first step on the path to conversion in Young Life circles is the apprehension of Christ as a friend."[37]

Before 1940 such a ministry strategy would be unneeded, as the self-chosen relationship did not yet exist with the same intensity. But with the loss of obligatory relationships due to the modernizing of the family, local community and society, as well as the effects of what Peter Berger has called "technical rationality" (i.e., using the logic of corporate bureaucracy to set terms for personal associations), self-chosen relationships became the only location for intimacy. Char Meredith, a Young Life biographer, observes: "Looking back now, it is easy to see that Young Life was fitting into an increasingly fast-paced society that was starving for the personal touch. This formation of friendships, this contact work that they were doing, had been given them to fill a great void in the lives of people."[38]

The success of Young Life's relational model of ministry was vast throughout the 1950s, 1960s and well into the 1970s. Astonishingly, there were no large conferences, rock festivals or larger-than-life personalities. Rather, every element of the ministry served the organization's singular strategy, offering intimacy through self-chosen relationships. As youth ministry moved into the 1960s and beyond, the model of relational ministry became "the" approach, the prominent model of ministry. With the simple strategic use of relationships, Young Life had become the leader of youth ministry.

1960-2000

Maybe it was the transition from black-and-white TV to color, but at least in my mind the 1960s seem very different from the 1950s. It feels as if the difference was not only the black-and-white television but also our black-and-white cultural conceptions. The 1950s may have nostalgically felt like paradise, but paradise won by painting the world and its problems black and white. It was in the mid-1960s that our black-and-white world was

---

[37]Cailliet, *Young Life*, p. 48.
[38]Meredith, *It's a Sin to Bore a Kid*, p. 61.

ruptured by a psychedelic wave of colors. The stiff world of the idyllic 1950s was cracked by a revolution from within its midst. People, most especially young people (teenagers), recognized that this monochromatic world was no paradise. In place of a black-and-white utopia arose a world of hyper-technological change, political skepticism and sexual revolution.

Adolescence. By the 1960s high schools were so entrenched within American society that it became hard to recall a time when it was not "the" location of American young people. But life inside the high school was beginning to change. The captains of cool were slowly losing their monopoly, and consumer culture was providing more choices in music, fashion and film. Hence, cool was defined subjectively by individuals. The football star may still have held the most esteem (cool) within the school and especially in the local community. But other adolescents, who defined themselves in opposition to popular "jocks," were also being seen as cool (at least to some adolescents). Long-haired rebels who smoked and played guitar soon made some girls swoon and won some guys' admiration. The distinct youth culture had fragmented.

Within the ethos of American life the nationalistic conservatism of the 1950s was abruptly wrestled into submission by the mid-1960s. All that had been held sacred (the flag, the faith, the family and the child) was churned by racial inequality, the Vietnam War, feminism, a sexual revolution and a drug-using youth counterculture. The government, religion and teenagers could no longer be trusted.

The technical rationality brought forth by modernization between 1940 and 1960 now burrowed itself deeper under the skin of American society, leading to a kind of consumer rationality whereby people encountered both institutions and individuals with consumeristic expectations. Service and quality became the expectations of adolescents and adults alike for their friendships, churches and youth ministries.

The fragmentation of youth culture was not the effect of consumer culture alone however, but was also fueled by the need for intimacy provided by the self-chosen relationship. Many adolescents in the 1970s, 1980s and 1990s decided it was a waste of energy to conglomerate cool; rather it was more advantageous to be concerned with a smaller group where one could stop chasing intimacy and start experiencing it. The high school students of the 1950s could pursue self-chosen relationships knowing that if it was not achieved the family was still capable of providing intimacy. Yet with the breakdown of the family structure and the escalation of cultural pluralism in the latter part of the twentieth century, seeking intimacy in the lotto of cool became too risky. Popularity was still the goal of the adolescent; without it no one would chance contact in the self-chosen relationship. But now popularity was a diversified label. Many adolescents still dreamed of being the most popular (because the most popular person controlled his or her own self-chosen relationship des-tiny), but this was allocated to only a fantasy of teen movies.

By the mid-1960s the adolescent was not only in his or her own youth culture but, it seemed, on his or her own planet. With the escalation of consumerism, the unified youth culture had fragmented into a hundred subcultures. Now parents and adults had to work not only to understand the distinct youth subculture but also its new subcultures. Most of the youth subcultures were antagonistic toward mainstream adult culture, making them not only confusing to but also repulsive for parents.

The momentum of youth culture's fragmentation into multiple subcul-tures came from the desire for intimacy in the self-chosen relationship. Yet the consumer culture provided distinct marks and labels (hippies, metal heads, punks, nerds, skaters, etc.) that allowed the adolescent diversifica-tion to take its unique shape. While adolescents, like adults, had an ex-panded view of the planet and its inhabitants in this period, they turned further inward into smaller cohorts to form distinction within plurality.

By the mid-1990s some began to wonder if the modern construction of adolescence had not become, in Max Weber's terms, an "iron cage," which young people entered but could never leave.[39] In a global world with plural choice, a small tribe-like community became essential to survival. Without this group youth are left intimacy-starved as connections in self-chosen re-

---

[39]Friedrich Schweitzer writes about the lengthening of adolescence: "Adolescence tends to stretch out more and more—with postadolescence as a new stage of the life cycle or just with young people not leaving adolescence behind" (*The Postmodern Life Cycle* [St. Louis: Chalice Press, 2004], p. 49). He continues, "Adolescence is no longer a well-defined period of transition with the task of preparing people for adulthood. Rather, adolescence has become a period of life in its own right. It has extended toward childhood and toward adulthood, thus turning into a protracted span of ten, fifteen, or even twenty years. Adolescence has become an ill-defined age with no clear beginning and without a clear end" (ibid., p. 55).

lationships become more and more difficult in a world of confrontational diversity and technical-consumeristic rationality.

American evangelicalism. With the breakdown of trust in authorities due to president John F. Kennedy's assassination, Vietnam, Watergate and social movements opposing the oppressive structures of society, American culture became skeptical of the benevolence of organized religion. In the place of a conservative ethos a national liberalism arose that desired openness and tolerance over rules and "oughts." The swelling of America's cultural liberal bent caused alarm for evangelicals. They had seen this story played out before; only forty years before conservative Protestantism had lost its voice in American culture. This time it would not go down without a fight. To counter the open pluralism that began to dominate America in the late 1960s and 1970s, evangelicals became involved in political organizations, hoping that, with the help of "godly" politicians, they could stand against the anti-evangelical (or what they called "anti-American") elements in the larger culture.

The deeper entrenchment of American culture in pluralistic openness led evangelicals to see American culture as hostile to their commitments. As D. G. Hart explains:

> The United States entered a new phase of cultural history in which Protestantism no longer yielded a common sense of purpose and set of standards as it once had. The resurgence of evangelicals in America . . . can be explained chiefly as a reaction to this situation. . . . [T]he change in America, from a Protestant to a post-Protestant society, made evangelicals appear to many as old-fashioned, if not a little obnoxious.[40]

This hostile interpretation deepened evangelical subcultural identity. Yet, unlike the fundamentalists of 1920s and 1930s, evangelicals chose to confront (and try to overcome) the hostile culture with two interconnected strategies.

First, continuing the successful evangelical use of the self-chosen relationship from the 1950s, evangelicals sought to mobilize individuals to befriend and convert others within the hostile culture. It was believed that with enough relational contact through the self-chosen relationship evangelicals could turn the tide of American culture. This strategy made com-

---

[40]Hart, *That Old-Time Religion in Modern America*, p. 147.

plete sense from a consumerist perspective. If evangelicals could sell enough individuals on the benefits of conservative Protestantism, its stock would soar and in turn the stock of the hostile pluralistic culture would plummet. Individual evangelicals were then encouraged to be sales reps for God and the evangelical faith.

If this sales strategy was to work, evangelicals would need an actual product to present to individuals. The local congregation, with its dynamic preaching, teaching, activities and music became that product. By providing for consumers' needs evangelicals believed that individuals would be more willing to allow them to provide for their spiritual needs. "As a result, the line dividing evangelicalism as a form of entertainment and a means of gaining new converts had become harder and harder to detect."[41] Christian faith, then, was an individual free-will choice that was presented through the self-chosen relationship.

The second strategy that evangelicals used to confront hostile culture was mobilizing individuals for political action. The goal of such groups (e.g., the Moral Majority) was to move individual evangelical Christians to convince Washington powerbrokers that it was advantageous for them to heed the concerns of evangelicals. The issues evangelicals stood behind (which they believed were under attack by a hostile culture) were individual moral choice issues like abortion, prayer in pubic school and creationist education. The danger of the new "liberal" attitudes and behaviors, from an evangelical perspective, was not only their immorality but also their threat to families. Evangelicals believed that the open pluralism of the last decades of the twentieth century was dangerous to their children.[42] But the greater danger was culture's penchant to subvert parental authority. Evan-

---

[41]Ibid., p. 190.

[42]The sexual revolution of the 1960s and 1970s was not simply a moral degradation of society in the eyes of evangelical leaders; according to D. G. Hart, it had far-reaching implications for how evangelicals would raise their families and propagate their values. Chastity and marriage were called into question by the relaxed sexual standards of the era, and the cultural understanding of femininity and childbearing "directly challenged the cult of domesticity" that characterized born-again Protestant culture (ibid., p. 150). Along with these perceived threats to the evangelical family came a rethinking of public education that threatened to sideline aspects of child development considered sacred by most practicing evangelicals. The Supreme Court ruling against the practice of prayer and Bible reading at the beginning of the school day was interpreted as anti-religious bias on the part of educators and many politicians. Evangelicals began to wonder whether the United States was any longer "a suitable place for rearing children" (p. 15).

gelicals mobilized politically to protect their rights to educate their own children in a conservative Protestant ethos. Yet this would take a cultural conversion because evangelicals were not willing to separate themselves or their children from culture. Evangelicals held that culture needed to be remodeled to support evangelical domestic desires.

If an individual politician could present him- or herself as godly (by supporting these evangelical concerns and speaking candidly about a faith commitment), then evangelical political coalitions would provide large blocs of votes. Evangelicals, then, tended to focus on individual moral choice and family values rather than larger structural issues (and evils) that affected individuals and families alike. Evangelicals believed that when people choose to act morally, society is less hostile, evangelical faith is secure and evangelical children are safe. To meet this goal it was necessary to elect "godly" politicians, but it was also vital that individuals participate by "selling" others, through personal testimony, on the value and importance of making an evangelical commitment. In this ethos, relational ministry offered a fragmented and consumer-driven adolescent culture with a chance to be in relationship with adult conservative Protestants who could steer them clear of the pitfalls of the hostile culture and fortify them in their subcultural identity.

Age-specific ministry to youth. Influential parachurch organizations continued to dominate age-specific ministry to youth throughout the 1960s and into the 1970s. But things were slowly changing. Young pastors were revisioning local congregations, working to make them more culturally relevant and therefore attractive within the religious marketplace. One important initiative that many evangelical congregations turned to was hiring a full-time youth worker. This often young, dynamic person, usually male, was solely responsible for the care, education and, most important, evangelization of the teenagers in his or her congregation and community.[43] The investments needed to hire and maintain such a person on the church staff were well worth the cost. Many parents feared the effects the

---

[43]This is not to say that the turn to local congregations was the end of parachurch youth ministry. Rather, many parachurch ministries continued to operate (though never at the staggering numerical success of the 1950s-1970s), and others were created to help network and train youth workers working in local congregations. The best example of this is Youth Specialties, a for-profit organization

moral and spiritual decay brought forth by a hostile, pluralized culture. The youth pastor, who was perceived as culturally relevant (cool), provided a conservative Protestant influence, which parents believed adolescents were not finding at school or in other institutions in the community. To find cool conservative Protestants who were interested and skilled at ministering to adolescents, local congregations began raiding parachurch staffs. Young Life and Youth for Christ workers were happy to take guaranteed salaries and be free from fundraising for a living.[44]

The new youth pastor was encouraged to implement the new church ministry in the same fashion as his or her former parachurch ministry. The relationship focus of many of the parachurch youth ministries in 1940s and 1950s slowly metastasized in the bones of youth ministry. The experts using the self-chosen relationship for ministerial gain were now practicing their expertise not beyond (or alongside) but within the church.[45] As the youth culture became increasingly fragmented, the relational forms of ministry that many of these youth workers had learned in their parachurch days were seen as advantageous in their new ecclesial setting. The model allowed them to enter intimate friendship groups through a relationship with church-attending youth. In a perceived hostile culture where adoles-

---

created to help church-based youth workers do effective ministry. It is not coincidental that this organization was formed in a time of the rise of consumer culture. Senter explains the birth of Youth Specialties, pointing, unknowingly, to their connection with the arrival of a hyper-consumer culture brought forth by globalization: "Though Yaconelli and Rice fought against the inconsistencies of the religious establishment continually, their visibility, creativity, and insights in the world of youth ministry soon made them part of a newly established power block. 'Ideas' were their commodities. Consistently, they generated programming ideas which had once been the domain of the para-church agencies and marketed them to every church youth worker in the nation. The net effect was a rapid and broad distribution of para-church ministry technology to people who were more interested in methods for keeping students active in youth group than in full-cycle discipleship" (*Coming Revolution in Youth Ministry*, p. 149).

[44]It was not only conservative Protestant churches who were hiring parachurch staff but also mainline congregations, leading the relational-ministry model deeper into the consciousness of youth ministry.

[45]These same individuals who made their way from the parachurch giants to the local congregation became the veteran youth workers who were given college and seminary positions as youth ministry professors. As youth ministry moved toward its professionalization, with its own degrees given by institutions of higher learning, these veteran youth works taught their students the same model of relational/incarnational ministry that they themselves had been using for years. This model of ministry then became "the" method of a successful youth worker in evangelical churches. Yet what is problematic is that few of these educators, because they lacked rigorous theological education themselves, looked critically at the practice to ensure that it had a dynamic theological foundation rather than merely being a cultural reaction to modernization.

cents encountered pluralism at every turn, relationship-centered ministries provided the greatest opportunity for impact.

Because adolescents were no longer chasing cool, the youth pastor could no longer focus only on the captains of cool but needed instead to exert relational energy into the distinct groups in the diversified youth culture.

But the church youth ministry had a silver bullet that the parachurch ministry did not—a large program budget. This large budget allowed the youth pastor to use consumer culture as a lubricant for relational contact. These large, cool, expensive youth-ministry-program productions served the purpose of relationship-building between the youth worker and adolescents (as well as the Christian teenager and his or her non-Christian friends). By providing cool outings and programs, the youth worker could present him- or herself as a "with it" and trustworthy individual with whom to risk relational contact. Both the larger evangelical congregation (through aerobics classes, contemporary music and lively preaching) as well as the youth ministry (through concerts, trips and exciting youth rooms) used their large budgets not for direct service to people, families and society, but rather as incentive for individuals to risk relational contact.

3

Our Relational Motivations

A few years ago my wife and I were blessed with the opportunity to spend six months traveling the world together. The first two and a half months we stayed in Melbourne, Australia. We had decided that we would not spend these few months as tourists but would do our best to actually live in Melbourne. So we moved into a flat on the campus of a local college, got our produce at the farmer's market and weekly took the tram to visit the local grocery store. We spent evenings in conversation with theology students, professors and locals (or, I must admit, watching Australian television). Yet the more that we tried to live normally in this new place, the more we realized how different from home this place was and how different we were from it. (And this was Australia, an Anglo-British colony, clearly there are far more different places, but this proves my point.)

After one evening my wife said matter-of-factly but profoundly, "I guess before coming here I never really thought about how much American culture impacted the way I saw the world and myself, but being here I can see for the first time how my culture has shaped me."

Spending these six months away changed both of us. Taking the time to look at the culture that was so much a part of us that we barely acknowledged its existence forced us into deep contemplation about who we were and who we wanted to be. The experience freed us from simply continuing with practices and perspectives that we had absorbed but may have been anchored more on the routines of culture than on truth.

In this chapter we will do much the same with relational ministry. We will examine how evangelical culture has determined the way we practice incarnational youth ministry. By stepping back and seeing culture's impact we will be more prepared to reimagine the practice (part two).

I have placed the sociological material presented in this chapter in conversation with interviews and focus groups I did with five youth workers and their adolescent students in Southern California. Choosing Southern California for both its influential evangelical population and organizations (Saddleback Church, Youth Specialties, Fuller Theological Seminary) as well as the pluralistic context of Los Angeles, I was introduced to five youth ministries recognized for doing the best relational/incarnational youth ministry in the area.[1] The objective of these interviews and focus groups was to investigate whether the sociological theories of the use of relationships in evangelicalism affected the practice of relational youth ministry, and to see whether those doing the best relational ministry were using relationships as a tool of influence or understanding relationships as the place of God's presence.[2]

CULTURAL ANALYSIS

A sociology of religion: American evangelicalism. Research partners Christian Smith and Michael Emerson present their sociological findings on American evangelicalism in two books, Smith's *American Evangelicalism: Embattled and Thriving* and Smith and Emerson's *Divided by Faith*. Both Smith and Emerson present evangelicalism as a vibrant, thriving cohort in American religious life. On six important sociological measures (adher-

---

[1]In order to identify five youth ministries to study I contacted the traditional hub of evangelical scholarship, Fuller Theological Seminary. Their Center for the Study of Youth and Family Ministry provided me with a list of local youth ministries that understood their approach as relational/incarnational. Each one was judged (by the people at Fuller) to be an exemplary case. In other words, these youth ministries and youth pastors were considered to be doing the best relational ministry to the knowledge of Fuller. Fuller's knowledge of youth ministries is expansive. From the inception of the their Center for the Study of Youth and Family Ministry they have been working with thousands of youth pastors on the West Coast and beyond.

[2]To read a fuller presentation of each congregation and methodology of the project see www.faithfulpractices.org/root.htm . Click the PDF file link for "A View from the Ground: Relational Incarnational Ministry in Five Evangelical Youth Ministries."

ence to beliefs, salience of faith, robustness of faith, group participation, commitment to mission, and retention and recruitment of members) they detected evangelicals to be faring much better than other religious groups.[3] Overall, Smith and Emerson found that evangelicalism is doing quite well within today's religious and cultural pluralism. As a matter of fact, Smith and Emerson hold that evangelicalism is not only faring well within a pluralistic culture, but is thriving because of it.[4]

Smith shows how this is possible through what he calls "subcultural identity theory." He explains: "A religious movement that unites both clear cultural distinction and intense social engagement will be capable of thriving in a pluralistic, modern society. Far from undermining the strength of religion . . . cultural pluralism and social differentiation of modern society provide an environment within which well-adapted religious traditions— like evangelicalism—can flourish."[5]

The roots of evangelical success in a pluralistic environment rest in the movement's historical commitment (see chaps. 1-2) to a position of "engaged orthodoxy."[6] Evangelicalism has striven since 1940 to uphold biblical Christianity while avoiding sectarianism by directly engaging American culture. For evangelicals the terms *engaged* and *orthodoxy* cannot be split. Evangelicals are not merely a group engaged in American culture and also holding to orthodox beliefs. Rather, evangelical engagement is engendered from its desire to protect the legitimacy of orthodox belief in a modernized and globalized world. Therefore, evangelicalism finds itself in a continual relationship of conflict and tension with and threatened by

---

[3]See Christian Smith's *American Evangelicalism: Embattled and Thriving* (Chicago: University of Chicago Press, 1998), p. 21

[4]Smith's theory is in direct contrast to Peter Berger and his student James Davison Hunter's "enclave theory," which argues that evangelicals are surviving because of their distance from the forces of modernity. Smith asserts, "Evangelicalism . . . is very much engaged in struggle with the institutions, values, and thought-processes of the pluralistic modern world" (ibid., p. 75).

[5]Ibid., p. 90.

[6]This term has been coined by Smith and Emerson. They explain, "By engaged orthodoxy we mean taking the conservative faith beyond the boundaries of the evangelical subculture, and engaging the larger culture and society. To be sure, for many non-evangelical Americans, this is controversial. For evangelicals, however, this engaged orthodoxy is part of their very identity. Evangelicals want their traditional faith to offer solutions to pressing social problems" (Michael Emerson and Christian Smith, *Divided by Faith: Evangelical Religion and the Problem of Race in America* [Oxford: Oxford University Press, 2000], p. 3).

American society. This has sociologically provided evangelicalism with strong margins that delineate who is adversarial and who is adherent, providing evangelicalism with a robust subcultural identity. Evangelicalism's tense relationship with pluralistic modernity has provided its adherents with both a distinct identity (belonging) and a strong purpose (meaning)—both of which are difficult to discover and maintain within the pluralism of a globalized world.

Evangelicalism provides its members with identity and purpose "by drawing symbolic boundaries [or margins] that create distinction between themselves and relevant out-groups."[7] Evangelicalism, then, can thrive within a pluralistic landscape not only because it is willing to engage others in encounters of tension and conflict but, more importantly, because it is willing to label them as outsiders. "Evangelicals know who and what they are and are not. They . . . define the frontiers beyond which one is not an evangelical."[8]

Through the recognition of an in-group and out-group, evangelicals fortify their boundary by providing a distinct identity ("You are a true Christian") as well as purpose ("We must help people come to this understanding and keep the world from abandoning the truth"). Because of evangelicalism's emphasis on personal choice, the in-group/out-group labeling is not seen by them to be divisive. Anyone is free to be part of the in-group; all he or she has to do is personally except Jesus as Savior.

Evangelicals classify the out-group and all other nonevangelical cultural constructions as "the world." Evangelicals recognize that they cannot escape the world; it surrounds them at work, in their neighborhoods, in politics and in the media (to name a few places). While being *in* the world is unavoidable, the evangelical believer nevertheless can be not *of* the world; he or she can avoid deriving identity and purpose from it. However, the godly life is not only about resisting the temptations of the world but working within the world for its redemption. Smith found that for most evangelicals, the way to labor for the world's redemption is by modeling a Christian alternative, which individuals have already internalized through

---

[7]Smith, *American Evangelicalism*, p. 91.
[8]Ibid., p. 124.

their distinct subcultural identity. Smith describes an "on-stage" mentality among evangelicals; many reported a sense of near-constant scrutiny by onlookers testing the validity of their "witness."[9]

In the evangelical youth ministries I studied in Southern California I found the subcultural identity theory to be functioning. All five youth pastors (although to varying degrees) understood the culture to be a hostile place. Gary, a veteran youth worker for an Assemblies of God congregation, saw culture as forcefully acidic to Christian commitment. Discussing the public school's distribution of pink bracelets for gay rights, Gary asserted, "The Bible says in the last days, evil will be considered good and good will be considered evil. And now if you don't wear the bracelets, they consider you to be intolerant, to be a bad person."

James, the senior high pastor of a megachurch, and Matt, a young pastor of a nondenominational GenX congregation, embraced culture but admitted that its impact on the youth they worked with was ultimately detrimental. Both expressed the spiritual possibilities within pop culture, but then concluded their comments by discussing its negative influence on adolescents. Matt stated, "But on the flip side, if our focus is Christian formation, the environment's probably not as welcoming to that." James's words are almost identical: "I would say those things [movies, music, TV] are shaping kids in the negative; I would say it's pretty influential."

Randy, an ex-Young Life area director who now serves a congregation in Sierra Madre, spoke passionately about the negative effects of consumerism, sex and pornography. He had a deeply prophetic stance against American culture. But this did not stop him from critically engaging it; rather, Randy admitted that other cultures are even more acidic to Christian faith. When they were asked to rate the culture on a scale of one to five (one being supportive to Christian faith, five being destructive to Christian faith) all youth pastors except Gary (he rated it a 5) rated it with deep qualifications. But in the end most saw it as a three. This shows their engaged orthodoxy in action. While all admitted to culture's acidic impact, they nevertheless were not willing to abandon it.

The adolescents I interviewed were not so nuanced in their thinking.

---

[9]Ibid., p. 135.

All believed that culture was not only hostile to their faith but was violently attacking it. Many spoke of the abuse and ridicule they received at school, from both staff and students, for their Christian commitments. Of course, some of the intense rhetoric and emotions within the adolescents' response must be understood alongside their developmental location. For many, their Christian faith served as the pillar on which they built their identity. When it was attacked, it no doubt felt violent. A girl from Gary's Assembly of God congregation, referring to her school, stated, "They're all, like, specifically against Christianity. Like, they'll accept any other religion except Christianity, and they say that, like, I am a Nazi and I'm a communist bastard because I believe in that. That's what they call me!"[10]

Not only do they perceive school as hostile but also pop culture. All adolescents spoke of the negative portrayals of sex, body image and cussing in movies, music, and TV. Many of the adolescents felt that the culture's demand for tolerance was intolerant to their faith. "They say, 'Well, be tolerant of gays,' and 'Be tolerant of this,' and I can't be intolerant. And everywhere you go, sex is advertised. Every song you hear on the radio, every commercial—it's like, sex." While feeling more battered by the currents of culture, they were nevertheless, like their youth pastors, unwilling to abandon culture but rather saw themselves in a constant conflict of participation and distinction.

The in-group/out-group dichotomy was also present. When Sam, an associate pastor who oversees the youth ministry in a Presbyterian church in an Orange County beach town, was asked about culture, he presented a balanced, reasoned response. He explained, "We saw it in the election didn't we? They sure didn't like it when Bush was saying he was a Christian; they were pretty hostile to that. But on the other hand, you see the Christian community stepping up when it comes to the tsunami, and people appreciate that." While this response was balanced, it rested on an in-group/out-group hermeneutic. Sam discussed the impact of culture by contrasting the Christian community with "them" (nonevangeli-

---

[10]I found comments like this in almost every focus group. Adolescents felt as if other religions were given latitude to express themselves, but not Christianity. Smith's research supports this; he noted the evangelical perception of a double-standard, with the common complaint being that "every . . . perspective existing is given fair time and a fair hearing, except the Christian perspective" (ibid., p. 140).

cals). This was seen even more pointedly in the adolescents in Sam's youth group. A high school senior stated, "The thing is, outside of this group, everyone else at our school is not a Christian." "Yeah," another girl continued, "like, some of my friends are like quasi-Christian. Like, you know, they go to Catholic mass and stuff, but I don't think they have the same kind of relationship with God that we do." The in-group/out-group dichotomy ran deeply throughout all five of the youth ministries I examined. It was so strong that even those trying to avoid it often fell back into such categories.

When it comes to engaging culture, almost all youth pastors and adolescents repeated the phrase "We must be in the world but not of it." It seemed that for both youth pastors and youth the key to engagement is critical discernment, parsing out what is and is not acceptable for Christians (the in-group). One adolescent called this his "crap filter." He explained, "I know that the Holy Spirit will instill certain things in me that filter out what is bad, so you can be in that environment and still not be of it. It's really hard, really hard, but it's possible. You have to have a firm foundation first, before you try that, or else you will be eaten alive."

When asked how a Christian can influence culture, the common response from both adolescents and their youth pastors was that culture is influenced through positive, oppositional modeling, that is, by being a good example (by influence).[11] Both the adolescents and the youth pastors supported Smith's assertion that evangelicals see themselves as on stage, always being watched. All agreed that direct, up-front sharing of the gospel was not as effective as modeling a positive and meaningful Christian commitment in a hostile world.

These responses reveal that these youth ministries were operating from something like Smith's subcultural identity theory. Thus it is logical to as-

---

[11]Smith discusses this "good example"-centered perspective in his own research around the issue of hell. "Of all the evangelical views concerning hell, however, the one most consistently expressed was that belief in hell most appropriately prompts one to pray for nonbelievers, live one's own life as a good Christian example, and occasionally try to slip in a word of encouragement to nonbelievers to consider faith in Christ. One Baptist man from South Carolina, for instance, said, 'It goes back to trying to be a model before them. I'm probably not—well I know I'm not—as active in trying to quote scripture and convince them of their sin as I ought to be. But my way is trying to hopefully let them see a little bit of Jesus in me' " (Christian Smith, *Christian America? What Evangelicals Really Want* [Berkeley: University of California Press, 2002], p. 86).

sume that subcultural identity was at work beneath their understanding and practice of relational ministry. Each of these youth ministries saw culture as hostile, operated from an in-group/out-group dichotomy and desired to engage culture through positive modeling of being in but not of culture. It may be that the subcultural identity of evangelicals was setting terms for incarnational practice. To see if this is so we must look deeper at what cultural tools evangelicals use to engage culture and provide their members with identity and purpose.[12]

Evangelical cultural tool kit. Smith and Emerson explicate what they see as the evangelical tool kit. It is from this tool kit, they assert, that evangelicals construct strategies of action which set the terms for their cultural engagement. While evangelicals may be aware of a number of possible ways to interact with the cultural world, the tools in their kit set the parameters for what they will actually do, for what actions they will take.[13] This is not to diminish the importance of theology, indeed their tool kit is shaped by their theology. According to Smith, the tool kit itself stems from the normative moral codes of individuals and groups. Therefore, it is from evangelicalism's lived theology; (this can be very different from academic or formal theology) that the tools are taken and then used in the contexts of ministry. A lived theology is how a faith community or group organizes its life. This organization may reveal more clearly than its stated theology its beliefs about divine revelation (God's action in the world). I must emphasize that lived theology, theology molded from the heat and pressure of practical experience in the world, forms the cultural tools that are used.[14]

The most utilized evangelical tools, according to Smith and Emerson,

---

[12]The phrase *cultural tools* or *cultural tool kit* comes from sociologist Ann Swidler and her important article "Culture in Action" and book *The Talk of Love*. For further discussion on the relevance of her position for this topic see Andrew Root, "A Critical and Constructive Examination of Relational/Incarnational Youth Ministry: Toward a Social Relational Practical Theology" (Ph.D. diss., Princeton Theological Seminary, 2005), chap. 2.

[13]Emerson explains this, "Ann Swidler argues that the cultural tool kit limits possibilities or, put another way, in providing a set of tools, it withholds them. For those we interviewed, the tools of individualism and personal relationships limited their ability either to recognize institutional problems or to acknowledge them as important" (*Divided by Faith*, p. 80).

[14]"Evangelicals . . . negotiate their lives with cultural tool kits containing a mix of tools that do not necessarily all work neatly together. Contemporary evangelicals are heirs of diverse historical and theological legacies, the multiple strands of which provide logics, impulses, and inclinations that often contradict each other" (Smith, *Christian America?* p. 189).

are what they call relationalism, free-will individualism and antistructural-ism. Evangelicalism has perceived itself as living in unsettled times since the nineteenth century. This has allowed for a great entrepreneurial spirit within evangelical ministry. Therefore its tool kit has been in a continual state of flux. But through all its innovations (see chaps. 1-2), relationalism, free-will individualism and antistructuralism have remained, due to the strategic benefits they provide evangelical engagement.

I observed all three of these operating in the youth ministries I studied. But in my research, relationalism was the tool most favored (for logical rea-sons; I was studying relational ministry). While free-will individualism and antistructuralism were present, they were often conditioned by rela-tionalism. For this reason I will give the greatest amount of attention to the cultural tool of relatonalism, without neglecting the others as they are laid out by Smith and Emerson.

Personal-influence relationalism. Smith and Emerson explain that the cultural tool of relationalism is born from the evangelical theological com-mitment to a personal relationship with Jesus Christ. Evangelicals believe that their personal relational connection distinguishes them from both nonevangelicals and non-Christians. This relationship is so central that it provides the core of the evangelical universe. Personal relationships guide strategies of engagement in all other structures of culture, whether in the family, government or larger society.[15] The goal behind this relationalism is what Smith calls "personal influence strategy." "This method is strategic in that it consciously attempts to influence others. It is relational in that it relies on interpersonal relationships as the primary medium of influence."[16]

Through personal connections and positive example, evangelicals be-lieve they can influence others toward the benefits and joys of being in a

---

[15]"Evangelicals see the relationalist strategy of social influence as part of what sets themselves apart from others." This strong self-understanding, Smith observes, allows evangelicals to distinguish themselves from fundamentalists, who are understood to be separatist and judgmental, and also to distinguish themselves from mainline and liberal Protestants, who are thought to place too much em-phasis on social activism and political process. Non-Christians, in the eyes of evangelicals, are naive in their trust in secular education and government programs. By concentrating their energies on per-sonal relationships as the venue for societal change, evangelicals understand themselves as allowing God to do transformative work through the relationship, and ultimately to change the culture "from the inside-out" (Smith, *American Evangelicalism*, p. 188).

[16]Smith, *Christian America?* p. 45.

personal relationship with Jesus. The advantage of this strategy, according to evangelicals, is not only changed lives but also changed social structures—"societal transformation" by "sheer demonstrational power."

This is so, Smith explains, because the lens of relationalism can reduce the complexities of a socially complex structure into mere matters of relational breakdown. Evangelical analysis and solutions to multidimensional social issues, according to Smith, are often one-dimensional.[17]

Of course, a one-size-fits-all relational approach to societal problems has also placed certain constraints on evangelicals when it comes to thinking through "useful responses and solutions to social, economic, political, and cultural problems." This is so, Smith explains, "because evangelicals typically view the complex, socially structured social world, which they hope to influence, through the simplifying lens of relationalism, they routinely offer one-dimensional analyses and solutions for multidimensional social issues and problems."[18] Ultimately it is believed "that people make wrong choices if they are not in proper relational contexts with others."[19] Emerson explains further, "Because evangelicals distrust basic human propensities (as the result of the doctrine of original sin), they view humans, if not rooted in proper interpersonal contexts, as tending to make wrong choices. For this reason, for evangelicals, relationalism moves to the forefront."[20] For adolescents living in a hostile culture, this is especially true.

It is no wonder then that relational ministry would be born from the cultural engagement of evangelicalism (as we saw in chaps. 1-2). As a model for youth ministry it was seen as an effective approach to reach adolescents in the modern world (due to the arrival of the self-chosen relationship), and it reinforced evangelical subcultural identity.

In the youth ministries I examined in Southern California, the strategy of personal influence relationalism was strikingly present. Gary, the veteran Assemblies of God youth pastor, was fully cemented in an instrumental relationalism. He believed relationships completely served the means of personal influence. This could be seen both in Gary's understanding of

---

[17]Smith, *American Evangelicalism*, p. 188.
[18]Ibid., p. 189.
[19]Emerson, *Divided by Faith*, p. 101.
[20]Ibid., p. 77.

why he operated from a relational model and the goals he hoped this model would meet. This approach to ministry is useful because it allowed Gary to break through adolescent skepticism and ambivalence; he explained, "Teenagers don't respect you because you're an adult, you have to earn it first." The relationships Gary built earned him the right to influence adolescents. Consistent with Smith and Emerson's findings, the influence Gary most desired to achieve through his relationships with youth was a personal relationship with Jesus. Gary stated clearly, "The goal in my relationship with you is that you come to know Jesus Christ as your personal Savior. That's why I am here. I tell kids . . . the whole purpose for my relationship with you is to make sure that you make heaven your home." The personal influence relationalism of Gary's ministry had greatly affected the adolescents in his group. In answering how Christians should interact with the world around them, more specifically with non-Christian friends, one girl stated, "If you have friends who aren't Christians, you have to make sure that you are a good influence on them rather than them being a bad influence on you. So make sure that you are not changing and make sure that you are, like, changing them."

Sam, the Presbyterian pastor in the upscale Orange County beach community, also operated from instrumental relationalism, though with less rigidity than Gary. The aim of his relationally focused ministry was modeling. "The purpose of relational ministry is that they [adolescents] see an authentic and genuine relationship with Christ in you." By being in relationship with an adolescent, the adult models a personal relationship with Jesus and therefore personally influences the adolescent in a similar direction.

The personal-influence modeling of Sam's ministry had been clearly understood by his committed adolescent leaders. "I just find it's a really awesome place to build relationships with the leaders, like I have someone to look up to, someone who can set an example for me. It's just, like, so much fun to be in a no-pressure environment." This personal-influence relationalism had burrowed so deeply into adolescents at Sam's church that they now saw "being a good example" as the only way to interact with the world. "I feel, like, just living my life the way I do, and let's say we're at a party and I don't drink, that would be an example in itself, I don't feel like I have to actually say anything because I think that would turn them off more. So, I think just living your life as a Christian is an example enough for, like, non-Christian friends."

The use of personal-influence relationalism can also be spotted within Randy's congregation in the foothills community of Sierra Madre. While Randy was able at times to critically spot the conundrums of a ministry model built from this cultural tool, he nevertheless was unable to free himself from it. Randy explained that the reason that youth ministry has turned to a relational-ministry approach is because it has the greatest potential to draw and retain adolescents (to influence them). Therefore, relationships, again, like with Gary and Sam, operate as an instrument for personal influence. Randy acknowledged just this point when he said, "What is the point of the relationship if, once you have it, you don't go anywhere with it? If you don't try to influence them?" The way to influence adolescents, Randy believed, is by the adult leader's modeling. By being "Jesus with skin on" through the relationship Randy believes adolescents will be affected.

The adolescents at Randy's church gave his relational ministry approach much credit for their Christian commitment. The element they found most helpful was the example Randy set for them. One adolescent explained, "Randy totally leads by example. He really exemplifies Christ. It's just an encouragement for me to see him, so that's what I want to model my life after, because he's just such an amazing person."

By Randy's personal relationship with these adolescents, he embodied the strategy built from the tool of relationalism; through a relationship of modeling the benefits of Christian living he had influenced them to seek this for themselves. Because of this, these adolescents (like all the adolescents that participated in focus groups from the five churches) saw example modeling as the best (and for many, the only) way to engage the world.[21]

Both James, at the megachurch in Pasadena, and Matt, at the nondenominational GenX congregation, were critical of many of the results of a

---

[21]"Most ordinary evangelicals believe and invest in building personal relationships, sharing their faith politely, setting good examples, and hoping the unbelieving world will see the truth and voluntarily respond with a changed heart" (Smith, *Christian America?* p. 49). I found this to also be true among evangelical adolescents. All saw the best, and really only, way to engage the world was through being a good example.

ministry that uses relationships for influence, but in the end both remained committed to a personal-influence, instrumental perspective. James explained that the goal of incarnational ministry was spiritual formation, but when pushed to explain what he meant, James fell immediately into the personal-influence strategy. He stated, "A kid will not look more like Jesus without the relationship. I'm convinced if they're going to follow Jesus in college and the rest of their lives, it will be because they had a relationship with one another and with somebody older who modeled that." Matt also seemed at first glance to avoid instrumental relationalism; he stated that the needs of adolescents should set the terms for youth ministry. Matt explained that one of these needs was a relationship with an adult. When asked what this relationship looked like, Matt's answer fell back into the personal-influence strategy; he explained that relationships provided adult modeling that could lead students into deeper committed faith and participation in the congregation.

While each of these youth pastors operated from an instrumental personal-influence strategy of relationalism, all, excluding Gary, were able for a time to escape its strictures. For instance, Sam, in Orange County, discussed how he allowed adolescents to see him in the weakness of his suffering as he grieved a personal tragedy. Randy, in Sierra Madre, described incarnational ministry as stemming from the anthropological need for relationships. He explained that relational ministry must be built on unconditional love, with the hope that adolescents themselves would become incarnational agents who engaged the world with compassion and care. This is quite different than personal-influence strategy. James, at the megachurch in Pasadena, discussed the need to create open spaces where mutual conversations could occur. And Matt, at the GenX congregation, asserted that relational ministry isn't so much an approach as an outflowing "of our convictions and theology of how church should be done."

Though these assertions were poignant and empowering to each of the youth pastors, they did not ultimately free any of them from operating from a position of instrumental relationalism, where the purpose of relationships is influence. Such comments revealed that they had the desire to free themselves from the rut of relationalism, and they could hypothetically imagine an incarnational approach not dependent on it. But in the end the tool of relationalism set the terms for their strategy of action, for their ministerial practice.

According to Smith and Emerson, however, relationalism is not the only tool in the evangelical tool kit. They also discuss free-will individualism and antistructuralism.

Free-will individualism and antistructuralism. For relationalism to exist with the power that it does, the tools of free-will individualism and antistructuralism must support it. Relationalism's personal-influence strategy is dependent on the belief that individuals are free to choose their own destiny. Evangelicals are committed to the American notion, Smith explains, that "individuals should not be coerced by social institutions . . . and particularly not on personal matters; that freedom to pursue individual happiness is a paramount good."[22] Therefore, evangelicals are not only free-will individualists but also antistructuralists, believing that individuals are supposed to be ultimately unconstrained to choose whatever life they desire. For the personal-influence strategy to work, it must be held that individuals are autonomous and completely free to make their own choices. Therefore the structures of society (political systems, bureaucratic agencies, even such things as racism and poverty) cannot threaten one's free choice.[23]

But this free-will individualism does not mean individuals are free from all accountability. Rather, as Emerson and Smith explain, "individuals do not simply have the freewill to make the choices they deem best. They are individually accountable to family, other people, and, most important, to God for their freely made choices."[24] Because of the evangelical commitment to an individualism that is free from all obligations but the accountability of relationships, they have little motivation to attend to issues of injustice in the structures of society. Rather, it is believed that through good relationships in families and larger society, social and systemic problems will take care of themselves. "Absent from their accounts is the idea that

---

[22]Smith, *American Evangelicalism*, p. 212.

[23]"Evangelicals typically underscored the uniqueness of each individual's involvement. As one man from a Congregational church said, 'Each person has to decide in his own heart what he or she ought to do'" (ibid., p. 199).

[24]Emerson and Smith, *Divided by Faith*, p. 77.

poor relationships might be shaped by social structures, such as laws, the ways institutions operate, or forms of segregation."[25]

Nevertheless, this does not mean that evangelicals avoid confrontation with the structures of society through political or institutional avenues. Rather, it means that even in this environment evangelicals often operate with a relationalistic perspective that believes the objective of political action is to clear the way for better relationships within society, uninhabited by its structures. Despite Smith's explicit attempt to steer the discussion beyond "interpersonal relationships and individual morality," evangelical respondents continued to form their responses around "merely improving the morality of individual businesspeople through the influence of personal associations."[26]

Free-will individualism and antistructuralism were apparent in the five evangelical youth ministries of Southern California. When I asked Gary, whose Assemblies of God congregation is located in San Gabriel Valley of Los Angeles, about his ministry to the neighborhood kids in his city, he mentioned that he had seen little direct change in their lives. When I inquired why he thought this might be, he explained that for most of them it had to do with the difficulty of their home life. As he unpacked this he mentioned no larger structural issues like poverty, welfare or unemployment. Rather, for Gary, the problem centered on poor relationships—like absent fathers or divorced parents—which had no connection to poverty, welfare and unemployment. Gary wasn't alone in this; no youth pastor I interviewed mentioned any structural issues as affecting the adolescents or communities in which they lived and worked.

Because of their commitment to a relational-based youth ministry of influence, they all placed a great amount of attention on the individual worship experience. The individual actions of raising hands, clapping and tearful singing have become the markers of serious faith. When discussing what they liked about their youth ministry, many adolescents mentioned "worship" (meaning time of singing), because of the way it made them feel.

In the same way, all the youth ministries participated in mission/service

---

[25]Ibid., p. 78.
[26]Smith, *American Evangelicalism*, p. 203.

trips. While it could be imagined that such a practice would lead to greater acknowledgment of the structures in society, it appeared that most often such trips reinforced antistructuralist individualism. When I asked adolescents about their experience, most expressed personal feelings of fulfillment. Mission trips were important for how they made the individual adolescents feel. Many of the mission trips were built around an antistructuralist, relational focus. Youth pastors and youth explained that the purpose of their mission trips was to build relationships and give back "because we have been given so much." All the mission trips focused on benevolent volunteerism, and none were directed toward countercultural activism.

All of the youth pastors' understanding of individualism and antistructuralism operated in the same way that it did for personal-influence relationalism. For a short time they were able to escape the rut only to fall back into it again. James, at the megachurch in Pasadena, is the best example. He passionately explained how his church, a large, white affluent congregation, was trying to recover a neighborhood presence within a poor Hispanic and African American neighborhood. James's initiatives for change surrounded structural realities. He explained the need for the church to hire staff that racially represents the neighborhood, and for a mandate that all church staff become bilingual. But when James was asked what would be tangible signs of progress, he did not mention things like economic improvement, a lower crime rate, improved schools or even more adolescents from the neighborhood attending college. Rather, James's hope was relational. He wanted to see neighborhood and church youth form such strong relationships with each other that one day they would be in each other's weddings.

SUMMARY AND CONCLUSION

Throughout this chapter we have seen relational ministry as an evangelical strategy designed to address the many challenges confronting evangelicalism in a modernized and globalized world. In chapters one and two we reviewed the historical forces that birthed relational ministry. From this vantage point we noticed that the practice of incarnational ministry has had more to do with cultural location than attention to the continued ministry of God in human history (theology). We saw that evangelicals give attention to context but rarely allow theology to enter into the conversation at a deep level. This means that relationships have been used for cultural leverage (getting adolescents to believe or obey) rather than as the concrete location of God's action in the world.

To examine how evangelical youth ministries are using a relational or incarnational approach we looked at evangelical youth ministries through the research of Christian Smith and Michael Emerson. Examining Smith's subcultural identity theory, we saw that the engaged orthodoxy of evangelicalism allows it to thrive in a pluralistic culture. By engaging culture through strong categories of in-group and out-group, evangelicalism provides its members with both identity and purpose.

The evangelical subcultural identity was strong in the youth ministries I examined. Both youth pastors and adolescents drew bold lines between believers and nonbelievers, church and world. To explain how evangelicals are engaging culture, Smith and Emerson present three essential evangelical cultural tools: relationalism, free-will individualism and antistructuralism. I believe that the contemporary practice of relational ministry is constructed from the tools of evangelical engagement, the most prominent of which is relationalism. According to Smith, and verified in my research, this tool is implemented through interpersonal relationships that model the benefits of Christian living. Relationships then are used as an instrument of personal influence. The tools of free-will individualism and antistructuralism are mobilized to support relationalism and its unquestioned objective of conversion through personal influence. This chapter brings us to the unavoidable conclusion that relational youth ministry is highly dependent on the use of influence for its effectiveness.

So what? What is the problem with having a little influence? What is wrong with youth ministry being used to influence adolescents toward some end? Is a focus on influence really life-threatening for relational youth ministry?

Suddenly, in the middle of an argument with my wife, I realized that influence was not only threatening but deadly to relational ministry. We were newly married and my wife was experiencing a crisis in her family of origin. As she shared her deep feelings of pain and suffering I found myself trying to fix things; I tried to influence her to see something this way or that, hoping it would solve her problems. Finally, exasperated with me, she stated in deep frustration, "Stop! Stop trying to fix things! I don't need you to fix this, I need you to be with me in it. Relationships aren't about making things better, they're about being together in each other's most difficult and painful moments; that's love."

Her words were transformative, not only to our relationship but also to how I understood incarnational youth ministry. I had been working so hard to make things better by influencing adolescents to do this or do that, to believe this or know that. But in the process I was more concerned with their decision, behavior or commitment than with their broken humanity that desired someone to share in their deepest sufferings through relationship. When I tried to influence them, I had neither the patience nor the vision to truly share in their suffering, to make it my own and to join my own broken humanity with theirs. I was so busy making assertions about heaven that I refused to see and accompany them in the darkness of their personal hells.

I have realized that a youth ministry of influence has very little to do with the incarnation. The incarnation is about a God who desires to be with us so fully that God becomes one of us in order to join us in the darkness of our personal and corporate hells. God became human to be with and for us, not to simply influence us toward this or that end. (This would actually be the heresy of docetism, which believed that Jesus only *appeared to be* human in order to influence us.) Evangelical youth ministry risks making relationships only about personal influence, worship about individualistic emotion, and mission about volunteeristic service that helps adolescents feel good but does not confront the systems affecting those needing help. The incarnation is not about influence but accompaniment. It is not about getting us right but bearing what is wrong with us, so that we might find that we are only right in the embrace of a God who loves so much to be with us!

Do our relational youth ministries take this form? Is the practice constructed more from this theological confession or from our conflicts within culture? Part one of this book asserts that too often it has been the latter. We need to reimagine the practice from a theological perspective so that it is no longer a tool for cultural assimilation through personal influence but the concrete location of Christ's presence in the world. Christ calls me into self-giving, suffering love for the adolescent, with no pretense or agenda. The theological construction is the objective of part two.

PART TWO

Every fall a flier found its way onto our church's bulletin. It was usually pink and had a large heart on one of the corners. It read, "The last Sunday of September will be Healthy Heart Sunday!" On Healthy Heart Sunday doctors, nurses and health professionals from the local medical center came to our church to provide free diagnostic health examinations. They would check blood pressure, do cholesterol tests and prescreen for diabetes.

But they actually did more. When they discovered a high reading from one or more of their tests, they would sit with the person and construct a lifestyle plan that included diet, exercise and medications. And it was all free! The idea, of course, was that more good could be done by going into the community to help people than by waiting for people to become patients.

In part one, I have argued that relational youth ministry has a high level of "influence" coursing through its bloodstream. If action is not taken, then such youth ministry runs the great danger of being more about cultural conflict than the concrete presence of God in the world. Therefore, part one is the warning of a physician: Your cholesterol is too high. You need to adjust your lifestyle or risk a massive heart attack.

It is *not* too late to reimagine relational youth ministry apart from personal influence. Part two does this very thing. It provides a new, healthier lifestyle plan. Because influence in relational youth ministry runs the risk of being more about cultural conflict than the concrete presence of God, this rethinking, this new lifestyle plan, must be constructed theologically. Therefore, part two will reexamine incarnational theology (or a theology of relationship) in light of the ministerial practice of relational youth ministry.

The health professionals that constructed new lifestyle plans for people at my church focused on three elements: diet, exercise and medication. In *The Word Made Flesh: Towards an Incarnational Missiology*, Australian missiologist Ross Langmead provides three elements for a theologically rich relational/incarnational ministry. He explains, "incarnational mission can be seen as (1) following Jesus as the pattern for mission, (2) participating in Christ's risen presence as the power for mission, and (3) joining God's cosmic mission of enfleshment in which God's self-embodying dynamic is evident from the beginning of creation."[1]

These three elements will guide our theological rethinking of relational youth ministry. Langmead has outlined a broad theological and biblical justification for incarnational ministry understood from the action of God in the world. I will not add to this. Rather, in chapters five, six and seven I will turn to one theologian who has been an inspiration to many Christians (both evangelical and nonevangelical) throughout the second half of the twentieth century, Dietrich Bonhoeffer.

Bonhoeffer's theology is particularly relevant for a theological rethinking of relational ministry because as a whole it is constructed around the threefold perspective Langmead has presented. A number of scholars have asserted that Bonhoeffer's theology asks three broad questions: Who is Jesus Christ? Where is Jesus Christ? What then shall we do? Bonhoeffer's questions have direct correlation with Langmead's threefold understanding of incarnational mission.[2]

In chapter four we will take up the question Who is Jesus Christ? Chapter five will address the question Where is Jesus Christ? And chapter six, What then shall we do? While these chapters will draw from Bonhoeffer, we will not lose our direct focus on relational youth ministry. Rather, each of these chapters will take the form of a conversation between a health professional and patient. While it is essential that the patient understand how certain fats

---

[1]Ross Langmead, *The Word Made Flesh* (Dallas: University Press of America, 2004), p. 8.

[2]"During his theological studies Bonhoeffer was already beginning to struggle with the question that increasingly dominated his theological reflection: 'Who is Jesus Christ?' For Bonhoeffer this always implied the further question, 'Where do we encounter him concretely?' " (John De Gruchey, *Bonhoeffer and South Africa: Theology in Dialogue* [Grand Rapids: Eerdmans, 1984], p. 20). These questions shaped Ray Anderson's course "Dietrich Bonhoeffer: Theology and Life" at Fuller Theological Seminary.

Threefold Understanding of Incarnational Mission	Three Questions of Bonhoeffer's Theology
1. Jesus as a pattern for mission ⟶	1. Who is Jesus Christ?
2. Participation in the presence of Jesus ⟶	2. Where is Jesus Christ?
3. Joining God's mission of enfleshment ⟶	3. What then shall we do? (ethics)

Figure 4.1. Langmead's three criteria and Bonhoeffer's three questions

affect the body or what the side effects of a medication might be, this theory must be placed in connection to the patient's life situation. Therefore, chapters five, six and seven will unpack Bonhoeffer's theology and then immediately apply it to the issue at hand, relationships in youth ministry.

Interacting with these three questions will reorient our fundamental understanding of the practice of relational/incarnational youth ministry. Instead of seeing relationships as leverage for personal influence, we will discover, through the theology of Bonhoeffer, a better understanding of both the incarnation and human-to-human relationships in what I have called "place-sharing" *(Stellvertretung)*.

When Bonhoeffer says that one person shall become another's place-sharer *(Stellvertreter)*, he means that one person must stand in the place of the other, acting fully on his or her behalf, like a noble leader for her citizens, a thoughtful teacher for his students or a loving father for his children. Place-sharing takes shape when we place ourself fully in the reality of the other, refusing to turn away even from its darkest horror. Just as Jesus incarnate, crucified and resurrected was fully our place-sharer, so we too, as Jesus' disciples, must ourselves become place-sharers, suffering with and for young people.

I believe that when we rethink and reimage relational youth ministry as place-sharing, we will be able to see human-to-human relationships as the location of God's presence in the world, and therefore honor the broken and yet beautiful humanity of adolescents (and ourselves!).

Chapters seven, eight and nine will focus on relationships as place-sharing and put them into action. Chapters seven and eight present a paradigm of relational transformation. This will show how human relationships of place-sharing are transformative to suffering people, and therefore it will reveal how relational ministry should be reimagined. To do this, chapters seven and eight will take a narrative shape. We will look at stories of two individuals who are transformed as another shares their place in the midst of their suffering.

Chapter nine will focus on moving incarnational ministers into engaging others within their own contexts. Turning to application, it discusses broadly how we can think about a relational youth ministry of place-sharing in our own congregations.

4

Who Is Jesus Christ?

I was in seminary when I first heard of Dietrich Bonhoeffer (1906-1945), the German Lutheran theologian and pastor. I had grown up in the Lutheran church and yet had not heard of him. But when I did, I was drawn to him like a magnet. Bonhoeffer directly uttered to me what I had known in my being for so long: life is hard, suffering is real, and life is filled with difficult choices.

I was (and still am) fascinated by how a man who confessed to be a pacifist pastor could willingly conspire to kill Hitler in the final days of WWII. What I realized then, and what is still so meaningful to me now, is that Bonhoeffer made this decision not through some moral loophole. Rather, he made this decision honestly, believing that it was the only way that he could truly (*truly* = in the imitation of Christ) share the place of those crushed by the wheels of the Nazi political machine. To Bonhoeffer, this was not a noble or innocent act, but it was a responsible one. It would be an act that would join his heart to those suffering in the deepest and darkest of hells. And Bonhoeffer believed it was the God of the cross (the crucified God, as Martin Luther had uttered) that called him this far.

In the shadow of Bonhoeffer's amazing biography it is often forgotten that he was one of the most promising theologians of his generation. As with all theologians, but most especially Bonhoeffer, it is difficult to draw a clear line between his life history and his theological thought. For Bonhoeffer, theology is constructed from within the concrete place of the theologian as he or she lives in the world, worships in the church and reads the Bible. For instance, though it is not explicitly stated, in *Discipleship* we can hear the palpable strain of frustration and fright scribbled from the hand of Bonhoeffer as the church in Germany enters a struggle (less than triumphantly, from Bonhoeffer's perspective) to maintain independence from Hitler's government *(Kirchenkampf)*. In *Ethics* we can hear the perplexed introspection of a man sorting through what must be done, and to what extent, now that he is no longer a pastor in the parish or a theologian in the classroom, but a double agent.

For Dietrich Bonhoeffer, life and theology cannot be separated; theology is constructed from within real life and existence. As we will see, Bonhoeffer came to this understanding because of his view of the person of Jesus Christ made known through the incarnation. This makes Bonhoeffer a valuable dialogue partner as we seek to construct a relational ministry that moves beyond seeing the incarnation as a tool to leverage cultural influence. Bonhoeffer is an ideal dialogue partner not only because of his theological thought on the incarnation but also because of his own relational practice of ministry with adolescents (for further discussion on this see the appendix).

To examine the potential of Bonhoeffer's theology for a reconstruction of incarnational ministry, we will explore the first of the three questions that make up Bonhoeffer's theology, Who is Jesus Christ?

WHO IS JESUS CHRIST?

Bonhoeffer writes that all theology and ministry, as well as faith itself, begins with the question *Who?* Who are you? Who is this Jesus from Nazareth? Often it is thought that theology begins with the question *How?* How is God present in Jesus? How is Jesus both divine and human? How does God atone for the world's sin in Jesus? How do I have faith in Jesus? But for Bonhoeffer, How? is a question of unbelief; it is the question of frozen theory that in the end makes no difference in the life of the individual or the world. You can answer all the above how questions and yet still not believe. You can even know how to have faith in Jesus and yet never move from knowledge to trust.

According to Bonhoeffer, How? is also the question of disobedience, because it costs me nothing. Knowing how God has atoned for the world's sin in Christ or how Jesus is both divine and human is simply knowledge—like knowing how to make pasta primavera or how to throw a curve ball. In the end it has little effect on my being, on my understanding of myself in relation to the world. In the end How? is an impersonal question; it keeps Jesus locked behind a theoretical equation. At its worst it allows me to possess Jesus; he is no longer transcendent or other, but because I know him in the "how," I can use him how I wish. He is not a person to me but my property. " 'How?' is . . . the 'serpent's question,' while 'Who?' is oriented toward transcendence and proves its asker ready to hear."[1]

Bonhoeffer explains that Who? is the question of faith; "Who are you?" asked the women at the well. Who? is the question of personal (relational) encounter. The who question acknowledges a present Christ who is calling you to join in God's mission in the world. The how question not only leads me away from the person of Christ but will ultimately lead me away from all other persons. But by encountering Christ in the Who? I am opened to the Who? of my neighbor. Clifford Green summarizes:

> If the proper question of Christology is "who is Jesus Christ?" this is a question which can only be asked to the Christ who is present. Christology is not concerned with an ideal of Christ nor with the historical influence of Christ, but with the resurrected Christ, the living God, who is really present. Furthermore, Christ is present as person not in isolation but only in relation to persons.[2]

WHY DOES THIS MATTER?

When asking the youth workers in chapter three for their theological justification for using relational youth ministry, all spoke in "how" language. With minimal nuance they explained that they did relational ministry because that is what Jesus did. Jesus became a pattern (and only a pattern, therefore foreclosing on Longhead's first element of incarnational mission) for how to do relational or incarnational ministry. They did not move be-

---

[1]Craig Slane, *Bonhoeffer as Martyr: Social Responsibility and Modern Christian Commitment* (Grand Rapids: Brazos, 2004), p. 168.
[2]Clifford Green, *Bonhoeffer: A Theology of Sociality* (Grand Rapids: Eerdmans, 1999), p. 209.

yond this pattern perspective into discussing anything about the living "who" of Jesus Christ.

When relational ministry looks to Jesus' life as a pattern for ministry and goes *no further*, it has slid into the how, and in doing so has turned from the who (we do ministry *how* Jesus did it; Jesus became incarnate, so that is *how* we do it; rather than, we go to *whom* Jesus calls us; we follow the one *who* gave his life for others). By mobilizing relational ministry from how, by stopping only at Langmead's first aspect of incarnational mission (Jesus as a pattern for mission), the who of personal encounter, of participation in the continued presence of Jesus, is squeezed out into a utilitarian pattern (Jesus did it this way so we should too) that can be duplicated but lacks the indwelling power and direction of God.

This does not mean that Jesus' ministry is not a pattern for our own ministry, but the pattern must be fueled by Who? rather than How? The pattern must be mobilized from the tutelage and direction of a present teacher who encourages and works alongside, rather than from the instructions of a step-by-step how-to book. A relational youth ministry of placesharing is practiced from the belief that Jesus is alive and active in world. This has even deeper ramifications that soon will be drawn out further. For instance, if our incarnational ministry is constructed solely from How? the goal of the practice can easily slide into figuring out how to get adolescents to participate, rather than discovering and supporting the distinct who that each adolescent is in his or her person.

If relational ministry is to move beyond its use as a cultural tool of influence, we must begin to reconceptualize the practice from the starting point of the who. But this has only helped us to know what question to ask—Who is Jesus Christ?—not what the answer might be. Bonhoeffer answers who Jesus Christ is: the incarnate, crucified and resurrected Godman. These three can never be divided; they must remain linked.

THE INCARNATE

Who is Jesus Christ? Bonhoeffer answers that he is the very incarnation of God in the world, meaning that God is in the world. The incarnation means for Bonhoeffer that there is no longer any reason to turn from the world to encounter God. Rather, God through Christ encounters humanity within creation through the humanity of Godself. The incarnation then means three things for Bonhoeffer.[3]

God has taken bodily humanity in its fullness. In taking on human form and surrendering to all that it means to be a created being (time, space and death), God reveals the depth of love and care God has for both humanity and creation as a whole. Though creation may be broken and humanity sinful, God treasures it enough to enter fully into it, to share its place. Therefore, because God has become human, all human beings find direct solidarity between their own being and God's.[4] "When the eternal Logos entered into the world and 'became flesh,' a solidarity was established between God and man at the level of actual humanity, not idealized humanity."[5]

The incarnation makes it clear that the only criteria for one to be known and loved by God is to be human. This means that the incarnation is not simply a strategy or plan God has used to rescue humanity or to influence us toward salvation. Rather, "what the incarnation reveals to us through the condescension of God to become flesh is the actual content of divine being itself."[6] God becomes incarnate in Christ not because it best meets God's goals and desires, but rather because God's heart yearns to be near to humanity. Bonhoeffer says, "It is true that all human beings as such are 'with Christ' as a consequence of the incarnation, since Jesus bears the whole of human nature."[7] Thus, through the incarnation there is a direct solidarity between human being and human being made possible by the humanity of God in Christ. Through the incarnation there is complete equality between persons. But this does not wipe away the need to confess and follow Christ, as if you could say, If all humanity is loved by God anyway, why should I love God or follow God? Rather, the followers of Christ

---

[3]These three points are taken from John Godsey, who has extracted them from Bonhoeffer's *Ethics* (see Godsey's *The Theology of Dietrich Bonhoeffer* [Philadelphia: Westminster Press, 1958], p. 270).

[4]Bonhoeffer explains further, "The incarnate one is the glorified God: 'The Word was made flesh and we beheld his glory.' God glorifies himself in man. That is the ultimate secret of the Trinity. The humanity is taken up into the Trinity. Not from all eternity, but 'from now on even unto eternity'; the trinitarian God is seen as the incarnate one. The glorification of God in the flesh is now at the same time, the glorification of man, who shall have life through eternity with the trinitarian God" (*Christ the Center* [San Francisco: HarperCollins, 1960], p. 105).

[5]Ray Anderson, *Historical Transcendence and the Reality of God* (Grand Rapids: Eerdmans, 1975), p. 253.

[6]Ray Anderson, *The Shape of Practical Theology* (Downers Grove, Ill.: InterVarsity Press, 2001), p. 115.

[7]Dietrich Bonhoeffer, *Discipleship* (Minneapolis: Fortress Press, 2001), p. 217.

are distinct not because they possess something others do not but rather because they are living directly from their encounter with (the who of) Christ, who sends them out to be led by Christ to love and serve the world.

The divine being cannot be found otherwise than in human form. The incarnation reveals that the concrete place where we encounter the *who* of God is in the nearness of our fellow sisters and brothers. But the presence of God in the nearness of the human other is hidden; Jesus' "presence is a hidden presence. This God-man, Jesus Christ, is present and contemporary in the form of the *homoioma sarkos* (likeness of the flesh), i.e., in veiled form, in the form of a stumbling block."[8] It cannot be said then that another person is God, but God is concretely present in the mystery of his or her humanity, which the incarnation calls me to love and encounter. We will explore this further in chapter five when taking up Bonhoeffer's question Where is Jesus Christ? What is important to see is that we encounter the *who* of Jesus Christ in this incognito, this hiddenness of a God in a manger.

In Jesus Christ humanity is free to be really human before God. Bonhoeffer has no room for religious mystical dreaming in which an individual strives to throw off his or her humanity and become something beyond it. Rather, for Bonhoeffer, God has created humanity to be human: even in humanity's disobedience and sin the incarnation of God within human history makes it clear that humanity is to remain human. Bonhoeffer states:

> God loves human beings. God loves the world. Not an ideal human, but human beings as they are; not an ideal world, but the real world. . . . While we exert ourselves to grow beyond our humanity, to leave the human behind us, God becomes human; and we must recognize that God wills that we be human. . . . While we distinguish between pious and godless, good and evil, noble and base, God loves real people without distinction.[9]

There is no shame in being human before God. The incarnation not only reveals God's commitment and love for humanity but also God's desire that humanity be freed from its sin and disobedience, which perverts

---

[8]Andreas Pangritz, *Karl Barth in the Theology of Dietrich Bonhoeffer* (Grand Rapids: Eerdmans, 1989), p. 138.
[9]Dietrich Bonhoeffer, *Ethics: Dietrich Bonhoeffer Works* (Minneapolis: Fortress Press, 2005), 6:84. Subsequent references to Bonhoeffer's *Ethics* refer to this source.

it into antihumanity. Our sin is not a product of our humanity, for we are created to be human with God and one another. Rather we are sinful when we deny our humanity (deny God and neighbor) and seek to live solely for ourselves, thus outside of our own humanity.[10]

The incarnation reveals that liberation can occur only through the human Jesus who lived in full obedience to the Father, and in so doing reveals what it is to be truly human. In becoming human, God brings forth both the reconciliation of humanity (be human as Jesus is human) as well as its judgment (there is no humanity outside the humanity of Jesus). In becoming human and desiring nothing other for humanity, we see the extent of God's being-for-us. It reveals that humanity "is no longer in any way isolated by [it]self, nor can [humanity] any longer be so regarded; 'in, with, and under' human reality we are encountered by the reality of God."[11]

WHY DOES THIS MATTER?

When the incarnation is discussed in connection to relational forms of youth ministry, it is often discussed as God's strategy or plan, making it possible for us to cut off the incarnation from the incarnate One. We often assume that being incarnate means being present in such a manner that we earn the leverage to influence others, as though God in heaven decided that incarnation was the best way to influence humanity. This position holds that God used God's humanity to convince people to accept God's message; it denies that the message itself *is* God's humanity. To think of the incarnation as a tool of influence is to deny the necessity of Jesus' humanity (as the heresy of docetism does; see the end of chap. 3). It would have been just as well if Jesus only appeared human—he only needed to be human *enough* to influence us. But Bonhoeffer has revealed that the incarnation is much more; it is not simply the strategy of God but the very heart of God for creation that opens the very being of God to humanity. If our humanity is to be transformed, we need a fully human God. We need a God who bears our reality and takes it fully into Godself. We need some-

---

[10]This is the view of both Augustine and Luther; both define sin as *cor curvum in se*, the heart turned in upon itself.

[11]Heinrich Ott, *Reality and Faith: The Theological Legacy of Dietrich Bonhoeffer* (Philadelphia: Fortress Press, 1972), p. 308.

one to accompany us (share our place) all the way to hell. Speaking of the incarnation as only a strategy for influence cuts free Jesus' humanity, making it possible for him to be only an idea, a logo, and not the *who* that encounters us within our human situation.[12]

The incarnation, then, is not about influence but about solidarity in common humanity, and so relational ministry should be the same. Relational ministries should avoid the temptation to use relationships to influence adolescents and instead see the mandate of the incarnation as the call to shared solidarity in common humanity. The adolescent is already ontologically (in their being) what God desires him or her to be: human. Relational ministry is about helping adolescents be authentic human beings as determined by the incarnate, human Christ. It joins them in full solidarity with humanity, helping them avoid and oppose that which dehumanizes, and helping them claim their humanity in worship and service of the human God.

Too often relational youth ministries stop with the incarnation, never discussing how the cross and resurrection affect ministry. Incarnation without cross and resurrection may be interesting and inspiring, but it's not the gospel. Humanity needs more than simple solidarity; it needs solidarity that leads toward transformation. Therefore, relational ministry must not only reflect on Christ's incarnation but also on the cross and resurrection. Todd Speidell states, "The incarnation testifies to God's identifying presence with us. . . . The cross presupposes the incarnation. . . . The incarnation leads to the cross, for God identifies with sinners from birth unto death, healing 'all that lies between.' "[13]

THE CRUCIFIED

When asking, "Who is Jesus Christ?" we cannot stop at incarnation, but

---

[12]Bonhoeffer explains the heresy of docetism: "Christ's manhood is a cloak and a veil; it is a means God uses to speak to men. But it does not belong to the essence of the matter. Jesus the man is the transparent cloak for God. This heresy is as old as Christianity itself." He continues, "One knows the deity already before he is revealed. One knows the truth already as a suprahistorical, absolute idea. When God is thought of as an idea, Christ must be understood as an appearance of this idea, but not as an individual. This heresy disregards the humanity in Christ" (*Christ the Center* [San Francisco: HarperCollins, 1960], p. 76).

[13]Todd Speidell, "Incarnational Social Ethics," in *Incarnational Ministry: The Presence of Christ in Church, Society, and Family,* ed. Christian Kettler and Todd Speidell (Colorado Springs: Helmers & Howard, 1990), p. 142.

in the same breath we must answer that Jesus Christ is the human God suffering and dying publicly on a piece of wood. For Bonhoeffer the cross means two things.

"The whole world has become godless by its rejection of Jesus Christ." God may be in the world, loving the world from God's very being, but as a penalty for God's love and solidarity the world in its radical penchant toward antihumanity violently placed the only true human on a dehumanizing cross of hatred and isolation.[14] The cross reveals the depravity of humanity cut free from the humanity of God. Therefore the cross is the wrath and judgment of God against humanity, which God takes upon Godself in Jesus Christ. Bonhoeffer states it this way:

> In the judgment of wrath on the cross, God had to deliver all of humanity unto death so that God alone would be righteous. God's righteousness is revealed in the death of Jesus Christ. The death of Jesus Christ is the place where God has supplied the gracious proof of God's own righteousness, the only place from that moment on where God's righteousness dwells.

Bonhoeffer fleshes out the ramification of this: "Now Christ has assumed our flesh, and in his body has borne our sin onto the wood of the cross (1 Peter 2.24). What happened to him happened to all of us. He took part in our life and in our dying, and thus we can take part in his life and his dying."[15]

Therefore, the incarnate, loving Lord suffers to the point of death. There is no avoiding this; to be near to the broken and sinful humanity of another is to expose your own humanity to the suffering of hurt, insult and violence. *To be incarnate is to be crucified.* (I doubt that many of us say this to our adult leaders!) The cross reveals a God who suffers, who is not disgusted by human deformity, disgrace or disease, but takes this upon God's person to suffer fully. Bonhoeffer says, "This love of God for the world does not withdraw from reality into noble souls detached from the world, but experiences and suffers the reality of the world at its worst."[16]

"The godless world bears at the same time the mark of reconciliation as the

---

[14]The subhead is a quotation from Godsey, *Theology of Dietrich Bonhoeffer*, p. 270.
[15]Bonhoeffer, *Discipleship*, p. 271.
[16]Bonhoeffer, *Ethics*, p. 83.

free ordinance of God." Suffering is truly suffering; it is as horrible and painful as can be imagined.[17] But it is shared suffering; to know God is to know Jesus Christ who suffers the severity of being human.[18] To encounter the *who* of God is to encounter God on the cross; it is to join God as God takes upon the suffering of the world as God's ministry to the world.[19] There is no reconciliation without the cross, and there is no possibility of being human as God intends by circumventing suffering. Bonhoeffer explains, "What happened to and in Christ has happened to all of us. Only as judged by God can human beings live before God; only the crucified human being is at peace with God. In the figure of the crucified, human beings recognize and find themselves."[20] We must follow the incarnate Christ as he walks into the center of the world's suffering. When we turn from the suffering of the world, we turn from the cross, which is to turn from the Christ who is found on the cross.

WHY DOES THIS MATTER?

By stopping at incarnation, we have been slow to see that relational youth ministry is about suffering with adolescents. Perhaps suffering has been ignored because relational ministry has been more about personal influence than place-sharing. And if we practice incarnational ministry from a posture of personal influence, then when an adolescent's suffering is present, an incarnational connection may not be made because the relationship becomes much more complicated and success more difficult to measure. For

---

[17]The subhead is from Godsey, *Theology of Dietrich Bonhoeffer*, p. 270.

[18]Bonhoeffer's thoughts at this point and throughout his theology are inspired greatly by Martin Luther's theology of the cross. Alistar McGrath presents the core of Luther's position: "The Christian is forced, by the very existence of the crucified Christ, to make a momentous decision. Either he will seek God elsewhere, or he will make the cross itself the foundation and criterion of his thought about God. The 'crucified God'—to use Luther's daring phrase—is not merely the foundation of the Christian faith, but is also the key to a proper understanding of the nature of God" (*Luther's Theology of the Cross* [Malden, Mass.: Blackwell, 1985], p. 1).

[19]"God is particularly known through suffering. . . . A fundamental contention of the *theologia crucis* is not merely that God is known through suffering (whether that of Christ or of the individual), but that God makes himself known through suffering. For Luther, God is active in this matter, rather than passive, in that suffering and temptation are seen as means by which man is brought to God" (ibid., p. 151). See also Douglas John Hall's work for an implication of the theology of the cross. (*The Cross In Our Context: Jesus and the Suffering World* [Minneapolis: Fortress, 2003] and *Thinking the Faith: Christian Theology in a North American Context* [Minneapolis: Fortress, 1991])

[20]Bonhoeffer, *Ethics*, p. 88.

example, in the midst of an adolescent's struggle with depression, a youth worker may see the depression as too overwhelming for the ministry to bear; it is likely to sidetrack the ministry and block the possibility for personal influence toward conversion. But this in fact is exactly where ministry lies; for in coming close to the adolescent's suffering, we come close to the cross of Christ. We must see that from a theological understanding of incarnation, suffering and relational ministry are inseparable. Following the incarnate Christ means following him to the cross. " 'Suffering with God' is part of the Christian vocation to discipleship. This entails a willingness to accept life's sufferings together with the joys, trusting fully in God and cooperating with Christ in the work of reconciling people to God and to each other by living an other-centered life of service."[21]

And it is not only entering *into* the suffering of the adolescent that is demanded but also suffering *from* the adolescent. We go to the adolescent knowing that we may be abused and ridiculed by him or her. "To participate in the ministry of God, we must proceed into solidarity and oneness with others, standing where our suffering and guilty neighbor stands, as God through Christ has stood and died buried alongside us, only thus revealing who God is."[22]

We should never assert, "This is not what I signed up for." Suffering with and at the hand of those to whom we minister is the call of the incarnation and crucifixion.[23] "As the Gospels make plain, to follow Jesus is to take up the cross and follow Jesus in conflict, suffering and possible loss of life for his sake (Mk 8:27-9:8, Mt 16:24-28, Lk 9:23-27, Jn 12:23-26)."[24] Bonhoeffer reminds us, "Just as Christ is only Christ as one who suffers and is rejected, so a disciple is a disciple only in suffering and being rejected, thereby participating in crucifixion. Discipleship as allegiance to

---

[21]Geoffrey Kelly, *Liberating Faith: Bonhoeffer's Message for Today* (Minneapolis: Augsburg, 1984), p. 79.

[22]Alan Lewis, "Unmaking Idolatries: Vocation in the *Ecclesia Crucis*," in *Incarnational Ministry: The Presence of Christ in Church, Society, and Family*, ed. Christian Kettler and Todd Speidell (Colorado Springs: Helmers & Howard, 1990), p. 112.

[23]"Conformation with Christ the Crucified requires readiness to absorb the suffering of others into one's own being—for Christ suffered 'the reality of the world in all its hardness'—and a commensurate acceptance of the world's fury so that when at last it exhausts itself, forgiveness might be offered and reconciliation accomplished" (Slane, *Bonhoeffer as Martyr* [Grand Rapids: Brazos, 2004], p. 190).

[24]Ross Langmead, *The Word Made Flesh* (Dallas: University Press of America, 2004), p. 51.

the person of Jesus Christ places the follower under the law of Christ, that is, under the cross."[25]

Our unwillingness to acknowledge the cross as well as the incarnation has deceived us into believing that we are justified in neglecting a great many adolescents who at first respond to our offers of friendship with ridicule and aggressive rejection. The incarnation has made these very children our responsibility, our beloved brothers and sisters. We must reach out to their humanity even if it means the suffering of our own humanity, for this is the way of the cross.[26] It may be that the reason they don't trust our offers of friendship is that they intuitively know that we are not willing to see, hear and accompany them in their deepest suffering. We have offered them trips to Disneyland, silly games and "cool" youth rooms, not companionship in their darkest nights, their scariest of hells.

THE RESURRECTED

If we stopped our understanding of the *who* of Jesus Christ at incarnation and crucifixion, we would surrender humanity as well as creation to fatalism. In the incarnation we see God's commitment to and love for humanity in the solidarity of God's own humanity. In the crucifixion we see God's willingness to suffer from humanity for humanity, bearing the suffering and death of estranged humanity, bearing the wrath and judgment of God for humanity. Stopping here would no doubt leave us with an intriguing story, but as Paul has said, we are still left in our sin. With no resurrection, there is no possibility for human transformation, meaning there is no hope for humanity to be freed from its destiny of estrangement and isolation revealed most fully in death. Rather, Bonhoeffer reminds us that the Incarnate and Crucified is the resurrected One. Christ as resurrected means two things for Bonhoeffer.

---

[25]Bonhoeffer, *Discipleship*, p. 85.

[26]"As Christ bears our burdens, so we are to bear the burden of our sisters and brothers. The law of Christ, which must be fulfilled, is to bear the cross. The burden of a sister or brother, which I have to bear, is not only his or her external fate, manner, and temperament; rather, it is in the deepest sense his or her sin. . . . In this way Jesus' call to bear the cross places all who follow him in the community of forgiveness of sins. Forgiving sins is the Christ-suffering required of his disciples. It is required of all Christians" (ibid., p. 88).

"Jesus Christ has overcome sin and death and . . . he is the living Lord to whom all power is given in heaven and on earth." Jesus is not only the suffering God but the Lord who has overcome the world by committing himself fully to it, suffering its estrangement unto death and then conquering its death with life.[27] Jesus Christ is Lord of creation and the true human because he has overcome the enemy of humanity, death. For it is the threat of death that deceives humanity into the sinful acts of self-determination and self-preservation, which lead to dehumanization and consequently estrangement from God, neighbor and creation.[28]

By suffering the fullness of death as a human and overcoming it, Jesus has bent humanity back to God, overcoming and transforming in his own person the human penchant for self-determination and self-preservation. Bonhoeffer states, "The love of God became the death of death and the life of this human being. In Jesus Christ, the one who became human was crucified and is risen; humanity has become new. What happened to Christ has happened for all, for he was the human being. The new human being has been created."[29] The resurrected humanity of Christ has crushed the lie that to be human is to be free from God and neighbor. In nearness to Jesus' resurrected humanity we are transformed to live free for God and others, proclaiming in our transformation the future of all creation.[30]

In our time, freedom is often understood through the lens of consumerism; with the right airline ticket or cell phone plan I'm free to go anywhere or talk to anyone anytime. Freedom *from* is the freedom to do whatever we want. However, if we are honest we will admit that consumeristic freedom feels more like captivity after a while. What Bonhoeffer desires here is that we see freedom not from a consumeristic but from a theological

---

[27]The subhead quotation is from Godsey, *Theology of Dietrich Bonhoeffer*, p. 270.

[28]Again this *cor curvum in se* of Augustine and Luther.

[29]Bonhoeffer, *Ethics*, p. 91.

[30]Here Bonhoeffer speaks more in-depth: "The earthly body of Jesus is crucified and dies. In his death the new humanity is also crucified and dies with him. Since Christ had not taken on an individual human being, but rather human 'form', sinful flesh, human 'nature', all that he bore, therefore, suffers and dies with him. All our infirmities and all our sin he bears to the cross. It is we who are crucified with him and who die with him. True, Christ's earthly body dies, but only to rise again from death as an incorruptible, transfigured body. It is the same body—the tomb was, indeed, empty!—and yet it is a new body. Jesus thus brings humanity not only into death with him, but also into the resurrection. Thus even in his glorified body he still bears the humanity which he had taken on during his days on earth" (*Discipleship*, p. 216).

perspective. From a theological perspective we are freed from sin and dehumanization to be with and for God and neighbor. This then leads to Bonhoeffer's second point.

Christ resurrected also means that the empty tomb "is the setting free for life in genuine worldliness." Following the One who has overcome the cross is to be free from the fear that suffering can destroy my humanity.[31] I can face the suffering of the world, I can face the world without trepidation, for it cannot destroy me. My destiny is determined not by my suffering but by the Lord who suffers with me, encouraging me to not fear the world, for he has overcome the world in suffering love. I then can enter the world in joy and service.

WHY DOES THIS MATTER?

The resurrected Christ has two important ramifications for relational ministries. First, it affirms that the very purpose of the practice (at least from a theological perspective) is not cultural assimilation into a Christian lifestyle but being transformed by the person of Christ. Most would agree with this, but we must guard against the danger of slipping into using relational ministry for the means of program participation, camp registration or moral rehabilitation. Bonhoeffer reminds us that the incarnation is about transformation; humanity is given the power to be human solely through the resurrected God. Thus we must recognize that in the practice of incarnational ministry we are involving ourselves in a practice of transformation. But we must be reminded that transformation happens in contact with suffering, not in avoidance of it, for resurrection is made necessary by crucifixion.[32]

Second, in facing the suffering of the adolescent we must remember that we cannot be destroyed by it. We often avoid entering into the depth of another's suffering for fear that proximity to his or her suffering will destroy us. We fear that in standing too close to sexual abuse, family neglect, eating disorders and drug involvement we will be sucked into a sinkhole of anguish that will strangle our own humanity.

---

[31]The quote in the subhead is from Godsey, *Theology of Dietrich Bonhoeffer*, p. 270.

[32]"Being conformed to the Risen One means living as a new person before God—but this is life in the midst of death and righteousness in the midst of sin" (Green, *Bonhoeffer*, p. 311).

Yet Bonhoeffer reminds us that the *who* of Jesus is not only the crucified but also the resurrected. In connection to Jesus' lordship our humanity is forever secure in his own humanity no matter how frightening, dirty and stomach-turning the other's suffering might be. "Fear not because I have overcome the world" (Jn 16:33). And even in the midst of the intensity of suffering, hope can never be destroyed. Through the resurrection we are promised that suffering is not eternal, that God will not only overcome evil and pain but will end it and redeem it in the fullness and finality of God's presence. This means that youth ministry is freed to be a bold kind of ministry, not cowering from possible suffering but standing firmly with and for others no matter the depth of despair.

Bonhoeffer has answered the *who* of Jesus Christ as the incarnate, crucified and resurrected God-man. We have also seen the ramifications of this for the practice of relational ministry. What Bonhoeffer would want us to understand from this discussion is that to know Jesus Christ as the incarnate, crucified and resurrected One is to know him not as a concept but as a person, a contemporary, living person who encounters us still today.[33] Bonhoeffer next asks, "If Christ is present, not only as power, but in his person, how are we to think of this presence so that it does not violate this person?"[34]

JESUS CHRIST AS PERSON

Now that Bonhoeffer has answered that Jesus is the incarnate, crucified and resurrected One, he would drive us deeper by reminding us again of the question Who *is* Jesus Christ? It's not, Who *was* Jesus Christ? If this were the question it would be possible to answer it in the same way: Jesus *was* the incarnate, crucified and resurrected One. But this is not the question. The question is, Who is this that encounters us (you and

---

[33]Anderson explains, "The continued presence and work of the Holy Spirit constitute the praxis of Christ's resurrection. This means that the truth of resurrection is not only the fact of a historical event but the presence and power of a resurrected person, Jesus Christ. The means by which Christ's work of making peace between humans and God does not take place through the application of methods, ideologies or even theories derived from Scripture. It is Christ himself who 'makes peace' through the praxis of his Spirit in a dialogical relationship with our truth and methods" (*Shape of Practical Theology*, p. 52).

[34]Bonhoeffer, *Christ the Center*, p. 45.

me)? Jesus is not dead but alive (he *is* resurrected and ascended), and as living person he continues in ministry, continues to be a contemporary to us in the world. As the *who* that *is* alive, he is a person. Bonhoeffer's commitment to the living, active Christ is seen in his discussion of discipleship.

> Discipleship is commitment to Christ. Because Christ exists, he must be followed. An idea about Christ, a doctrinal system, a general religious recognition of grace or forgiveness of sins does not require discipleship. In truth, it even excludes discipleship; it is inimical to it. One enters into a relationship with an idea by way of knowledge, enthusiasm, perhaps even by carrying it out, but never by personal obedient discipleship. Christianity without the living Jesus Christ remains necessarily a Christianity without discipleship; and a Christianity without discipleship is always a Christianity without Jesus Christ.[35]

Jesus Christ is not a phantom or essence, but a person that meets my very person as other. The person of Christ may be the ascended person, now in the world through his Spirit, but he nevertheless remains person, bound by his own humanity to mine.[36]

But what kind of person is he? This leads us back to the answer Bonhoeffer has just provided: he is the person who is incarnate, crucified and resurrected, true God of true God. As the kind of person who is incarnate, crucified and resurrected, we discover he is who he is alongside and for us. Jesus remains in his present person, even today, the incarnate, crucified and resurrected One. He continues as the one who is incarnate for me, crucified because of me and resurrected despite me, and he is all of this for me. This leads Bonhoeffer to assert that Jesus Christ is ontologically (in his very being as incarnate, crucified and resurrected) for me

---

[35]Bonhoeffer, *Discipleship*, p. 59.

[36]"Bonhoeffer chooses Luther as his theological predecessor in this regard, for 'Luther tried to interpret the presence of Christ from the Ascension.' In this way Luther was able to speak of Christ as our contemporary. Though Bonhoeffer does not directly acknowledge it, Luther left his mark upon him in yet another way. The presence of the Crucified and Risen One in space and time, *hic et nunc*, means that even today Christ participates fully in the ambiguities of human life. That is, just as his historical presence 'in the likeness of sinful flesh' (Rom. 8:3) once veiled God in his glory, so too the resurrected Christ deigns, even chooses, to come to the world incognito. Here Luther's *theologia crucis* is woven into the fabric of Bonhoeffer's Christology" (Slane, *Bonhoeffer as Martyr*, p. 172).

(pro me). Jesus Christ is the person who from eternity has been for me. Yet as living person, though he is for me, I can never possess him as if I own him, like I can an idea. Like all persons he escapes capture; the reservoirs of his being are too deep, too beautiful and too mysterious for me to cage. And his person most especially cannot be captured, for unlike all others he transcends space and time as spirit.

While Christ is for me, he is not for me alone but for all others as well. He is the incarnate, crucified and resurrected One to all others. And in being for others, he is at the same time for me; he makes it possible through his own person for me to meet, know and love other persons in the world. The *who* of his person continues to encounter the *who* of every person. This makes the person of Jesus Christ, according to Bonhoeffer, the man who is for others. By becoming incarnate, crucified and resurrected he has given his very person for the persons of the world.[37]

WHY DOES THIS MATTER?

At its core, relational ministry is about persons. It is not about strategies of ministry (*how* ministry is done) but about the person of Christ, who meets the persons of the world as the incarnate, crucified and resurrected One. Bonhoeffer reminds us that because Jesus is person we are no longer allowed to separate our commitment to our ministries and faith from the adolescent persons we encounter. Bonhoeffer states boldly, "We are not allowed to separate God from our sister or brother. God does not want to be honored if a sister or brother is dishonored. God is the Father. Yes, God is the Father of Jesus Christ, who came to be brother to us all."[38] We have too often forgotten that Christ is calling us to join him in *his* ministry to and for concrete persons in the world. If we are to minister to adolescents in an incarnational manner, we must minister to them as persons encountered by the person of

---

[37]Karl Barth holds to a position very similar to Bonhoeffer's. He states, "If we see Him alone, we do not see Him at all. If we see Him, we see with and around Him in ever-widening circles His disciples, the people, His enemies and the countless millions who have not yet heard His name. We see Him as theirs, determined by them and for them, belonging to each and every one of them. . . . What emerges in it is a supreme I wholly determined by and to the Thou" (*Church Dogmatics* 3/2 [Edinburgh: T & T Clark, 1960], p. 216).

[38]Bonhoeffer, *Discipleship*, p. 123.

Christic.[39] We must see them not as consumers of our program or even our faith, but as beautiful and mysterious individuals who, even at this moment, are held by God who is for others, for adolescents. Bonhoeffer states beautifully:

> The disciples view other people only as those to whom Jesus comes. They encounter other people only because they approach them together with Jesus. Jesus goes ahead of them to other people, and the disciples follow him. Thus an encounter between a disciple and another person is never just a freely chosen encounter between two people. . . . Disciples can encounter other people only as those to whom Jesus himself comes. Jesus' struggle for the other person, his call, his love, his grace, his judgment are all that matters.[40]

The incarnation is not a metaphor but the very ground of our being, the place where we meet the person of Christ as *who*, where we encounter the incarnate, crucified and resurrected One. The relational minister is called to live conformed to the incarnate, crucified and resurrected person. This happens as we seek the person of Jesus within the world loved by Christ (incarnate), who suffers in complete solidarity with those in it (crucified) and proclaims in word and deed that all which threaten to destroy them (and us) has been overcome in the risen humanity of Godself (resurrected).

This moves us past the rigidity of the subcultural identity that we saw in chapter three and its need to label boldly who is in and who is out. Because Jesus is the person who has loved all in the suffering solidarity of his own humanity there is no out-group, according to Bonhoeffer. God has made neighbor of enemy and friend of stranger.[41] By seeing relational ministry as partic-

---

[39]Bonhoeffer states in *Ethics*, "In becoming human, he put himself between me and the given circumstances of the world. I cannot go back. He is in the middle. He has deprived those whom he has called of immediate connection to those given realities. He wants to be the medium; everything should happen only through him. He stands not only between me and other people and things. He is the mediator, not only between God and human persons, but also between person and person, and between person and reality" (quoted in Slane, *Bonhoeffer as Martyr*, p. 178).

[40]Bonhoeffer, *Discipleship*, p. 170.

[41]"There is no part of the world, no matter how lost, how godless, that has not been accepted by God in Jesus Christ and reconciled to God. Whoever perceives the body of Jesus Christ in faith can no longer speak of the world as if it were lost, as if it were separated from God; they can no longer separate themselves in clerical pride from the world. It is nothing but unbelief to give the world . . . less than Christ. It means not taking seriously the incarnation, the crucifixion, and the bodily resurrection" (Bonhoeffer, *Ethics*, p. 67). Ray Anderson explains further, "Therefore, this movement of God 'outside of himself' to become flesh, and so bring estranged humanity into eternal and perfect unity with himself, demands that we now understand the nature of God in such a way that 'outside of' is also 'within' " (*Historical Transcendence and the Reality of God*, p. 179).

ipation in the person of Christ in the world, relationships in youth ministry are freed from being only tools to strengthen subcultural identity and are seen instead as the place where we experience God's presence in the world.

From a sociological standpoint we may argue that losing the in-group/out-group labels will hurt the vitality of religious groups in our pluralistic culture. But what makes the subcultural identity theory potent is that it provides a unique identity and purpose in a culture that is confusingly pluralistic. What Bonhoeffer has presented can allow for just such an identity and purpose, yet in such a way that there is no evil out-group and solely righteous in-group. From Bonhoeffer's perspective the disciple, the follower of Christ, is distinct, for he or she has given him- or herself over to Jesus to be conformed to his own person as incarnate, crucified and resurrected. The disciple is unique because he or she follows Jesus into a divisive world to stand for its solidarity, to suffer with a world that knows only strife and to proclaim hope and life to a world that is locked in cycles of dread and death. Those who follow the living Christ have both *identity* as his disciples and *purpose* as they follow him into the world, taking his form as the incarnate, crucified and resurrected. There is no need for in-group/out-group distinctions, there are only those who follow and serve and those who are also loved and cared for as unique persons encountered by Christ. Therefore the disciple is distinct as the one who loves the world as Christ does, empowered by the person of Jesus. Relational ministry, then, is not about a strategy of influence but about persons being conformed to the person of Jesus as incarnate, crucified and resurrected, and going into the world to join the *who* of Christ as incarnate, crucified and resurrected.

5

Where Is Jesus Christ?

RELATIONAL MINISTRY AS

PARTICIPATION IN GOD'S PRESENCE

A number of years ago I heard a preacher discuss how every morning he sat alone in a room and demanded that God speak to him. I listened as he told the group that it never failed, that every morning he heard God's voice directing him into a new day. I'm sure this person didn't mean that he heard God speak audibly, but he was sure that he heard God, that he communed with God's presence.

The next morning I gave it a try. I quieted myself, breathed in and out, calming my mind and preparing myself for prayer. Then, I said it, "God speak to me; your servant is listening!" I waited. "God speak; your servant is listening!" I waited. "God, I really want to be in your presence. Speak to me!" I waited. I must admit that I'm not a patient person, but after fifty minutes I had lost the little patience that I possess. "God! Speak!" I shouted in frustration like I was demanding a stubborn Labrador to come and sit.

The preacher had assured me that communing with God's presence was easy. All I needed to do was ask. But I neither felt the presence of God nor heard God speak.

I have felt God's presence and embrace in times of solitude and prayer. But more times than not I've found myself wondering if I was hearing God or myself, if I was in the presence of God or the presence of my imagination.

I first read Bonhoeffer with these questions in my mind. I was shocked by his dogged desire to discuss what he called the concreteness of God's revelation (the concreteness of God's presence). While he affirmed and encouraged people to pray individually and in solitude (see *Prayerbook of the Bible* and *Life Together*), Bonhoeffer sought to place God's presence somewhere other than in our subjective and individualistic experience. Instead he placed God's presence in the social experience of community, in relationships.

It is interesting that none of the youth pastors I interviewed (see chap. 3) spoke about relationships being the place where we meet the presence of God, the place where God embraces us. Rather, it seemed relationships only served as tools to convince adolescents that they should seek a subjective and individualist faith experience by themselves. But what if we followed Bonhoeffer's thought and understood relationships in youth ministry not as influencing tools but as the concrete presence of God in the world? How would that change the practice of relational/incarnational youth ministry? To see the possibility I will delve into Bonhoeffer's second question, Where is Jesus Christ?

WHERE IS JESUS CHRIST?

We have begun to understand how fully and dynamically Bonhoeffer sees the contemporary presence of Christ in our world as the person who *is* incarnate, crucified and resurrected. The *where* of Christ already presupposes the *who* of Christ as the One we encounter, for if Christ were not the One who is still active in the world, to ask where he is present would be meaningless.

All of the youth pastors I interviewed discussed how Jesus was a model or pattern for ministry (yet not in the manner of incarnate, crucified and resurrected as we have discussed), but there were few to no comments on *where* they understood the continued ministry of Christ to be present. The sole attention to the pattern of Christ has often caused relational ministry to focus almost exclusively on getting adolescents to accept the message of Christ rather than participating in the living, active presence of Christ. Relational ministry is not about getting someone to accept a message (an idea) but about participating together (one to another) in the presence of

God.[1] For relational ministry to be more than just a tool for cultural purposes (acceptance of an ideological position) it must be conformed to the person of Christ *who* is incarnate, crucified and resurrected, and calls us to participate in his own person through our person.

But this leads us to ask the more concrete question that Bonhoeffer would desire, Where do I encounter this one to whom I am called to conform? To move beyond its one-dimensional form, incarnational youth ministry must work theologically to articulate where it understands the presence of Christ to be and how persons participate in his presence.

Bonhoeffer has provided his own answer, which I believe is helpful to youth workers. He answers that Jesus is present to us in two interconnected locales, one is the church community and the other is within the world, standing alongside and with distinct persons. For Bonhoeffer, these two locales are inseparable, for both church and world exist under the sole lordship of Christ. Nevertheless, they are distinct. The church is the community of saints and sinners, *simul justus et peccator* (i.e., each member, and the church as a whole, is both saint and sinner simultaneously), that partakes in Christ through a shared life of mutual care and love through sacrament and preached word. The world is the universal community of persons that God, in the person of Christ, has reconciled to Godself. It is the place where the person of Christ remains in ministry, drawing creation toward its eschatological fulfillment.

For Bonhoeffer the tissue that holds church and world together, maintaining their connection, is the reality of relationship (sociality). Only through relational bonds with others do we discover the distinction of our own *who*, our own existence as a person. We always discover who we are alongside other people; we find our shortcomings, gifts and perspectives as we live with others as family, friends, colleagues and neighbors. We are social beings, there is no escaping this. And as we have seen, God too, in Jesus Christ, is person.

---

[1]Heinrich Ott fleshes this out helpfully: "What we have to preach is not 'must accept Christ,' for how could one accept a Christ whom at the time one does not know at all, who at the time is only an empty name? That would only be law. Rather we have to preach to the people that Christ is already there. That alone is Gospel. To preach the Gospel means to demonstrate the testimony to Christ in every human situation" (*Reality and Faith* [Philadelphia: Fortress Press, 1972], p. 436).

Therefore, Bonhoeffer holds that the concrete place of God's revelation (the place where God reveals Godself and is present to us) is within personal encounter, shared relational bonds of *I* and *other*. Because Jesus Christ is a living person who is ontologically (in his very being) *pro me* (for me and you), he stands beside each of us. So to be in relationship with another is to encounter Jesus Christ who is beside and for us. This happens, Bonhoeffer maintains, within the relationships of persons meeting persons in church and world. In relationships God, in Christ, is concretely present, and thus the very core of one's humanity is transformed. For Bonhoeffer God's revelation is ultimately a social reality, a relational encounter.[2] We will see how such an understanding of the *where* of Christ affects relational ministry as we flesh out Bonhoeffer's perspective on church and world.

THE CHURCH COMMUNITY

It is quite odd that a Lutheran child from a secular family who rarely attended church would choose to be a theologian and to write a doctoral dissertation on the church. But that is just what the nineteen-year-old Dietrich Bonhoeffer did. Many believe that the inspiration for this project came from an extended trip abroad with his brother Klaus to Italy. It's been reported that Bonhoeffer spent a number of afternoons in Rome, sitting and watching as pilgrims made their way to the Vatican. Returning home to begin his doctoral studies, the topic of the church became his passion.

Bonhoeffer's interest was not so much in the historical or biblical understanding and confessions of the church, but in the church's contemporary life, the church as it is found in the world. Therefore, Bonhoeffer presented what he called "a sociological examination of the church." But this too may be misleading. Bonhoeffer had no charts of statistical analysis that we often expect today within a sociological project. There were no case

---

[2]"In Bonhoeffer's theology, the presence of Christ is described in a very deliberate and comprehensive phenomenology of sociality. Revelation is an inherently social event, which occurs in a human community of persons; it is inseparable from, and is directed to, the concrete modes of being in human personal, communal, institutional, and political life. The outcome of revelation, consequently, is a new social form of humanity in which love liberates people from dominating and exploitative power over others to the freedom of being with and for others" (Clifford Green, *Bonhoeffer: A Theology of Sociality* [Grand Rapids: Eerdmans, 1999], p. 2).

studies or sight observations. What concerned Bonhoeffer in this work was neither the historical and biblical confessions nor the empirical and societal interactions of the church. Rather, Bonhoeffer's concern was with the inner life of the church community and how this inner life was the place of God's revelation (presence) in history. This focus can be seen in the word Bonhoeffer chose for the church in *Sanctorum Communio*. Instead of using the German word *Kirche* ("church"), Bonhoeffer uses the word *Gemeinde* ("community" or more precisely "church community").[3] By using the word *Gemeinde* Bonhoeffer's concern is with the inner life of the church community as the place where Christ is concretely present in the world. Bonhoeffer states this bluntly: "Community with God exists only through Christ, but Christ is present only in his church community, and therefore community with God exists only in the church."[4]

For Bonhoeffer, Christ becomes concretely present within the church as the community hears the preached word and shares the sacraments together.[5] Bonhoeffer explains:

> I hear another man *[sic]* really proclaim the gospel to me. He extends to me the sacrament: you are forgiven. He and the community pray for me, and I hear the gospel, join the prayer, and know myself in the word, sacrament, and prayer of the community of Christ to be bound with the new humanity, be it now here or elsewhere, borne by it, bearing it. Here I, the historically whole man, individual and humanity, am touched.[6]

For Bonhoeffer, Christ is not present as a kind of invisible entity, as if we could leave an empty chair and say, "Jesus sits there." Rather, for Bonhoeffer Christ is present in the spirit of relationships that hold the com-

---

[3]If it was solely "community" Bonhoeffer would have used *Gemeinschaft*, a word English readers will recognize from Ferdinand Tonnies *Gemeinschaft und Gesellschaft* (New York: Harper Torchbooks, 1957). Rather, by using *Gemeinde* Bonhoeffer is nuancing the term with a more distinct ecclesial focus.

[4]Dietrich Bonhoeffer, *Sanctorum Communio: A Theological Study of the Sociology of the Church* (Minneapolis: Fortress Press, 1998), p. 158.

[5]Miroslav Volf expresses the essential importance of community much like Bonhoeffer: "Because the triune God is not a private deity, one cannot create a private fellowship with this God. Fellowship with the triune God is therefore at once also fellowship with all other human beings who in faith have surrendered their existence to the same God" (*After Our Likeness* [Grand Rapids: Eerdmans, 1998], p. 33).

[6]Dietrich Bonhoeffer, cited in John Godsey, *The Theology of Dietrich Bonhoeffer* (Philadelphia: Westminster Press, 1958), p. 69.

munity together as they love one another through the sharing of the sacraments and submission to the Word of God. It is in persons meeting persons, in relationships, that the concrete presence of Christ is experienced. But "Bonhoeffer is far from arguing that wherever people experience something they call 'community' they are in some way experiencing Christ. The Christian community is constituted by the communal presence of Christ in Word and sacrament in the church."[7] Word and sacrament give the church its distinction within the world, but relationship, person meeting persons, reveals its solidarity to the world.

Therefore, because Bonhoeffer holds that Christ is not an invisible entity (not the invisible person in the chair) but is concretely present within the social life of the community (through relationship), when someone is invited into its life, he or she is not only sharing in the community but also sharing in the person of Christ. Thus his or her very being, very person, is transformed. "What it means for Christ to exist as community is that the I is opened up to be with and for the other. . . . Life together establishes and restores our genuine humanity as individual persons, even as our individuality attains authenticity only in life with others."[8]

Yet there are two dangers Bonhoeffer would want us to steer clear of. First, such a perspective on the church does not mean the church is perfect or free from sin, corruption or idiosyncrasy. Rather, the church is always the community of saints and sinners simultaneously, *simul justus et peccator*, never one without the other. Because Christ is not invisibly sitting in the empty chair, he cannot be controlled, made into a mascot or simply ignored. He is always judging the church for its sin, calling it to conform to his own person.[9] When the church refuses to conform itself to the incarnate, crucified and resurrected Christ, becoming instead a place of hatred, power plays and abuse, it is no longer the church (or it is the church in

---

[7]Green, introduction to *Sanctorum Communio*, p. 16.

[8]Charles Marsh, *Reclaiming Dietrich Bonhoeffer: The Promise of His Theology* (New York: Oxford University Press, 1994), pp. 76, 141.

[9]Green explains further, "The peccatorum communio lives on in the sanctorum communio; the church is the kingdom of Christ in history, not the eschatological kingdom of God. So the Spirit cannot be identified with the objective Geist of the church, nor Christ with the Kollektivperson of the church; Christ is indeed present in and as the church, but in a form which continually encounters it, breaking it up and building it up" (*Bonhoeffer*, p. 60).

name only), for its collective relational life is contaminated with dehumanization. For Bonhoeffer, the church is only the church of Jesus Christ if it
is the church that is for others.

This leads us into Bonhoeffer's second concern. If the church is to be
the concrete place of Christ in the world, the church must refuse sectarian
exclusion from the world. Rather, just as the community is upheld by the
distinct relationships of people within the church, in the same way the
church community, to remain community, needs the world to serve as its
counterpart, the place where the church discovers its own distinction in
care, service and love for the world.[10]

THE WORLD

This leads us to Bonhoeffer's second answer to the *where* of Jesus Christ.
The second locale of the concrete presence of Christ is in the world.[11]
From Bonhoeffer's perspective the way the church can be conformed to
Christ and therefore avoid being corrupted by a world of deceit, violence
and evil is to stand completely for this world. In being for the world the
church is completely different from the world, showing its difference from
the world in its commitment to the world.

The church does not possess Christ, as though he were caged within
its walls of polity and practice. Rather, Christ calls the church to follow
him into the world in loving service. And by serving the world—in the
form of incarnate, crucified and resurrected—the church, the disciple,
encounters the concrete *where* of Christ, who stands with and for those
in the world ("Whatever you did for one of the least of these . . . you did
for me" [Mt 25:40 NIV]). Then just as the church is the concrete place of
Christ's presence because of its social/relational life, so too is the world.
As the disciple encounters unique persons in the world, standing with

---

[10]"It is not only that the world needs the church in order to have Christ. The church also needs to be
in relation to the world in order to know Christ and in order to be the body of Christ. Formation of
Christ in the world does not take place apart from the world" (Ray Anderson, *The Shape of Practical
Theology* [Downers Grove, Ill.: InterVarsity Press, 2001), p. 118.

[11]"In Christ we are invited to participate in the reality of God and the reality of the world at the same
time, the one not without the other. The reality of God is disclosed only as it places me completely
into the reality of the world. But I find the reality of the world always already borne, accepted, and
reconciled in the reality of God. That is the mystery of the revelation of God in the human being
Jesus Christ" (Bonhoeffer, *Ethics* [Minneapolis: Fortress Press, 2005], p. 55).

and for their humanity, he or she can be confident that within the relational encounter Christ is concretely present. Christ is not present as the other person, but because Jesus is the person *who* is incarnate, crucified and resurrected, he stands in between my person and the person I meet in the world. He is in between because he stands for and alongside the other, just as he stands for and alongside me *(pro me)*. Quite literally, that which I do unto the other I do unto Christ. Therefore, relationships of persons to persons within both the church and the world become the concrete place of Christ's presence.

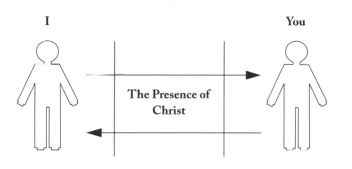

Figure 5.1. The concrete place of Christ's presence

WHY DOES THIS MATTER?

Relational youth ministries have often neglected the importance of the church community, and by doing so have unknowingly become irrelevant to the world and impotent to stand for it. We can trace this neglect back to its birth in parachurch organizations (see chap. 2). The ministry models that have migrated from parachurch organizations to the church often do not have a deep understanding of the church. But as we have learned from Bonhoeffer, the church is essential for relational ministry.

An adolescent must be led into the life of the congregation; he or she as a distinct person must come into intimate and intense contact with other distinct persons in the congregation, and with the world through the congregation. It is not enough for the youth ministry to be a satellite community connected to but not integrated with the life of the church community. In the same way, relational mission (or outreach) to adolescents outside the church is only possible from within and by the church community. As Bonhoeffer states, "Where the body of Christ is, there Christ truly is. Christ is in the church-community, as the church-community is in Christ (I Cor. 1:10; 2 Cor. 6:16, 3:11). 'To be in Christ' is synonymous with 'to be in the church-community.' "[12] When an adolescent who is unconnected to the church is cared for by a youth worker as a friend, this is the work of the whole *ecclesia*, for it is from the community that the minister is sent and to the community that he or she will return.

When the minister returns, the adolescent will accompany him or her, and the community will need to make a place for the adolescent. The adolescent may refuse church participation or even hate it, yet this is irrelevant, for in connecting to us as a friend, the adolescent in the world has been attached to the community. Realizing this theological truth, the community must make a place for the adolescent even if doing so causes the community to suffer (e.g., in rage the adolescent lashes out at it). This is the cost of conformation to the incarnate, crucified and resurrected One.

Only the community has the ample resources to help adolescents who suffer in severe circumstances. The community's greatest assistance is to provide a new social context that speaks to the adolescent's present social situation, offering words and acts of hope. The community promises that fatalism will not swallow the adolescent, for if it is to swallow the adolescent it will have to swallow the community also. This would be an ontological impossibility because the spirit of Christ is present within the community, meaning fatalism and death have been conquered once and for all in the humanity of the resurrected Christ. The church is an eschatological community that offers the adolescent more than a model; it provides an actual reality, its own spirit-filled life.

Relational ministry presupposes suffering; when we are called to go, we must give our very selves to others, for this is following the Crucified. The depth of adolescent suffering in our time will inevitably produce defensiveness, suspicion and a lack of commitment. Without the community, we are

---

[12]Bonhoeffer, *Sanctorum Communio*, p. 140.

likely to compromise ourselves or give up altogether for fear of greater suffering and abuse. But when incarnational action is shared by the minister and the church at large, both the youth worker and the suffering adolescent are upheld.

The spirit of Christ is found within the community. Therefore, abandoning the community to minister alone means abandoning Christ. Such action can only represent the incarnation as "pattern"; in the end there is no power for transformation because we have lost the concrete presence of Christ. When we abandon the community we lose the context of relationship necessary for transformation and change, and by abandoning the community we will inevitably abandon the world.

I AND YOU

Bonhoeffer understands both the church and the world as the fundamental locations where persons meet persons in relational connection. Because Jesus is person he encounters persons through other persons in both the church and the world. The church, from Bonhoeffer's perspective, is not primarily a social institution or a place where individuals come to receive absolution; rather the church is the community of persons who witness in their own transformed humanity to the person of Christ, who is found concretely as persons meeting persons in worship and sacrament. The world, for Bonhoeffer, is not ultimately constituted by political ideologies or economic systems; rather the world is the place where stranger and neighbor meet as persons. Therefore, Bonhoeffer answers that Jesus Christ is present (where?) within the church and the world, but only insofar as the church and the world are places of relationship, places where I meet you.[13]

The meeting of I and you (relationship) is the place where we encounter the living presence of Christ, because it is the place of transcendent other-

---

[13]It must be stated that the I and you are not only individuals meeting individuals, but for Bonhoeffer I and you also constitute collective communities that interact with other communities or groups in relationships. I focus mainly on individual-to-individual relationships, but it is possible to think of individuals as collective persons. This would have some connection with Stanley Grenz's understanding of the ecclesial self as presented in *Social God and Relational Self* (London: Westminster John Knox Press, 2001).

ness.[14] The transcendent is that which is outside or beyond humanity's grasp; it that which is other than my own being. For something to be transcendent means that it is beyond me and other than me. In encountering that which is transcendent my very being is called into question because I meet that which has no correlation to me. Bonhoeffer is following Karl Barth in holding to a wholly other God who transcends (is beyond) all human thinking, socializing or feeling. These categories (or any other) cannot capture God, for God transcends them.

Yet, because Christ is the incarnate one who is crucified and resurrected, Bonhoeffer contends that God's transcendence must therefore be historical; it must confront humanity within humanity's experience of time and space, but in such a manner that God remains transcendent and other. Bonhoeffer contends that the place of God's transcendence within human history is found solely in the *person* of Jesus Christ. God has chosen to make Godself known as personal, for the inner life of the Trinity as Father, Son and Holy Spirit is constituted by persons in relation to one another. Therefore, Bonhoeffer holds that it is the other person (or human neighbor) who confronts me within my existence, and in so doing demonstrates his or her otherness from me (his or her transcendence). Because Jesus Christ is person (both in the inner life of the Trinity and within human history), we experience, according to Bonhoeffer, the transcendent otherness of God as we encounter the otherness of our human neighbor as person.[15] Therefore, it is within the relationship between I and you that we

---

[14]Emmanuel Levinas has gone to great lengths in his work to show that others meet me in the actuality of transcendence. Peter Sagwick fleshes out Levinas's position: "What we encounter in the world as radically or 'absolutely' other than us are other people, the 'Other' as an individual. Taken together, I and the other do not form a unity or totality. I am related to the other—who is a stranger to me—in virtue of the fact that I have no control over them. . . . Over him I have no power. He escapes my grasp by an essential dimension, even if I have him at my disposal" (*Descartes to Derrida* [Malden, Mass.: Blackwell, 2001], p. 80). Levinas states in *Totality and Infinity*, "Man as Other comes to us from the outside, a separated—or holy-face. . . . This surplus of truth over being and over its idea, which we suggest by the metaphor of the 'curvature of intersubjective space,' signifies the divine intention of all truth. This 'curvature of space' is, perhaps, the very presence of God" (*Totality and Infinity* [Pittsburgh: Duquesne University Press, 1961], p. 29).
[15]Bonhoeffer states, "There is no relation to men without a relation to God, and no relation to God without a relation to men, and it is only our relation to Jesus Christ which provides the basis for our relation to men and to God. Jesus Christ is our life, and so now, from the standpoint of Jesus Christ, we may say that our fellow-man is our life and that God is our life" (quoted in James Woelfel, *Bonhoeffer's Theology* [Nashville: Abingdon, 1970], p. 67).

come up against the living God.[16] In standing with and for the other person whom Jesus Christ stands beside, I encounter Christ as I see the mystery of other's humanity, as I recognize that I cannot possess him or her, but must love him or her as I confess the love of Christ for us both. I encounter the presence of God because in encountering the other I meet the one who is for and with him or her.

Where then is Jesus Christ? He is in the concrete place where the *I* meets the *you*, where persons meet persons. Green states, "The socioethical relation to the human 'other' is precisely the form in which people encounter the divine 'Other.' . . . God is not immanent in us, but is present to us in the social relationship. The transcendence of God means God's presence as 'Other.'"[17]

WHY DOES THIS MATTER?

It has been a common mistake in the practice of relational and incarnational ministry to assume that the relationship is a tool to influence the adolescent to know and accept Jesus Christ. We become friends in relationship so we can move the adolescent beyond a relationship with us and into a relationship with Jesus. In such a practice the relationship does not matter so much as the end to which the relationship leads. But the Scottish philosopher John Macmurray says poignantly, "This is the characteristic of personal relationships. They have no ulterior motive. They are not based on particular interests. They do not serve partial and limited ends. Their value lies entirely in themselves and for the same reason transcends all

---

[16]Bonhoeffer explains, "The social basic category is the I-You-relation. The You of the other person is the divine You. Thus the way to the other person's You is the same as the way to the divine You, either through acknowledgment or rejection. The individual becomes a person ever and again through the other; in the 'moment'. The other person presents us with the same challenge to our knowing as does God. My real relationship to another person is oriented to my relationship with God. But since I know God's 'I' only in the revelation of God's love, so too with the other person" (*Sanctorum Communio*, pp. 55-56).

[17]Green, *Bonhoeffer*, pp. 35-36. Green continues, "We do not deal with an invisible God in an invisible world of our wishful fantasies; God is met and heard only in the real world where human, personal wills encounter one another; God is to be sought in the real experience of historical, social, ethical existence. Furthermore, . . . the purpose of the divine presence is precisely to renew the personal and corporate life of human sociality. Human personal being, then, derives ultimately from the personal being of God. If God has been philosophically described as absolute Geist, Bonhoeffer insists that God, as well as human beings, must be fundamental as Person" (ibid., p. 36).

other values. And that is because they are relations of persons as persons."[18]

Using relationships as an end is a mistake because it assumes that there is a third thing (a relationship with Jesus) that can be attained outside of the relationship between I and you. According to Bonhoeffer there is no such third thing: "One does not love God in the neighbor, nor are neighbors loved to make them Christian—neighbors are loved for their own sake, and in this love of the human companions one serves the will of God."[19] The way to Christ is through the other, the neighbor. Bonhoeffer asserts, "I do not love God in the 'neighbor', but I love the concrete You; I love the You by placing myself, my entire will, in the service of the You. . . . The person who loves God must, by God's will, really love the neighbor."[20]

To assume that there is a third thing, that a relationship with an adolescent is the means to another end, is to deny both the transcendence of the adolescent and the transcendence of the person of Christ. The transcendence of the adolescent is lost because he or she is only important inasmuch as he or she comes to know and accept the gospel message. His or her unique humanity, which the adolescent has made open to us, has little value in and of itself, for what is important is not what is shared within the relationship but what end the relationship moves toward.

In such a perspective the transcendence of Christ is also lost, for his concrete place with and alongside the other as person is lost, and Jesus becomes a disconnected entity with no concrete place to encounter me as the Lord and Judge who is other than me and my ideas of him.[21]

Relational ministry, then, should not be about a third thing but only about meeting Jesus Christ in the reality of his person, who is found within relational bonds with the adolescents with whom we minister. Therefore, helping adolescents come to faith and move into discipleship is not about a program of conversion, it is never about closing the deal or moving them forward; it is not about helping them "get it" (whatever "it" might be). It

---

[18]John Macmurray, *Reason and Emotion* (London: Faber & Faber, 1935), p. 101.

[19]Green, *Bonhoeffer*, p. 58.

[20]Bonhoeffer, *Sanctorum Communio*, p. 169.

[21]God's transcendence is lost because God becomes an added-on entity, as Ray Anderson explains: "God, therefore, is not a reality 'added to' the social relation, but the reality of God constitutes that relation; consequently, God, man and community intrinsically cohere in the concrete social relation" (*Historical Transcendence and the Reality of God* [Grand Rapids: Eerdmans, 1975], p. 77).

is only, most beautifully and powerfully, about being together, sharing life before God and understanding that in our shared connection of common humanity Christ is present. As Ray Anderson has stated, people are "up against God himself when Christ meets [them] at the centre of a . . . relationship."[22] No tricks or techniques are needed, only the willingness to be oneself alongside the adolescent. Relational ministry is about relationships, not because they involve adolescents in programs, not because in a hostile culture relationships mediate the gospel message, not because relationships can make adolescents into supercommitted lifelong believers. They may help in some if not all of these areas, but *the theological commitment to relationships in relational ministry should be solely because in our connection one to another as I and you Christ is concretely present.*

The ultimate danger of the "third thing" is that it has little room for transformation that can affect the core of the adolescent's self. If the relationship exists for only the third thing and not the concrete humanity of the other, it is ultimately cheap grace because it costs me nothing of myself; it makes no demand that I open my own being to the other. We are transformed (changed) only when we truly encounter otherness. When we encounter the other, we come up against that which we cannot possess, that which is completely other than our own being.

By recognizing the transcendent otherness of the adolescent in his or her mystery that cannot be possessed, I am awakened to the uniqueness of my being. I recognize that I am free to be my unique self but only insofar as I am free to be for the other, for this other has become the boundary by which I know myself.

Therefore, a "[hu]man becomes an I through a You," says the great Jewish philosopher Martin Buber.[23] Only in connection to this other, as I act with and for the other, I become an I and discover the depth of my gifts, abilities and worth. Culture and society may try to tell me many things about who I am ("Girls can't do that," "Blacks commit crimes," "Your test scores say you're

---

[22]Ibid., p. 85.

[23]Martin Buber, *I and Thou* (New York: Charles Scribner's, 1958), p. 80. Buber continues this thought, "Not through such a deduction but only through genuine intercourse with a Thou can the I of the living person be experienced as existing" (*Eclipse of God: Studies in the Relation Between Religion and Philosophy* [Amherst, N.Y.: Humanity Books, 1952], p. 40).

stupid," "Poor people are lazy") but these are abstractions; they have no correlation with reality because they deny the unique person. It is only in the context of relationship, of I and you acting with and for each other, that I discover that what culture or society has spoken is a lie; the other person reveals my true self as he or she becomes the one I relate to within a relationship. This is not to say that some "relationships" might not be destructive and abusive. But these connections are not, from a theological perspective, relationships, for they have destroyed the transcendence of the other (see chap. 8).

The you, then, exists as the boundary or barrier that I need to discover who I am. I realize that I am I and you are you. By recognizing in social bonds that the otherness of the you is my barrier, I recognize that the other's humanity must be respected as a place made sacred solely by the person of Jesus Christ. By maintaining this barrier in my meeting with the you of another, I am encountering otherness that transcends me, and in so doing, it transforms me. *Up against the barrier that is my neighbor, I discover my own limitations; I discover that I am a person in need of relationship with others and God. The barrier must be maintained if I am to know myself in relation to God and neighbor.* I have crossed the barrier when I no longer see the other as other but as a tool that I can use for my own purposes. Seeing the other in this manner denies his or her transcendence and in so doing denies God's. Therefore, there is an ethical dimension to relationships between I and you. For Bonhoeffer it is not enough to recognize that my own being is constituted only alongside the other, but rather in recognizing this I am called to reach out in acts on behalf of and with this other that has become my barrier.

The incarnational minister is relational not only because he or she goes but also because he or she goes as a barrier. In relating to adolescents we help inform them of their distinct gifts, abilities and worth from within the relationship.[24] But also as boundary we confront all actions and attitudes within

---

[24]We may wonder how such a perspective is honest to the adolescent's developmental location. It has been believed, through the work of Erik Erikson and others, that in adolescence individuals work to form a unique, distinct identity. This therefore has the result of making adolescents very concerned about themselves, leading some to believe that a kind of (healthy) self-centeredness happens at this time of life. This self-centeredness may be ground for encouraging adult and adolescent social connections, and not settling for *only* adolescent-adolescent relationships. Because of their developmental stage, adolescents may be growing into social-ethical relationships and not yet completely competent to take them on. Nevertheless, to grow into them, they must experience them. According to Erikson, adolescents intensely seek out relationships to discover who they are in the context of their society.

the adolescent that are born from the belief that other persons have no transcendent quality but can be manipulated or abused as he or she wishes. Therefore, the relational minister says both yes and no to the adolescent: Yes, you are lovable, for I love you. Yes, you are valuable; look at how you have helped me. Yes, you do have much to offer; look at how you have enriched my life. No, you cannot treat me like that; I am person, I deserve your respect. No you cannot say that to him; he is a person, see how that hurt him. No, you cannot do that; it will hurt you and maybe others. *Relationships, if they are true relationships, demand judgment and confrontation.* But harsh judgment and militant confrontation can never lead to relationship.

As barrier, the relational minister operates in both an open and closed manner in relationship with the adolescent. It is often wrongly assumed that a good youth worker is totally open to the adolescents he or she ministers to. But this views relationships as an instrument (for the good sales rep is always available to his or her clients) and not as the place of God's transcendence. *The youth worker's openness to the adolescent must be balanced with closedness.* As Bonhoeffer says, "The 'openness' of the person demands 'closedness' as a correlative, or one could not speak of openness at all."[25] We must be able to say, "Sorry, I am on vacation. I will get back to you." "Please don't stop over at dinner time, my family and I are eating." "It is late. Call me in the morning." Or simply, "I am not available, I need some time away." To be closed to the adolescent is to be *for* the adolescent. In being closed, we allow the adolescent to recognize us as other, not a personal possession but a distinct human being who is complicated and beautiful in our own right. Being able to say no to young people communicates that ministry is person to person and not producer to consumer. This open-and-closed balance is no doubt hard to strike, and it is often more of a dance than a science. Its core belief is that ministry should be a humanizing activity, both for the minister and the one being ministered to. If at any point we feel as if our own person is being lost in another's demands (understand

---

[25]Bonhoeffer, *Sanctorum Communio*, p. 74. Good definitions of *open* and *closed* is given in footnote 19 in *Sanctorum Communio*. "By 'open' Bonhoeffer means the capacity and necessity of a person to participate in sociality with others. 'Closed' refers to the unity, integrity, and irreducibility of the person; it indicates the otherness of the other, guarding against the totalization of idealist thinking. 'Openness' does not mean merged into a supra-individual unity, nor does 'closedness' mean shut off from interaction with other persons" (ibid., p. 67).

this as different from doing things we don't want to do), we must say, "No. Stop! This is closed to you." (This will be fleshed out more fully in the narratives in chaps. 7-8.) *By experiencing youth workers as closed, adolescents are able to recognize their openness as a gift of transcendent wonder.*

Of course this open-and-closed dynamic of shared relationship makes it impossible for an individual to enter into such relationships with all or most of the adolescents in a youth ministry. Such relationships demand a commitment from youth workers, adult leaders *and* the whole congregation (see chap. 9). Lacking the open-and-closed balance, many fatigued youth workers have tried to move beyond relational ministry. Yet, if we can live and minister as persons who are both open and closed to the other, we cannot only avoid moving past relational ministry but actually (some of us for first time) move into it.

ANTHROPOLOGY IN LIGHT OF THE NEW HUMANITY

In seminary I deeply wanted to feel and know God, but I found myself beaten down by my constant striving. I participated in disciplines of prayer, Bible memorization and more, and yet found myself feeling increasingly trapped by these practices rather than experiencing the freedom of the gospel. I was sitting in one of Professor Ray Anderson's classes when he read and explained a quote from Bonhoeffer. He said, "We are called to be human as Jesus Christ is human, we are not to deny our humanity but to live in the world as whole people, as human beings." I had been taught to avoid or suppress my humanity by being spiritual, and with Bonhoeffer's words and Anderson's explanation the freedom of the gospel washed over me. I could embrace the world, myself and my suffering. Not only could I embrace it, but I could experience God in it. I realized that in my youth ministry I was much more concerned about the adolescents being spiritual than being human, being holy than being honest. I decided to minister to their humanity by being human myself.

Because of the incarnation of Christ, our life objective is to be truly human as determined by the humanity of God in Jesus Christ (see chap. 4). In being the one who is incarnate, crucified and resurrected Jesus overcomes all that separates humanity from God and humanity from humanity, therefore restoring relationship (I and you) to the core of humanity.

Bonhoeffer states, "Christian life means being human in the power of Christ's becoming human."[26] This means that *to faithfully live our life as a human being—to live as we were created to live—is to live in an open-and-closed relational connection to another, where one person becomes the barrier to the other.*

It is from this open-and-closed life, according to Bonhoeffer, that God is in relationship with humanity. In the Garden of Eden, God creates Adam from the dust; Adam is a creature of the earth and God is the earth's Creator. There is a closed dynamic, God is unmistakably other than Adam; God is Adam's Creator. Yet, although Adam is created from dust and completely other than God, God speaks to Adam, inviting him into fellowship with God. Adam is the only creature of the earth that can hear God speak. Therefore, God is open to Adam. But in being open to Adam God sets a barrier at the center of the Garden (the tree of the knowledge of good and evil) to remind Adam that God is the *I* and Adam is the *you.*

Adam must never cross the boundary, for in doing so he would do the impossible, make God his object, no longer an I to Adam's you. This in turn would destroy relationship, cutting Adam off from the source of life, leading to death. Therefore, there is no humanity outside of relationship with God. This has led Bonhoeffer, as well as Karl Barth, to assert that the image of God *(imago Dei)* within humanity is constituted by relationships: "In the image of God he created them; male and female he created them" (Gen 1:27). Therefore, to be human as God intends is to be in relationship with another.

To be human as God intends is to live as a distinct person who is for and with other distinct persons in the power of the humanity of Jesus Christ. This human life as God desires is possible only through the new humanity of the present Jesus Christ, who is making us new in the I-you connection of human relationship. Bonhoeffer explains that

> human beings are not transformed into an alien form, the form of God, but into the form that belongs to them, that is essentially their own. Human beings become human because God became human. But human beings do not become God. They could not and do not accomplish a change in form; God

---

[26]Bonhoeffer, *Ethics*, p. 159.

changes God's form into human form in order that human beings can become, not God, but human before God.[27]

As Ray Anderson has said powerfully, "The incarnation did not 'Christianize' humanity, it 'humanized' humanity. Humanity in its concrete and historical form as creaturely existence is brought back into its contingent relation to God and to the other as the concrete neighbor."[28]

WHY DOES THIS MATTER?

Relational ministry has too often been seen as an *ought*. The practice has become a kind of badge of commitment, identifying who is doing proper youth ministry and who isn't. Those taking the personal risks and entering high school campuses or other adolescent gathering places are seen as successful. Yet for many, such as those who are either not outgoing (and maybe introverted) or uncomfortable in the adolescent world, this ought-based relational ministry has become a burden. Incarnational youth ministry can induce a vicious cycle of guilt, *I should be spending time with kids, but I just don't want to.* The burden becomes heavy to bear because it is never over; adolescents always seem to need more relational bonds, and once one group graduates there is a new group of students who need relational contact.

It may be that relational ministry has become a burdensome "ought" because it has become a tool for ministry rather than the ministry itself. In other words, relational ministry is something that youth workers *do* rather than something that youth workers *are.* To see ministry as such an ought is to separate it from its direct connection with our common humanity, with our anthropological make-up. Relational ministry should not be practiced as an ought but from the core of ourself.

Youth ministry that is practiced from one's anthropological center (*who one is*) places our authentic humanity before the adolescent, allowing the adolescent to see our joys and sufferings. Its goal is not working to convert adolescents. Rather, it is to point the adolescent to yourself, to your humanity, saying, "Come close, be near to me, see my broken humanity, understand what it means for me to be human. As you do, you are invited to

---

[27]Bonhoeffer, *Ethics*, p. 96.
[28]Anderson, *Shape of Practical Theology*, p. 139.

tell me what it means for you to be human; what are your worries, joys and dreams?" When we practice relational ministry as human beings, and not as super-youth workers, we are free to say, "That is enough, I'm done for now, I shared myself with you and now (with no guilt) I need time to myself. I want you to know me, but I too must know myself. So I need space."

Practicing relational ministry from the core of our humanity is empowering because we were made for just such relational connections. Practicing youth ministry as human beings (not superpastors) can free us from the burden of the *ought*, which too often is tethered to the old humanity.[29] This is not to say that relational ministry is not costly. As we open our humanity to another, it is left precariously vulnerable to be hurt or misunderstood. But this is the call of those *who* follow the true (new) human being, Jesus Christ, *who* offers his humanity for us that we might be human.

Practicing relational ministry in the *where* of Jesus Christ, practicing it in the confession of the continued presence of Christ with and for us, means avoiding the strictures of relationalism. *Relationalism* is a strategy used to personally influence someone to participate in a cultural group. It therefore has little concern with meeting persons in the shared relations of our common humanity. Bonhoeffer would ask us to leave behind our relationalistic strategies in recognition of our call to live in the church community, which is in the world and is constituted from the I meeting the you in the new humanity of Jesus Christ. He would call us to see relationships beyond personal-influence relationalism and instead as the core of our very being, as the place where God concretely meets us in the world. Relational ministry is more than influencing adolescents; it is sharing in I-you relationships where Christ is present. It is being truly human alongside and for the adolescent, and in so doing calling the adolescent to be human, which is made possible by Jesus, who is incarnate, crucified and resurrected.

---

[29]The old humanity is more often about self-preservation (*how* to keep our job by making adolescents like us) or self-determination (*how* to create the kind of ministry others will admire).

6

What Then Shall We Do?

I had just returned home from a seminary semester of reading Bonhoeffer. I met with a friend who was still attending the Christian college I had graduated from just a year and a half earlier. When I asked how school was, she confused me by telling me that her parents had just split up, which had caused her deep pain. She explained that in the midst of the pain she had started smoking cigarettes again (something she hadn't done since her junior year in high school) and had spent a few nights sipping wine and beer—all of which were against her school's lifestyle statement. She realized that this was stupid, but her rebellious acts seemed to keep her from crumbling under the pain of her parents' separation.

She explained that she finally talked about this with her roommate, who happened to be a resident assistant at the school. Her roommate responded with compassion, hugging and praying with her. However, the next morning my friend received a phone call from the dean of student life who wanted to talk to her about her drinking and smoking, reminding her that these were violations of the school's lifestyle statement. My friend was crushed; she had opened herself up to her roommate, who she thought was her friend.

After a humiliating conversation with the dean, my friend returned to her apartment to find her roommate. She asked her why she shared their conversation, why she turned her in. Her RA roommate explained that it was her Christian duty to be a person of integrity. She had to uphold the morals and rules of the institution; it was ethically the right thing to do, the RA explained. My friend shot back, "You mean to tell me that Jesus is more concerned about morals than me? You're telling me that you can claim you have some kind of integrity and yet you can betray my deepest sufferings? I thought you cared about me, and it appears all you cared about was being pure and holy. Is that really the gospel?"

As she shared this, my mind raced to Bonhoeffer. If Christ really was the incarnate, crucified and resurrected One who was found with and for us in human-to-human relationships, then what should we do? It appeared to me that my friend's roommate had failed to see that who Jesus Christ is and where he is present is in our being with and for each other, not in upholding a moral principle. For Bonhoeffer, ethics is based in personal relationships, not in oughts and musts. What then shall we do? Bonhoeffer wrote and shouted with his own life that we must become place-sharers; we should enter deeply into each other's lives for only their sake, knowing that in so doing God in Christ is present to us both.

Bonhoeffer explained that if our relationships are to be something more than leverage to influence people in the direction we want them to go, then they must take the form of place-sharing.

The third question of Bonhoeffer's theology is, What should we do? which lines up nicely with Langmead's third element of incarnational mission: joining God's mission. As Bonhoeffer stated throughout his theology, it is never enough to only know the *who* and *where* of Jesus. We must act; we must take responsibility as we are called into the continued ministry of God in the world. This then is about ethics, how we should act and live in the world. But Bonhoeffer is not concerned with an ethic of right and wrong, but an ethic (action in the world) that participates in the *who* and *where* of Jesus.

Bonhoeffer provides three overarching themes that give shape to his Christocentric ethic, or action of place-sharing. They are (1) correspondence with reality, (2) taking on guilt and (3) freedom. Bonhoeffer believes that these ethical components tend to the concrete lives of those in the world (the penultimate), and by doing so they move toward the fulfillment of God's ministry to the world (the eschatological or ultimate).

Too often relational youth ministry has had little to do with ethics, little to do with the continued eschatological mission of God. The focus has been on getting adolescents saved or committed rather than on standing responsibly for them in ethical action on their behalf, and in so doing pointing to an eschatological (ultimate) hope.

PLACE-SHARING

From start to finish, the concept of relationship is the essential component of Bonhoeffer's theology. He has shown that not only do we concretely meet the incarnate, crucified and resurrected One in human-to-human relationships, but as human beings we are created for just such relational encounters. Yet for Bonhoeffer it is not enough to simply acknowledge the other, recognizing that the other is present as a fellow human being. This is not relationship, for it has yet to lead toward ethical place-sharing.

To truly live as a disciple of the incarnate, crucified and resurrected One, we must not only acknowledge the present humanity of the other but also enter into a relationship where we share the place of the other. It is not enough to simply meet the other in a kind of benign relationship—being nice, sharing a laugh and being happy that the other person is present—while ignoring the other's poverty (emotional, financial, spiritual, cultural or physical) and pain. To stop here is to stop short of relationship. Rather, relationship, empowered by the humanity of God, demands action that is responsible for the very humanity of the other. Therefore, to be in a relationship is to take full responsibility for the other, standing in his or her place, becoming his or her advocate.

For Bonhoeffer, place-sharing is asymmetrical; it may be a one-way street. It does not wait or even expect the other to repay place-sharing; rather, I offer my ethical action from the core of my humanity with no expectation of return.[1] The fabric of relationship is spun by such ethical ac-

---

[1]This asymmetrical ethical perspective is not only Bonhoeffer's position but also Emmanuel Levinas's. Colin Davis explains, "It would be a mistake for me to respect the Other because I expect anything in return: my obligation and responsibility are not mirrored by the Other's reciprocal responsibility towards me. This asymmetry is consistent with Levinas's conception of the Other: to insist on symmetry or reciprocity would be to imply that I was empowered to speak for the Other, that the Other belongs to the same species or genus as myself. But for Levinas the ethical relationship entails an obligation which is incumbent on me alone; no power forces me to act in moral ways" (*Levinas: An Introduction* [Notre Dame, Ind.: University of Notre Dame Press, 1996], p. 52).

tions where I not only acknowledge the other's reality but vicariously enter into it, standing with the other, offering my own humanity as companion through the severe storms of existence. But place-sharing demands even more. It demands not only that I place my own humanity in the path of the other's personal storms, but that in so doing I make it my responsibility to see the other through the storm to calm waters. Place-sharing demands that I stand so close to the other that his or her reality becomes my own, his or her suffering becomes mine.

While relationships built on place-sharing may seem to destroy the open-and-closed dynamic, it actually fortifies it. For in place-sharing I take the self of the other into my own self. In doing so I do not lose myself, but rather my relationship with the other person becomes the data I use to know myself. Place-sharing has nothing to do with enmeshment, for if I lose myself in my relationship with the other I can no longer be his or her advocate; I can no longer stand for the other (or vice versa) because my own distinction has been swallowed. Place-sharing demands that I be completely *other* than the other (closed) while being completely for the other (open).

As Bonhoeffer understands it, in a relationship bound by place-sharing, a person is transformed (for he or she finds his or her own distinct person). For in becoming the advocate for the other, my very concept of myself within the world is changed; I become the one who is for this particular other, his or her person has direct impact on my own unique person. In the same way the other's person is drawn into transformation, for as I stand alongside the other, he or she must make room for me in the midst of his or her reality. Therefore, to be the barrier to another, I must become the other's place-sharer, combining my own person with the person of the other. While place-sharing seems radical and difficult, Bonhoeffer reminds us of its concrete place within our reality, he reminds us that place-sharing is the fabric of relationships:

> Individuals do not act merely for themselves alone, each individual incorporates the selves of several people. . . . [For instance,] the father of a family . . . can no longer act as if he were merely an individual. In his own self, he incorporates the selves of those family members for whom he is responsible. Everything he does is determined by this sense of responsibility. Any at-

tempt to act and live as if he were alone would not only abdicate his responsibility, but also deny at the same time the reality on which his responsibility is based. For he does not cease to be the father of a family; rather, instead of being a good father, he is now simply a bad one. He is a good father if he takes on and acts according to the responsibility reality places on him.[2]

The life of place-sharing is a life of selflessness; it is overcoming the self-preservation and self-determination of the old humanity in the new humanity constituted by actions with and for the other. As Bonhoeffer says, "[place-sharing] and therefore responsibility is possible only in completely devoting one's own life to another person. Only those who are selfless live responsibly, which means that only selfless people truly live."[3]

This is not selflessness that in effect says, "Because I am for you, I have no idea who I am, I have given up my own person to be for your person." This would be enmeshment, which loses the open-and-closed balance. It then could not be the will of God, for in it the person's own humanity is lost. Rather, it is a Christocentric selflessness that states, "Because I am completely for you, I know concretely who I am; the more I stand in for you the more I know myself." By being place-sharer to the other, by standing with and for the other, I represent his or her humanity before God and at the same time represent God's humanity to the other. In becoming the other's place-sharer I stand where he or she should stand but cannot (and he or she will do the same for me).

Therefore, in a relationship composed by place-sharing we take on the new humanity. Place-sharing then is the ultimate (or eschatological) reality of humanity, for it is humanity acting for humanity in the power of the new humanity of Jesus Christ. By becoming another's place-sharer, by becoming his or her advocate, the other and I live toward the eschatological fulfillment. In being another's place-sharer the meeting of our concrete persons becomes a concrete reality of hope—a foreshadow, though ever broken, of the way life will one day be in the full presence of God, who is the true place-sharer.

Of course, a person can never in his or her own power be selfless and

---

[2]Dietrich Bonhoeffer, *Ethics* (Minneapolis: Fortress Press, 2005), p. 221.
[3]Ibid., p. 259.

therefore place him- or herself in the new humanity. The action of place-sharing is radical and difficult, that is why, according to Bonhoeffer, it can never be done from within our own power but only from the power of One who is already present acting as place-sharer for all humanity, Jesus Christ. Taking the form of the incarnate, crucified and resurrected means entering the lives of others at the level of place-sharing, acting as one who is responsible for the full humanity of the other. Therefore, to be conformed to Christ is to be place-sharer to the other, for Christ is place-sharer to all humanity. Ignoring place-sharing, that is, imagining that you need not be responsible for the full humanity of the other, is to deny Christ, for it is believing that you can know Christ without following Christ (this is cheap grace).

WHY DOES THIS MATTER?

Relational ministry has very seldom been discussed or taught within the context of place-sharing. Relational connection is rarely approached from the level of ethical action. When discussing the practice of relational ministry we infrequently recognize adolescents as those who place an ethical demand on us to be responsible for their very humanity. We often neglect to understand that their suffering is an invitation to enter gently into relationships of place-sharing. Too often youth workers have been led to believe that they are responsible solely for the spiritual development or commitment of adolescents, and perhaps certain moral behaviors that are seen as detrimental to adolescents' spiritual growth. When responsibility is discussed within youth ministry it usually focuses on the leadership and direction of the program or maybe the safety of adolescents on an outing or trip. Rarely discussed is our vicarious responsibility for the full humanity of the adolescent.

When we fail to discuss the youth worker as an ethical actor for the very person of the adolescent, we fail to provide adolescents with a message of hope. We may have taught them that God cares and that their sufferings can be brought to the foot of the cross, but have we placed ourselves at the foot of this same cross, saying, "Let me carry your pain with you, and in our mutual suffering God will minister to us"? Practicing relational youth ministry as place-sharing means opening our arms and saying, "I will bear this load with you. Fear not, you are not alone. God is near to us, for Jesus is your true advocate. Let us together hope for God's return."

We know that our platitudes are unhelpful, but we often pull them out anyway when we are at a loss for words. It is time to place them on the shelf, for the place-sharing youth minister can no longer rely on them. When seeing the severity of the adolescent's situation, youth workers can no longer say, "Take it to God." "Just keep praying. Remember that God is working on you." "Just remember God loves you." Such comments are often used to avoid responsibility. "Take it to God" can mean "Please don't involve me." "Just keep praying" might convey "It's up to you alone, find your way out of this because it isn't really suffering, it's God making you better." And "Remember that God loves you" says "You're alone. I want nothing to do with this, but I don't have to feel bad because God is involved." Rather, the relational minister who is a place-sharer will state, "Bring it to me." "Come, I will pray with you." "Remember that I love you. Look into my eyes and see that I care. Feel my compassion and support; know it is a sacrament of God's love in Christ, which points to a time when you will hurt no more!"

Bonhoeffer teaches us that the incarnational youth worker must become a place-sharer to adolescents, for in such relationships persons are transformed by the presence of God in the humanity of Jesus Christ. But, we may ask, what is the shape of place-sharing, and how does it stay faithful to the open-and-closed dynamic? Place-sharing corresponds to reality and takes on guilt (being open), and does this in freedom (being closed).

CORRESPONDENCE TO REALITY AND TAKING ON GUILT

For Bonhoeffer, place-sharing finds its shape as it is molded around reality itself. Acting ethically as a place-sharer means acting in correspondence to reality. This means two things for Bonhoeffer; first it means that *the place-sharer meets the other with eyes wide open.* We work to take in the whole reality of the other, pushing ourselves to stand vicariously in the place of the other and recognizing the multiple pressures and experiences the other confronts in our complicated globalized world. The place-sharer sees the other in his or her numerous dimensions (both culturally and psychologically); the place-sharer understands that multiple systems affect the way persons understand themselves and their world. The place-sharer who corresponds to reality sees that persons are not only free but are affected by their unique psychological situation as it is affected by the forces and powers of culture.

The true place-sharer meets the other knowing that economic systems, family structure, governmental policies, societal perceptions and religious background affect the distinct humanity of the other. To act ethically as place-sharer is therefore to act in a manner that takes responsibility for the other within *and* in conflict with these multiple structures. But it is not enough to merely recognize these systems and the effect they have on the adolescent. We must enter them through our relationships with adolescents, suffering the many ways these systems can abuse their humanity. The place-sharer then takes responsibility for poor schools, violent neighborhoods, broken families, racism, sexual abuse and the deep psychological trauma (depression, anxiety, etc.) brought forth by these systems or by random biological occurrence (e.g., schizophrenia). "The responsible [person's] actions must correspond with reality if they are in fact to be responsible."[4] Therefore, "It is a duty of the Christian to face reality and to stand firm by it."[5]

Yet the place-sharer is not responsible to somehow fix these structures in his or her own power. Rather, the place-sharer responsibly enters into these cultural systems, speaking of their dehumanization and inequality, acting to reconstruct them in a more humanizing fashion. In the same way he or she takes responsibility for the other's psychological trauma, not in order to heal it but to feel the full depth of the trauma; being responsible to the point of not allowing the trauma or neurosis to determine the humanity of the other.

By taking on responsibility in correspondence to reality, the place-sharer, according to Bonhoeffer, inevitably takes on the guilt of the other. Bonhoeffer realized in his own time that to truly act for the Jews and others being destroyed by the Nazis, he would have to take on guilt. To responsibly oppose the dehumanizing system on behalf of the other, he

---

[4]Larry Rasmussen, *Dietrich Bonhoeffer* (Nashville: Abingdon, 1972), p. 42.
[5]Heinrich Ott, *Reality and Faith* (Philadelphia: Fortress Press, 1972), p. 299.

would have to lie and maybe even participate in the assassination of Hitler. These would be guilty acts, but Bonhoeffer believed that to be their place-sharer he would have to bear such guilt.

Our own time may not be as dramatic, but standing with and for anyone at any time causes us to take on guilt. This may not be the guilt of lying or killing a fascist dictator, but it is the guilt of connecting ourselves so closely to others that when they make poor choices such actions may reflect on us. If our objective is to be perceived as innocent and uncontaminated, then place-sharing may be impossible.

People do things, say things, think things that are embarrassing and erroneous, and ignorant perspectives and actions become attached to us. "Because you hang out with these adolescents you must be their drug dealer," or worse, "you must be a pedophile." Or we might be found guilty by association, "Danny is a racist. I bet you are too, or maybe you taught him these views." "You allowed a depressed, unstable youth to come on our backpacking trip. Now he has had an episode and ruined the trip for everyone else." According to Bonhoeffer, being a place-sharer entails taking on guilt, for in becoming the other's representative the other's guilt becomes my own.

> Because Jesus took the guilt of all human beings upon himself, everyone who acts responsibly becomes guilty. Those who, in acting responsibly, seek to avoid becoming guilty, divorce themselves from the ultimate reality of history, that is, from the redeeming mystery of the sinless bearing of guilt by Jesus Christ, and have no part in the divine justification that attends this event. They place their personal innocence above their responsibility for other human beings and are blind to the fact that precisely in so doing they become even more egregiously guilty.[6]

For Bonhoeffer, there is also a second way that the place-sharer corresponds to reality: *confessing (proclaiming) that Jesus Christ is Lord of the universe, that no reality exists outside of him,* that is, all reality is solely constituted by Jesus Christ. This is actually the primary way, for we can only be a place-sharer through the humanity of Jesus Christ, who in his person has become reality itself. This means that place-sharing demands proclama-

---

[6]Bonhoeffer, *Ethics,* p. 234.

tion. It demands that place-sharers speak of the life and work of Christ. But such speaking must be personal; it must be born from the desire to share in each other's place.

Therefore, to correspond to reality is to submit ourselves fully to the present person of Jesus Christ, who is active in the multiple realities of the world, taking them into himself, drawing them into one reality (one narrative) that is bound by his person and leads to his eschatological fulfillment. But to correspond to this reality that is Jesus Christ, we must be place-sharers with others in a world of multiple systems and situations (therefore Bonhoeffer's first and second points are intricately linked). When we submit to the true reality of Jesus Christ, we embrace reality as a place-sharer to another just as Jesus is to all humanity; and to be place-sharer is to take responsibility for all that affects the other. The first and second components of corresponding to reality are a continuous circle. In order to correspond to reality we must behold it from the eyes of the other, standing in a place to see and then bear the cultural systems and psychological situations in which the other lives.[7] But one can only do so by confessing that such systems and situations are subordinate to the reality of Jesus Christ, for there is no way to the other but through Jesus.

Everything comes under the lordship of Christ. Only that which is part of the new humanity and will continue to the end of the age is real. All else will pass away. Therefore, our cultural systems and psychological situations may be powerfully threatening and affect us greatly, but they are not real because they have not bowed to the person of Jesus Christ, who is the real One.[8] The very power of these systems and situations rests in their unreality; they deceive us into believing that we can determine who the other is by cultural definitions ("You're poor" or "You're Mexican") or by psycho-

---

[7]Ott explains it this way, "That is, for Bonhoeffer ethical behaviour is on the one side behaviour in keeping with reality and on the other conformation with Christ. The two are one and the same thing" (*Reality and Faith*, p. 278).

[8]Bonhoeffer states passionately, "Everything that actually exists receives from the Real One, whose name is Jesus Christ, both its ultimate foundation and its ultimate negation, its justification and its ultimate contradiction, its ultimate Yes and its ultimate No. Trying to understand reality without the Real One means living in an abstraction, which those who live responsibly must always avoid; it means living detached from reality and vacillating endlessly between the extremes of a servile attitude toward the status quo and rebellion against it. God became human, taking on human being in bodily form, thus reconciling humanity's world with God" (*Ethics*, p. 262).

logical situation ("You're sick," "You're crazy," "You're not to be trusted"). But this is not who the other truly is; he or she cannot be determined for all time by his or her cultural locale or psychological state. Rather their (our) identity is determined solely by the humanity of God in Jesus Christ. Cultural and psychological characterizations are not real because they are not bound in the structure of persons, but are held together by ideas. Therefore, they exist to perpetuate these ideas, not to uphold the humanity of the other. Only Jesus can lead persons into the new humanity, toward eschatological fulfillment, and thus only Jesus is real.

When the place-sharer enters the other's situation fully, facing cultural and psychological definitions with him or her, the determinative power of the other's reality (unreality) in cultural systems or psychological situation is broken. Then the other can begin to recognize his or her place in the true reality of the humanity of God.

WHY DOES THIS MATTER?

Corresponding to reality in this fashion means that the youth minister must recognize that adolescents are not solely individual wills that can simply choose this or that action. We have too often done this. We have asked adolescents to make faith commitments or behavioral changes without recognizing how they have been shaped by cultural locale and psychological conditions. If we are using relationships to merely influence adolescents, then we might assume that they can freely choose faith (like they choose which soda to drink). But this free-will individualism does not correspond to reality. The relational minister must recognize that cultural and psychological factors greatly affect adolescents. For instance, a boy who has been shuffled from home to home in his short thirteen years may have a hard time opening up and showing appreciation for a youth worker's relational contact. He may not trust anyone and may push the youth worker away to avoid being abandoned by another person. Or he may test the youth worker's commitment, verbally abusing and ridiculing the youth worker to see whether the youth worker's dedication will withstand the harsh behavior.

Corresponding to reality, the youth worker will try to compassionately understand the larger structures that affect the adolescent. The youth worker will know that the adolescent's behavior is tied to these systems and is not merely expressing his free will. The incarnational minister will recognize that more than one system (e.g., family) is affecting the adolescent. In getting close to the adolescent the youth worker discovers that this young man has been sent from home to home and family member to family member because no one can afford to keep him. The textile factory jobs that allowed his family to live in the lower middle class for decades have been moved overseas, leaving the family jobless. The boy's father left home to find work and has not returned, calling his family only twice in six years. His mother, a devout Catholic, divorced his father and tried to support herself and her son on the minimum wage set by the government and found it impossible to make ends meet. The local Catholic parish provides food for those in need, but because of her divorce she feels too ashamed to use it. With no options, she sent her son to live with her mother, who is living off of the social security and small pension of her late husband, who worked sixty years with no promotion (and only one raise) because he was Latino. All of these systems affect the adolescent, and the relational youth worker must recognize and take responsibility for them by calling attention to them and, with the church community, calling for justice. The call for justice must not be shouted above and beyond the adolescent but with and for the adolescent. The place-sharer must be brave enough to stare down the adolescent's reality, saying, "I see your suffering. I see how horrible it is, but I am not scared, for Jesus has claimed us. Come and be near to me, and together let's speak out against the injustice in your reality."

Doing youth ministry as a place-sharing requires corresponding to reality, seeing and entering the multiple systems and situations that affect adolescents. It must be reiterated, however, that correspondence to reality is not giving attention solely to these structures, but to the concrete persons who live within these structures. It is coming so close to the other that we feel the full weight of these structures on our own humanity. And in feeling its weight, we assert, "This is a heavy burden. Let me carry it with you, but let's remember these systems and situations cannot determine our humanity. Only the true human can do this, that is Jesus Christ." To join the continued ministry of God in the world we must become place-sharers and enter these very systems with and for the other, recognizing that in so doing we are following the incarnate, crucified and resurrected One—Jesus Christ.

FREEDOM

If place-sharing were only correspondence and acquiring guilt, it would be radically open, having no closedness to maintain the relationship of I and you in otherness (transcendence). With no corresponding closedness, place-sharing is a burden too heavy to bear, crushing our own person. Yet, for Bonhoeffer, place-sharing not only corresponds to reality and takes on guilt, but such actions are done in and through the freedom of our common humanity. Acting as a place-sharer is a radical step, but only because it moves away from the old humanity of self-centered bondage and leaps into the new humanity of freedom. According to Bonhoeffer, a person becomes himself or herself with and for others.[9] Place-sharing entails acting with and for others as a distinct person. It is action that connects our humanity with the fullness of reality, for it is done in the freedom of the person of Jesus Christ, who is reality. There are no *oughts* or *musts*, persons are free to be persons, but we are only free because we have followed the free One, Jesus Christ, who has overcome all that imprisons humanity. Jesus never loses his freedom in his own bodily life of responsible action. Rather, the more he lives with and for the other, the more it becomes clear the he is *the* distinct human being who is also God, unique from all others. The deeper he enters responsible action, the clearer it becomes that he is a distinct person who is the Son of God, who has freely given his life in place-sharing for all. Bonhoeffer explains:

> In the language of the Bible freedom is not something that people have for themselves but something they have for others. No one is free "in herself" or "in himself"—free as it were in a vacuum or free in the same way that a person may be musical, intelligent, or blind in herself or in himself. Freedom is not a quality a human being has; it is not an ability, a capacity, an attribute of being that may be deeply hidden in a person but can somehow be uncovered.

---

[9]"Importantly Christ as the source of the social relation energizes the vicarious fulfillment of the other's claim, which means that I am able not only to be free for the other, but to be free from the bondage of the I, and thereby am able to give myself to the other" (Charles Marsh, *Reclaiming Dietrich Bonhoeffer* [New York: Oxford University Press, 1994], p. 75).

. . . [Freedom] is a relation and nothing else. To be more precise, freedom is a relation between two persons. Being free means "being-free-for-the-other", because I am bound to the other. Only by being in relation with the other am I free. . . . [I]t is the message of the gospel itself that God's freedom has bound itself to us, that God's free grace becomes real with us alone, that God wills not to be free for God's self but for humankind. Because God in Christ is free for humankind, because God does not keep God's freedom to God's self, we can think of freedom only as a "being free for."[10]

Therefore, because this freedom is won solely by the person of Jesus Christ, it is a freedom for others, a freedom born from place-sharing. "Bonhoeffer understands freedom not in the modern, secular, and consumerist sense as countless choice"; from this perspective freedom is not freedom but bondage, for we are walled in by self-centered options. Rather, Bonhoeffer views freedom "in the classical Christian way which extends from Paul through Augustine and Luther to Karl Barth—as freedom to do the good, that is, ultimately, freedom to love God and neighbor. Accordingly, freedom and responsibility mutually imply each other."[11] Again, the more I am for others, through the humanity of God, the more I become my own distinct person connected and upheld by others. I am therefore *free* to be *me* alongside and for others.

WHY DOES THIS MATTER?

In the freedom of place-sharing there is both a no and a yes, or both judgment and mutuality. In the freedom of place-sharing I am obligated to oppose all actions and behaviors that would imprison the other or myself. In relationship with adolescents the relational youth worker, in freedom for both oneself and the adolescent, must be able to assert, "No. Stop!" When confronting drug use, serial sexual behavior or violence, for example, the place-sharer must say no, judging the activity or attitude. He or she does so in being free for the adolescent, for dehumanizing activities or attitudes will inevitably lead to a loss of freedom in the tangled web of self-centered (self-destructive) pursuits.

---

[10]Dietrich Bonhoeffer, *Creation and Fall: A Theological Exposition on Genesis 1-3* (Minneapolis: Fortress Press, 1997), p. 163.

[11]Clifford Green, *Bonhoeffer: A Theology of Sociality* (Grand Rapids: Eerdmans, 1999), p. 320.

In being with and for others as place-sharer, the youth worker takes on the responsibility of helping the other maintain or find freedom in the person of Christ. Some have been deceived into believing that relational youth workers may never make judgments on the actions or activities of adolescents, believing that making judgments will destroy the relationship. But this is erroneous, for relationships are upheld in the freedom of responsibility. Relations are lost when adolescents are imprisoned in dehumanizing activities and attitudes, because without freedom there can be no true relationships. But the fact that there is only freedom through the person of Jesus means that freedom is not freedom to do whatever we want; rather true freedom is freedom to be a human being through the new humanity of Christ, which means being for others in responsibility. If an adolescent has caged him- or herself in dehumanizing actions and attitudes, he or she must be confronted, for to ignore this is to ignore the concrete humanity of the adolescent.

In the freedom of place-sharing there is also the yes of mutuality. In being close to the other I must open up myself to the other. I am free to do this in the way and at the time that I desire, but to truly be for the other I must allow the other to hear and see my own suffering, pains, joys and celebrations. We meet adolescents not only to know them, but that adolescents might also know us, seeing our own humanity in our distinct sufferings and joys. Such mutuality is bound in freedom. My secrets can (and must) remain my secrets. No other person has control over my distinct humanity. But to be human, to find my person in the person of Christ, I must eventually, from my freedom, reveal my unique person to the other. Too often incarnational ministry has flowed in one direction. We have asked adolescents to let us come close and know them, but we have failed to reciprocate. At times we have demanded that they open up, with no mutuality. John Macmurray explains: "If I know you, then it follows logically that you know me. If you do not know me, then necessarily I do not know you. To know another person we must be in communication with him, and communication is a two-way process. To be in communication is to have something in common."[12]

---

[12]John Macmurray, *Persons in Relation* (London: Faber & Faber, 1961), p. 169.

One-way demands to know someone violate the freedom of place-sharing. In freedom, place-sharing allows the other to know me, respecting my distinct boundaries, and subsequently inviting the other to reveal and make him- or herself known. Therefore, place-sharing demands that in my freedom I make myself known to the other by being with and for the other. Adolescents may choose to remain closed to us due to their harsh realities or developmental locations, but this is of secondary concern to we who have become place-sharers. Our primary concern is freely making our humanity available to adolescents, inviting them to respect and honor our distinct boundaries while sharing in their unique suffering and joys.

CONCLUSION

An examination of Bonhoeffer's theology through his three overarching questions—Who is Jesus Christ? Where is Jesus Christ? and What then should we do?—has revealed the possibility that relational youth ministry can be practiced from a rigorous theological perspective that avoids the cultural baggage it has accumulated. We have seen that Bonhoeffer's answers to these three questions fit well with Langmead's threefold criteria for incarnational mission and make helpful corrections to many of the presently thin conceptualizations of relational ministry. (See figure 4.1, p. 83.)

Langmead's first perspective—Jesus as pattern for mission—has been a staple of relational ministry for decades. All the youth pastors I interviewed explained that their justification for using an incarnational approach was because "that's what Jesus did." Yet by unpacking Bonhoeffer's answer to "Who is Jesus Christ?" we have deepened this from simply mimicking a pattern to experiencing the living Christ as not only incarnate but also crucified and resurrected. Rather than seeing Jesus as simply a pattern to copy (as though this were possible), through the theology of Bonhoeffer we have seen that Jesus is a person, the true person. Thus the pattern we follow is that of persons meeting persons in the reality of Jesus Christ. Because Jesus is *the* person (true God and true human), all reality is borne in his person.

Langmead's second perspective—participation in the continued presence of Jesus—is conspicuously absent from much of the literature on relational youth ministry and was not mentioned by the youth pastors I interviewed.

Through Bonhoeffer's theology we saw that Jesus Christ is a *who*, a person who encounters others. Therefore he is present, but where? Bonhoeffer answers this through his theology of relationship. He asserts that God in Christ is concretely present in the church and the world, where persons meet persons in being with and for each other in the construct of I and you. Therefore, I experience the transcendent otherness of God in my encounter with the other person. When I act with and for you, God meets us both. And as Christ meets us in the relationship of I and you, each person is transformed, for we have encountered each other in the reality of Jesus Christ, changing us into the human beings we were created to be.

Finally, Langmead says incarnational mission is "joining God's mission in the world." All the youth ministries I interviewed had components of service and mission, but there was little that connected these programs to the eschatological future toward which God is moving humanity and creation. Bonhoeffer addresses Langmead's third component by answering "what then should we do?" Bonhoeffer asserts that we should act ethically as responsible place-sharers for our neighbor. Because God in Christ is the true place-sharer for humanity and creation, we must participate in God's ministry of place-sharing by becoming, in the power of Jesus' person, place-sharers ourselves. Joining God as place-sharers for humanity means we join God's eschatological mission in the world.

What then does it mean to see the practice of relational ministry through the theology of Bonhoeffer? We should not view ministry as a practice in which youth workers influence adolescents, making the relationship a means to a greater end. Rather, we should see ministry as the location where unique persons encounter fellow persons. Therefore, relational ministry, from a theological perspective, is not about influence but transcendence, about concretely experiencing the otherness of God within my concrete relational bond to the adolescent. "God's transcendence is not remote otherness or absence; God's otherness is embodied precisely in the other person who is real and present, encountering me in the heart of my existence with the judgment and grace of the gospel. In this way Christ is present *pro me*, for me."[13] The I-you relationship of person meeting person

---

[13]Clifford Green, "Human Sociality and Christian Community," in *The Cambridge Companion to Dietrich Bonhoeffer*, ed. John De Gruchy (London: Cambridge University Press, 1999), p. 124.

is the place where the transcendent otherness of God encounters us both. It is the concrete place where God is revealed to us (the place of God's revelation).[14] Green says, "Christ is present in human form—in the 'other' as the form of revelation and transcendence."[15] Relationships with others lead to our mutual transformation into the new humanity of Jesus Christ. It is then through person-to-person relationships that we, together, overcome that which threatens to destroy our humanity.

Relational youth ministry then is much more than one of many strategies for influencing adolescents for spiritual growth and religious commitment. Relationships are the concrete place where we meet the transcendent otherness of God in God's revelation and subsequently become place-sharers for young people.

Youth ministry, like all other ministry, is persons meeting persons in relationships bound by responsibility, for it is here that we meet Jesus as other. In the next chapter I will present a paradigm constructed from the theological discussions of chapters three through five. We will explore how persons meeting persons is transformative at both the existential level (Who am I? Why do I exist?) as well as the cultural level (What is my environment? How do I deal with it?). Ultimately, we will see how relationships of place-sharing can be the concrete place of encountering God, affecting our very being in the world.

---

[14]"Revelation is a social reality. God cannot be understood in isolation from humanity, and human beings cannot be understood individualistically" (Green, *Bonhoeffer*, p. 84).
[15]Ibid., p. 182.

7

How Place-Sharing Works

One of my students recently gave me an article from *Glamour* (I promise I'm not a regular subscriber) called "Why I Went Hungry," an autobiographical piece by a woman named Alison.[1] On a summer morning when she was fifteen, her world crumbled with the ringing of her door bell. As she was finishing a bowl of cereal and dreaming of how to busy herself on a rainy summer day, she heard a blood-curdling scream. Running to the door she found her mother on her knees. Two men, dressed in gray rain coats, were holding their hats uncomfortably. "What's wrong?" she asked. "The one on the left told me that Roy [her older brother] had been involved in a fatal accident."

The family was devastated by the death of Alison's older brother. Her father was inconsolable, simply repeating Roy's name over and over as he wept. The mental image of such family suffering and the profound experience of the loss of a sibling became a lasting memory for her.

The grief never left her family. To deal with it Alison started an odd ritual. She started eating only half of every meal. Deep in her subconscious she imagined that she could save the second half for her brother. She had spent her life sharing food with him, and now having it all to herself felt

---

[1]Alison Smith, "Why I Went Hungry," *Glamour*, May 2005, pp. 220-24.

like a violation of his memory. By the time Alison graduated from high school she was 5'6" and 85 pounds.

Leaving high school and home didn't change things. Alison spent her first three and a half years of college hiding half of her food as a sacrifice to her wounds of grief. During her senior year of college, Alison began eating her evening meal with her roommate, Katie. Katie began to notice that Alison never finished all her food. Asking about this, Alison assured Katie she was not hungry. The next evening the same thing, half the food left untouched.

Katie pressed the issue, and Alison burst into tears and told Katie of her brother's death. Then silence, broken eventually by Alison as she told Katie the whole story—about Roy's death, about her family's enduring grief. "I'd been saving food for him all these years, thinking this would keep him close to me."

Katie listened in silence to Alison's story. The next day she took Alison to dinner saying "You've got to learn to finish what you start." Alison ate, feeling as though she betrayed her brother's memory with each bite—but she ate her entire meal. Katie sat with her, grieving alongside her, offering silent encouragement through her presence.

Over the months that followed, they continued to eat together. Alison cried as she ate, but she also told Katie stories about growing up with and then losing her brother. Katie shared stories about her family as well, even painful stories about her challenging relationship with her parents. Before long the meal would be over, and Alison's plate would be clean. "I would . . . wonder out loud, 'Where did the food go?'"

This is a beautiful story of Katie being a place-sharer for Alison. Over a period of months Alison learned that sharing memories with another gave them more permanence: "The closer I got to Katie, the closer I got to Ray."

Why was Katie's relationship of place-sharing so transformative to Alison? Using Bonhoeffer's theology, I have argued that relationships are the place of God's concrete presence in the world. But how and why are human-to-human relationships of place-sharing transformative? In this and the next chapter I will attempt to answer these questions.

When thinking of relational ministry in terms of place-sharing, there are three overarching components that must be considered: (1) the person, (2) culture and (3) transcendence/revelation. In the last three chapters we allowed Bonhoeffer's three questions (Who is Jesus Christ? Where is Jesus Christ? What then should we do?) to lead us into a theological understanding of relational/incarnational youth ministry. In this chapter and the next, the three components of person, culture and transcendence/revelation will help us develop a picture of relational transformation.

We need to remember, though, it is only a picture. While pictures reflect something true, they are perspectival, coming from a certain angle of vision. Some may argue that I distinguish too clearly between person and culture. While I am committed to their mutual distinction, the margin that separates them in this paradigm is for the sake of clarity.

To bring my paradigm of transformation to life I will present it piece by piece using two narratives. The first narrative will be the story of fifteen-year-old Kelly and her youth pastor, Mandi; the second will feature twenty-year-old Will and his counselor and friend Sean. Kelly and Mandi are not real people. Their story is a conglomerate of anecdotes from my own and my students' ministry experience as well as from interviews with youth pastors. Nevertheless, because their stories are formed from these experiences, they are "real," or say something true. Will and Sean are not real people either; they are two characters from the Academy Award-winning screenplay *Good Will Hunting*. I have chosen these two narratives to give life to my paradigm of relational transformation. The first narrative (Kelly and Mandi) reveals how a youth worker's actions to be a place-sharer can transform an adolescent, leading to a life of discipleship. The second narrative (Will and Sean) shows the mutuality of the actions we can take for the other. Because it is a written screenplay, it also displays person-to-person dialogue that so vividly illustrates Bonhoeffer's theology.

Like building a house, I will lay out the frame of my paradigm, nailing each section together part by part: person, culture (chap. 7) and transcendence/revelation (chap. 8). I will use the two narratives as sheetrock and plaster to transform the skeletal structure into a home full of life.

By the end of these two chapters I hope that you will not only have a deeper theological understanding of a relational youth ministry of place-sharing but also a picture of how this ministry (conceptualized through Bonhoeffer's theology) is transformative to persons in their cultural situation, through the transcendent otherness of God in Christ.

THE PERSON

James Loder may give more attention to the issue of transformation than any other theologian. After experiencing his own transformational moment during a near-fatal car accident, Loder devoted the rest of his career to articulating the multiple dynamics of transformation through theology and the social sciences. What is particularly interesting is Loder's discussion of the inner dynamics of the existential life of the person, which helps us understand the unique inner shape of persons.

Loder asserts that there are four dimensions within a person: the "lived world," the "self," the "void" and the "holy." We often understand the inner shape of the human, or what Loder calls the human spirit, in a two-dimensional way, seeing the human only in correlation to the world and the self. But if our understanding of a person is to be truly theological, we must see the inner structure of the human in all four dimensions, including the void and the holy. He explains:

> The first two dimensions have to do with the human spirit, because the human spirit describes how we create and compose the world in a human sense. What we want to do is shift to a frame of reference that includes these first two dimensions, but then goes beyond them to include the whole scope of human existence.[2]

The self. Loder's first dimension is the self. The self is most basically the irreducibility of the I. "No matter what you understand about me, you will never understand what it is for me to be me."[3] To make this point more concrete, Loder shows the irreducibility of the I, of the self, by discussing Wilder Penfield's neurological experiments. Penfield was the first neurologist to do open-skull experiments with patients who were conscious. As Loder explains, by touching the brain Penfield could find the location of memories. When he touched one part of the brain, the patient would hear music; if he touched another part the patient would smell a certain odor. Yet what Penfield could not find (and is essentially significant to Loder) is the cerebral location of the I. When the brain was touched the patient would state, "You did that. I didn't." This pushes Loder to assert, "What

---

[2]James Loder, "Educational Ministry in the Logic of the Spirit" (Princeton University, 2001), chap. 5, p. 23.
[3]Ibid., chap 5, p. 25.

Penfield observed here . . . was the dual nature of self-relatedness as packed into a single symbol, 'I.' "[4] There is within the human a unique self-relatedness, for it is only I that understands what it means to be me.[5] This self-relation is the first dimension of the inner life of the human person.

The lived world. The second dimension is the lived world. Here the self works to build an environment in which the self can exist. It is a world created from the perceptions and understanding of the self; in other words, it is the creation of the self to find a place for the self. This is not to say that the lived world is a schizophrenic dream, but that it remains an operation within the self. Loder explains, "What the self does is repeatedly compose the world. You live in a world—not a world that is out there, but a world that you compose from what is out there. I'm not saying there is nothing out there. I am saying what is out there is something you constantly construe in order to make the world livable."[6]

The self is always at work recomposing and revising this world to make sense of new ideas, issues and experiences. What we think is "out there," while truly in one way or another being so, is more rightly within us. We understand it only as it is arranged in correlation with our self. Loder explains, "Reality 'out there,' as we normally speak of it, is an elaboration on, but not the foundation of, the lived 'world'; it is a reflective objectification of whatever lived 'world' one may spontaneously compose."[7]

Loder has shown that it is an ontological necessity to continue to form and reform a lived world. We receive data to form this environment from the surrounding "outer world," but we have a world only as we compose it around the dimension of the self. Hence, healthy life itself is an adaptation, for without the environment the self has no context to understand and relate to itself. This then means that the locus for change (for transforma-

---

[4]James Loder, *The Transforming Moment* (Colorado Springs: Helmers & Howard, 1989), p. 77.
[5]While seeing the beauty and power of this self-relatedness, of this irreducibility of the I, we must also see how it confronts humanity with a problem. Drawing from Kierkegaard, Loder explains, "As open to its world, to its embodiment, to new meaning and purpose, the self is extremely vulnerable; it experiences what Kierkegaard called 'the dizziness of freedom' and out of this dreadful condition it will fall into false grounds for securing itself, paradoxically attempting to establish its integrity of openness by locking it into universal systems of value or doctrine, enclosing it in a presumably 'open community' or by exercising a compulsive openness emulating Protean behavior" (ibid., p. 79).
[6]Loder, "Educational Ministry," chap. 5, p. 27.
[7]Loder, *Transforming Moment*, p. 72.

tion, whether good or bad) must come through the dimension of the "lived world," for it is only through this dimension that the self is given a new context to understand and relate to itself.

The void. The third and fourth dimensions of the inner reality of the human make Loder's understanding unique and explicitly theological. The third dimension is the "void." While the self is an irreducible I, which is always forming and reforming a lived world, it also must face its existential state, that it is not immortal. It must face with each new day the truth that it is one day closer to its slide back into nonbeing.[8] This void, Loder explains, is not only outside us but also within us. Therefore, when the void shows itself, it sends tremors to the core of our being because it speaks a language we know and dread. If the lived world is the locus of change and transformation, then the void is that which propels us to move, to act, informing and reforming the world around its haunting cackle.[9] When the void reveals itself, we must try to reconstruct our actuality in such a way that the monster is pacified and the person is upheld.

Practically, the void takes many different forms in our lives, from conflict to loneliness, from estrangement to abuse. All such experiences are stringent reminders of death, which is the present raging of the void within us. Loder explains:

> The void, then, is the third dimension of being human, but it has many faces, such as absence, loss, shame, guilt, hatred, loneliness, and the demonic. The void is more vast than death, but death is the definitive metaphor; "nothing" in itself is ultimately unthinkable, but death, shrouding all our lived "worlds," gives our clearest picture of nothing.[10]

The holy. The final dimension in Loder's understanding of the person is

---

[8]"Both these dimensions [the self and the lived world] of human beings are weak with respect to the third, the possibility of annihilation, the potential and eventually the inevitable absence of one's being. I will discuss this dimension under the rubric of the 'void,' because this is the end result of each human being, implicit in existence from birth and explicit in death. The 'void' is understood as the ultimate *telos* toward which all experiences of nothingness point; 'nothingness' refers to the 'faces of the void' taken collectively" (ibid., p. 70).

[9]"If the lived 'world' is the context of transformational knowing, and the self is 'the knower,' the face of the void intruding into the two-dimensional existence of the self-world is the 'conflict' that moves transformational knowing into action. . . . The void is implicit the moment the lived 'world' is ruptured and the process of transformational knowing begins" (ibid., p. 81).

[10]Ibid., p. 84.

the holy. There is something within the self that understands that the void, though real and unavoidable, will not and cannot have the last word. There is simply a transcendent impulse within humans. This transcendent impulse allows humans to understand themselves as distinct selves, critically reflect on their lived world, be fearful of the void and yet still hope for salvation in some form. Yet Loder's understanding of the holy is not a natural theology (such as Karl Barth accused Emil Brunner of having), an *analogia entis*, but is rather the other side of the reality of the void. Just as we intuitively understand that we were created from nothing and will return to it, we find this to be a problem and seek (vigorously) for an answer or solution to the problem. "The reason we do not cease to live," Loder explains, "is the deep sense that we are not merely three-dimensional creatures."[11] We have no direct knowledge of what the holy might be; rather the holy is an inclination within us that longingly hopes for liberation from the void and its fatalism (see fig. 7.1).

The first two dimensions, the "self" and the "lived world" are depicted as squares because they are sustained within the inner reality of the human. The other two dimensions, the "void" and the "holy," encompass the whole of the person, for they affect both of the other two dimensions. Therefore, they are not squares but left free of shape within the person because though they come from outside the person, in affecting the person they become part of the person.

The relevance of this for relational ministry is that these multiple dimensions are operating within each adolescent we encounter. Each adolescent has a tacit and dynamic (ever-changing) way of understanding him- or herself. The adolescent asserts, "I am this kind of person." Being that kind of person the young person lives in ways congruent with his or her self-understanding. (This is the lived world.) These lived-out conceptions of the self confront daily the reality of emptiness and death, forcing the self and lived world to compensate for the void's hauntings. And yet even in the midst of the frantic adaptive compensation of the self and the lived world to avoid the pitfalls of the void, the person still has hope, asserting, "Though I am this person and live this way, I hope I can be like this and

---

[11]Ibid., p. 85.

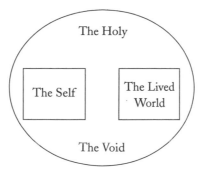

Figure 7.1. Loder's four dimensions of a person

live like that." Such is the way of all persons; we hold a loose but powerful conception of who we are, living in a manner congruent with this understanding through the ever-present realities of death and hope. This process dawns in more directly cognitive ways in early adolescence as the young person searches for an identity, but it remains a continuing process, as postmodern life-cycle theorists have recently argued.[12]

TWO NARRATIVES: KELLY AND MANDI, WILL AND SEAN

Kelly met Mandi (a youth pastor) when Kelly had just turned fourteen. Kelly's family moved into a townhouse adjacent to Mandi's. Mandi often noticed Kelly playing with her brothers and sister, and at times just hanging out on the driveway or front steps of her house. One day, needing help carrying the garbage cans to the curb, Mandi asked Kelly, who was sitting on the stoop, to give her a hand. From this short encounter Kelly and Mandi began waving to each other and sharing quick hellos and goodbyes.

Soon Kelly was stopping by Mandi's a few times a week. They would sit at Mandi's kitchen table and talk over soda and pretzels. It came out very quickly in their conversations that Kelly struggled in school. Kelly suggested that she was stupid because she had a hard time reading, got bad

---

[12]See Kenneth Gergen, *The Saturated Self* (San Francisco: Basic Books, 1991).

grades and was made fun of for the way she talked. Kelly defined her "self," her unique I, as stupid. Mandi always noticed heaviness in the way that Kelly carried herself. The unshakable depression of being stupid (as she understood her "self") gave Kelly a slouched, slow appearance. This definition of her unique "I" greatly affected her lived world. She explained to Mandi (in a round-about way) that she dreaded school and lacked the confidence to try new things or even to articulate her thoughts. The void had grown large in her life.

When Mandi asked if Kelly was ever scared by the thought of going to high school, Kelly spat back, "I don't think they'll let me go. I think they'll hold me back." When Mandi asked her if she thought that was fair, Kelly responded, "I am stupid. I don't think I could do high school work." Yet, even through the dark clouds of Kelly's understanding of herself and her environment, rays of hope beamed through. When Mandi questioned Kelly about what she wanted to do when she grew up, in an absurd inconsistency that Mandi nevertheless thought was truthful, Kelly responded, "I want to be a teacher; I think I will go to college and then become a third grade teacher." The holy was still stirring within her.

Will and Sean have been meeting for a number of months. Sean is Will's court-appointed therapist, but Sean isn't all that interested in being Will's doctor; he'd rather be his friend. Will began seeing Sean only to stay out of jail. Though Will looks and acts like a blue-collar thug, he is a mathematical genius able to intuitively solve problems and equations that even the greatest minds at MIT struggle with. He doesn't see himself as a genius but as a tough and fearless blue-collar kid from South Boston. But underneath his hard exterior is a vulnerable self who feels unlovable and unwanted.

Will, it seems, tries to hurt others before they can hurt him. He has built his lived world around this understanding of himself. He has refused to grasp his God-given talents and has chosen instead to commit himself to the rough life of urban Boston, working construction, drinking with his friends and fighting. The void is raging within Will; he has refused to allow himself to be truly known and in so doing has pushed away his girlfriend, Skylar, who loves him deeply.

But the holy too is present as Will probes, through conversations with

Sean, for answers about love and commitment. Sean's own understanding of his unique self has recently been shaken. He has lost his wife to cancer and is having a hard time seeing himself as anything other than depleted, beaten and finished. His lived world has been torn to pieces; he is left wondering who he is now that he is no longer lover and husband. His loss has kept him from reentering his vocation as a counselor to war veterans. He feels adrift in his grief. The void meets him in the deafening silence of an empty apartment as he returns from work. Yet, through the fatigue of sadness Sean can still find the energy to hope. The holy is still present: he has reached out to Will, a young man from his own neighborhood of South Boston.

Will, Sean, Kelly and Mandi (though we have not gotten into Mandi's background) all have deeply imbedded conceptions of themselves. Will sees himself as unlovable and vulnerable to be hurt by others, Sean sees himself as grief-stricken and lost, and Kelly sees herself as stupid and worthless. These self-understandings lead them to live in certain ways within their unique worlds. Will drinks and fights, refusing to use his talents. Sean sits alone in his apartment, stewing in his own thoughts, coming to grips with his belief that the best part of his life is over now that his wife is gone. Kelly walks into her classroom with her head down, hoping that if she can make herself small enough she can avoid the many flying daggers that accompany the social embarrassment of slurred speech and stuttered reading. She moves through her day in apathetic slow motion, presenting heavy shoulders, self-protective scowls and half (most often sarcastic) smiles. Though all three have deep hopes, they spend most of their time running from the void. Will pushes against a void of abuse, Sean fears being swallowed by loneliness, and Kelly feels sucked in by the undertow of worthlessness.

If they are to experience transformation, their very complicated four-dimensional persons will need to encounter deep change. Each one's unique I will need to redefine itself. Their lived worlds will need remodeling. The void will need to be silenced and scolded to take its place respectfully. And they need to allow the holy to speak truthfully, liberated from unrealistic dreaming and connected to the unique I in the lived world. But of course Kelly, Will and Sean (as well as Mandi, for that matter) are not solely influenced by their inner perceptions and how they live out these perceptions. But these very perceptions are engendered from their day-to-day living in the pressures and flows of culture. If they are to be trans-formed, it will not only address the existential core of their self but also confront how culture affects them. This leads us to the second major com-ponent of a relational transformational model of place-sharing: culture.

CULTURE

The structure of culture. According to Ann Swidler, culture is "the pub-licly available symbolic forms through which people experience and ex-press meaning."[13] Yet people do not experience and express meaning within culture per se but rather through multiple sectors which, when held together in aggregate, are labeled culture. Meaning is experienced and expressed as people live as members of families, participants in the economy, citizens in governments and members of religious groups. This means that culture is not a simple whole but is made up of overlapping systems that mutually penetrate and affect each other.[14] These systems or sectors are the structure of culture. They are family, economy, govern-ment, society and religion.[15]

All cultures, in one way or another, consist of these five sectors, yet the meaning they have and the way they are practiced are unique to location and time. For instance, both ancient Israel and Victorian England had family structures, but these shared structures were understood and prac-

---

[13] Ann Swidler, *Talk of Love: How Culture Matters* (Chicago: University of Chicago Press, 2001), p. 12.

[14] The Italian Marxist Antonio Gramsci developed the idea of the sectors or systems of a culture while writing in one Mussolini's prison cells. See his multivolume work *Notebooks from Prison*. For a more manageable version see Antonio Gramsci, *Selections from the Prison Notebooks* (New York: Interna-tional Publishers, 1971).

"The five basic sectors often overlap; they reinforce one another; they inevitably interpenetrate one another. In a myriad of ways, they mutually influence one another" (Max Stackhouse, "Religion, Society and the Independent Sector: Key Elements of a General Theory," in *Religion, the Independent Sector, and American Culture*, ed. Conrad Cherry and Rowland Sherill [Atlanta: Scholars Press, 1992], p. 14).

[15] These sectors or systems are from Stackhouse's "Religion, Society and the Independent Sector," in *Religion, the Independent Sector, and American Culture*, AAR Studies in Religion, ed. C. Cherry and R. A. Sherrill (Atlanta: Scholars Press, 1992), pp. 11-30. I have termed Stackhouse's political sector "government" and his cultural "social." *Culture*, up to this point, has been my blanket term for the interaction of these sectors, and I will remain committed to this understanding. I will refer to all five sectors together as the "cultural field." Hence, it was important to change the terms to avoid confu-sion. For an explanation on why I place religion under the cultural field, see Karl Barth's *Epistle to the Romans* and Bonhoeffer's *Letters and Papers from Prison*. Both theologians show that this category is too weak to be all-encompassing.

ticed much differently (the most obvious difference being polygamy and monogamy). The uniqueness of location and time informs and directs the particular practices. Therefore, each of the five structures of culture are bound by ideological hegemony.

Each society has a loosely agreed upon ideal understanding and practice within each sector.[16] For instance, in the United States there is an ideal family form: two parents and two or three children living under one roof (until the children reach the age of eighteen). These ideologies are not frozen but are ever-changing (sometimes with more frenzy than others; this is what Swidler means by "settled and unsettled times" in her article "Culture in Action").[17] For example, while the two-parent, two-children ideology remains operative in American culture, it is slowly evolving, making it more common (and acceptable) to be a family in which mom and dad are not married, or the children are not the product of the present relationship, or the married couple is of the same gender, or older children remain in the parents' home as young adults. The ideologies of the five sectors are always in the process of change and adaptation. They are considered hegemonic because their evolutionary change is a product of interactions within the cultural setting and evolve as individuals and groups discover new meanings. The change is not a product of direct coercion by the powerful (at least not in most democratic nations) but happens as individuals and collective groups renegotiate meaning.[18]

For the sake of our picture of relational transformation I have labeled these five sectors as "the field of cultural totality." The word *totality* is used deliberately because of its connections with the thought of Emmanuel Levinas (the justification for this label will be seen more clearly as our picture takes shape).

These five sectors greatly influence our being, for better or worse. As we

---

[16]These ideologies are constructed around moral codes of right and wrong. For further discussion see Christian Smith, *Moral, Believing, Animals* (London: Oxford University Press, 2003).

[17]Ann Swidler, "Culture in Action: Symbols and Strategies." *American Sociology Review* 51 (1986): 271-86.

[18]For further discussion of hegemony from this perspective see Gramsci, *Notebooks from Prison*. For a helpful overview of Gramsci see Roger Simon, *Gramsci's Political Thought: An Introduction* (London: Lawrence & Wishart, 1982), and Paul Ransome, *Antonio Gramsci: A New Introduction* (New York: Harvester Westsheaf, 1992).

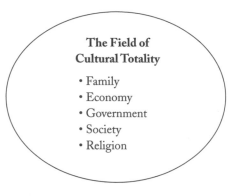

Figure 7.2. The field of cultural totality

interact within them we are given direct data about ourselves. From our acceptance or confrontation with these ideologies we receive information to construct our four dimensions (the self, the lived world, the void and the holy). The cultural field may lead us to believe that we are entirely defined by the ideologies of the five sectors. Thus the ideologies are not experienced the same way by everyone; our experience of the ideologies is shaped by our own situation and person. For instance, when the dominant ideologies of our culture idealize rich, white, Protestant consumers with well-adjusted and active children, one's very person (in its four dimensions) must deal with the incongruity between the ideologies and his or her actuality. So, if a man is summarized as a poor, Catholic, Mexican, illegal day worker, with six hungry mouths to feed, his logical response might be, "I am a failure, and I'm ticked off (the self). The world is a cut-throat place, and to survive I must do the cutting first (the lived world). I will join a gang and sell drugs so I can make money to feed my family (the hope of the holy), but if anyone threatens me I'll kill 'em (the void)."

There is a reciprocal nature to the dynamic between persons and culture. Just as our situation shapes how we experience culture, so the cultural field shapes how we know ourselves. My own subjective experience of the cultural field shapes my history, molding my interpretation of the family I grew up in, the money and education I have, my place in society, and the faith community to which I belong. These ideologies are nonontological. Though they have a strong influence on my being, they only determine who I am as I take them into my person (which is my being) in the four dimensions. Therefore a person living in the same cultural situation as the poor, Catholic, Mexican, illegal day worker may choose not to join a gang.

As the picture shows, the person (in his or her four dimensions) stands outside the cultural field. This does not mean that individuals stand outside culture (for this is not possible); rather it shows that each individual has his or her own subjective experience of the ideologies of the five sectors. Everyone is locked within culture, but as Swidler has shown, people interact within culture in different ways.

Following the diagram's arrows we see a data stream from the five sectors to the individual's unique history; this history then leads directly (following the next arrow) to the person and his or her four dimensions. Therefore, the four dimensions of the person are constructed and revised

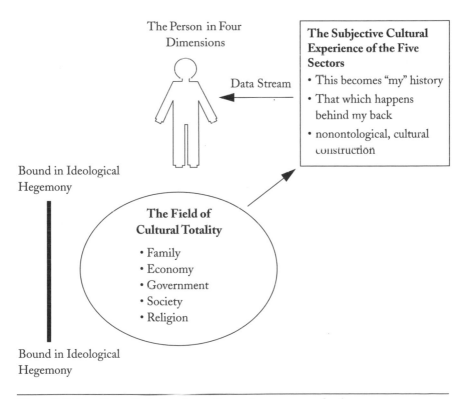

Figure 7.3. Paradigm of relational transformation: person and culture

from the data received from the cultural field.

KELLY AND MANDI, WILL AND SEAN

Kelly had her own unique interactions with the ideologies of the five sectors. Mandi had noticed both Kelly's mom and dad coming and going from their home; they appeared to be a normal family (mom, dad and four children). Kelly spoke of her parents in typical adolescent fashion; at times she criticized them for their lack of understanding, while at other times she spoke appreciatively of them. But what started as another typical conversation soon shattered Mandi's idea of the normalcy of Kelly's family. In the midst of discussing Kelly's long brown hair, Mandi asked, "Is your mom's hair naturally blond or does she dye it?" Kelly at first answered directly, "I think it's always been that way." But then in a half whisper, as if wanting to say it out loud but fearful that in so doing the earth would shatter, Kelly looked down and said quickly and quietly, "She's not my real mom. I mean, she is my mom, but I wasn't her baby."

After some gentle probing, Kelly explained to Mandi that her biological mother was actually her present mother's sister. When Kelly was two, her biological mother was arrested for possession of crack cocaine and had been in and out of jails and treatment centers ever since. Kelly's aunt, now her mom, took Kelly from Phoenix to Los Angeles to raise her. Kelly had not seen her biological mother since; her only contact had been two cards and a strained phone call. When Mandi asked if she ever talked to her dad, Kelly responded, "No one knows who he is." Mandi figured Kelly was the result of an addict needing a quick fix.

Kelly explained to Mandi further that her two older siblings were the children of Kelly's aunt and another man who moved out when Kelly was eleven. Her new dad, who had been living with them for two years, moved in when Kelly's mom (aunt) became pregnant with his child, her third child. Kelly was the only child in the home who had no direct biological connection to one or the other parent. Mandi asked her if this made things difficult, if she felt like they treated her differently. Seeming not to want to answer, Kelly looked up quickly and forcefully stated, "Sometimes," and then changed the subject. Mandi wondered how much Kelly's feelings of worthlessness were tied to being abandoned by her biological mother and feeling different from her siblings (family sector).

Economic pressures also affected Kelly; her mother was the breadwinner, working as a sixth grade teacher, but to supplement her salary she tutored at a local center after school hours. This kept her away from home until 7 p.m., making her unavailable to her own children. Kelly's (present) father worked odd construction jobs; some months he made a lot of money and other months he made none. The lack of extra income made it impossible for Kelly to receive the speech therapy she needed to correct her lisp. From third to sixth grade Kelly was provided speech therapy in school, but with recent school budget cuts such help was no longer available. Kelly felt like the only good thing she had in her life was her friends, and to keep them (she believed) she needed to have cool clothes and nice things (like an iPod) (the economic and governmental sectors).

She also believed it was important that her clothes revealed her recently developed figure. She had begun to be noticed by boys and liked (and hated) the way she felt when they looked at her. Once when Mandi asked Kelly to describe her friends, she explained, "Most of them are Mexican like me; we hate all those white b****es because they think they're all that." In further discussions Mandi learned that Kelly had experienced (a fair number of times) "mean girl" racism when she walked alone in the halls, one girl stating, "Hey look, it's that stupid Mexican girl that can't read. She's stupid like all Mexicans" (society sector).

Kelly's family never went to church. But Kelly had gone two times at Christmas when the family was visiting her grandmother in Phoenix. Kelly's family had a number of icons of the virgin Mary and one of Jesus in their home. When Kelly asked her mom why they had them, she shot back, "Because they make me feel good, and if anything bad happens I can pray to them." When bad things happened to Kelly or she felt really bad about herself, she tried praying. But, as she explained, "it never helps" (religion sector).

Will is an orphan. We don't know if he has ever seen either of his parents, but we do know that his foster father beat him mercilessly, sometimes with a belt, sometimes with a stick, but most often with a wrench. He now lives alone in a small, run-down apartment with no family (family sector).

Like most people in his neighborhood Will is living paycheck to pay-check; he feels a knot of resentment when he thinks of the packed class-rooms of Harvard and other institutions. He knows he is smarter than all of them, and yet because he lacks a rich father and a trust fund he is on the out-side looking in (economic sector). But Will isn't really trying to get into college; rather he is trying to stay out of jail. He has had a number of run-ins with the legal system and has a checkered past of stays in juvenile hall and probation. He is patriotic like most in his neighborhood; he loves baseball and respects the flag, but has little trust of the government. For instance, he has refused to take a government job, believing that in the end the government looks out for itself and those with money, and his buddies in his neighborhood will be left holding the bill (government sector). Will has a potent understanding of the haves and the have-nots, and it seems to enrage him at times (societal sector). His neighborhood is saturated in an Irish Catholic spirit. However, Will never attends church. Yet he recognizes how Irish Catholicism has influenced him and his neighborhood (religion sector).

The ideologies of the five sectors of culture in actuality are not easy to differentiate. For instance, determining what is an economic issue and what is a family issue is almost impossible. Nevertheless all are present in the lives of Kelly and Will. These ideologies provide direct and powerful data that shapes who they believe they are. Their histories—their understanding of their own unique places in the flow of the five sectors—have been molded by these cultural forces. For instance Kelly is the daughter of an addict and lives with her aunt in a lower-middle-class home with no money for speech therapy. She dresses to please the boys, has experienced harsh racism and is not involved in a faith community but her mother prays to icons. Kelly's person in the four dimensions (of self, lived world, the void and the holy) confronted this history. Who she is, how she lives in the world, the threats of nothingness, and the strength to hope are all constructed from her unique history, her own *Sein* and *Zeit* (being in time) in the five sectors. Like Kelly, Will too constructs his unique I and lived world around data he receives from the five sectors of culture. His place in the world throws him into the hands of a choking void; he must wrestle free from its grip to find the strength to hope. His poverty, family abuse, outcast status and distrust of authority have dynamically affected his person.

If another person were to stand in and become a place-sharer to either Kelly or Will, he or she would have to understand the five sectors of culture and how they uniquely affect Kelly and Will. But we must ask, Is this (the data they receive from the five sectors and their response to it) *it?* Is that all that Kelly or Will is? Are they not more?

AGENCY IN CULTURE

Up to this point I have laid out the multiple sectors of culture and discussed how the ideologies of these multiple sectors influence a person in his or her unique location within culture. Yet, this picture of culture is incomplete. Persons are not only affected by culture but together with others in community (either tightly or loosely bound) also change culture. Collective units of individuals (who often share a common history) shape culture through their actions and practices. These actions and practices of cultural engagement are strategic and most often are learned and created within these collective units.

Culture is made up of structures; it is also made up of agency, of individuals and groups acting within culture. While those who make up these groups do not share exactly the same financial situation, position in society or family background (demographics), they often share a certain perspective on the ideology of each of the five sectors.[19]

People do not form collective groups simply because they are similarly affected by culture. They are born into collective groups—neighborhoods, congregations and families. These groups provide symbols, stories and worldviews that give perspective to the ideologies, helping individuals understand who they are in the context of the five sectors. For instance, a girl born into an anti-establishment, antigovernment family in the mountains of Montana may hear stories of how the government is unjust and is planning to use mind-control to ruthlessly govern it citizens.[20] These stories

---

[19]To this end demographics may be an issue; people who have a shared ideology of money and family may choose to live in a certain neighborhood and attend a church that reflects who they understand themselves to be by affirming the ideologies to which they are committed.

[20]Family can be seen as both an ideological sector and a collective unit. There is a cultural ideology of the way family should be or what constitutes a family, but there is also the life of the family that provides stories and myths which teach each member the truth, lies or danger of the other ideologies, including that of family.

and myths would both affect the way she saw herself in the context of the dominant ideologies as well as provide her with strategies of action that could be taken in opposition to the dominant perspective. Fortified by the stories and myths of the collective unit, she would see her unique history as one of oppression by the American government. This would influence her understanding of herself in the four dimensions. But it would do more; the collective unit would also provide a tool kit (to use Swidler's phrase) of possible actions to be taken in engagement with the dominant ideologies. Therefore, she may choose to bomb a government building, begin stock-piling weapons or simply vote in a certain manner. The collective unit provides a lens to see the dominant ideologies of the five sectors in association to herself, and also provides tools created from a shared tool kit to engage these dominant ideologies. The tool kit provides her with strategies of action to engage these five sectors, working to either maintain their ideological shape or change them to be more appealing and accepting of the collective unit.

Therefore, our picture needs some updating (see fig. 7.4). The rectangle of history needs expanding, thus a dashed line creates two sections. The top portion remains the person's subjective cultural experience of the five sectors; it remains the person's unique history. However, the section below the dashed line is the collective unit to which the individual belongs. (I recognize that in a complicated globalized world individuals belong to more than just one collective unit.) Following Swidler and others, the picture presents individuals as constructing strategies of action from within distinct collective units in culture. These collective units may not be as clearly defined as the examples previously used. Nevertheless, individuals need interactions within collective units, however they are formed, to provide them with a tool kit.

Between the dashes separating the rectangle are arrows, two going down and two going up. The arrows illustrate the flow of impact. The arrows pointing down represent how our subjective history links us to a collective unit (i.e., people who see the world similarly because of similar experiences in culture). The second set of arrows illustrate how the collective unit, through its stories and myths, frames our unique history, helping us make sense of our place in culture. The data stream that had led from the

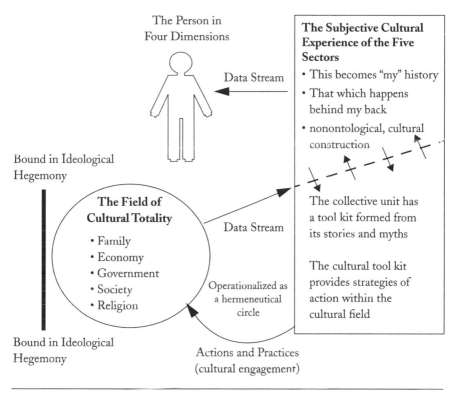

Figure 7.4. Paradigm of relational transformation: person, culture and agency

five sectors into the person's history now touches the dashed line. This signals that the ideologies of the five sectors give data both to our history, causing us to adapt our four dimensions to this history as well to the collective unit, leading the collective unit to form strategies of action from its own tool kit in interaction with these ideologies. The ideologies are bolstered or discarded depending on their ability to serve the collective in its interaction with the five sectors.

Below the arrow of the data stream is a curved arrow, originating from the collective unit and its tool kit and pointing into the five ideological sectors. This arrow represents the actions and practices of cultural engagement used by the collective unit. These actions and practices are constructed from their collective tool kit with the objective of working to change the ideological hegemony of each sector. For instance, from their biblical commitments evangelicals have judged the family to be under attack. Using their tool kit, they have formed strategies of action to halt the ideological changes to the family and to replace them with their own version of family.

The arrow going from the five sectors to the dashed line and the arrow going from the collective unit to the five sectors have formed a kind of misshapen oval. Inside this oval I have written "operationalized as a hermeneutical circle." This suggests that the ideologies of the five sectors are influenced by the actions and practices of cultural engagement. When affected they often (maybe only minutely) change their ideological shape (this is their hegemonic essence in Gramscian terms),[21] providing new information to the individual's history and the stories and myths of the collective unit. These revised ideologies present new actions and practices, formed from new strategies within the collective. This is to show that collective units have the power to influence culture through their engagement, ultimately revealing that the individual person is not simply a spectator in culture but is rather a player.

NARRATIVE OF KELLY/MANDI AND WILL/SEAN

When Kelly turned fifteen, things abruptly changed. Mandi had been meeting with Kelly for informal conversations for about six months, and they had become good friends. Mandi had thought of Kelly as a young girl; she had watched her play in the sandbox with her younger brother and have water fights with her older siblings and neighbors. Mandi recognized that Kelly had a number of issues she would need to deal with, but Mandi wasn't ready for the speed at which they escalated. Kelly had a number of important friends when she was in eighth grade; but in ninth grade these friends, as well as a few older ones, became Kelly's life. According to Kelly, her friendship group was the most important thing to her. When Kelly brought her friends to her house, Mandi would walk over and meet them. As Mandi got to know them, she realized that Kelly and her friends shared a similar background. Most came from single-parent homes and lived in lower-class to lower-middle-class families, and all were Hispanic. The girls loved hip-hop, swooned over tattooed, shaved-head gangbangers,

---

[21]I am referring to Antonio Gramsci, who asserted that cultural change occurred through the process of hegemony, where those in power entered into a give-and-take association with others.

and loved to watch romantic comedies. They shared loose stories and myths of the way the world was. These stories and myths (which they, of course, learned from a number of sources like media, relatives, older siblings, etc.) helped them form a tool kit of actions and practices to be used in their interaction with the five sectors. For Kelly these actions and practices included taking drugs, having sex, shoplifting, yelling at her teachers and blatantly disobeying her parents.

From Mandi's perspective this was more than peer pressure, this was a group of girls with a shared vision of the world who engaged this world tenaciously. These actions were strategic; they confronted ideologies of authority, wealth and importance. Of course, for Kelly, the tools that her collective unit provided did not help her deal with the brokenness of her four-dimensional person. While allowing her the activity to ignore her brokenness, they nevertheless fed the void, allowing it to grow stronger within her person.

Will may be an orphan, but even so he has a family; his family is his group of three friends (Chucky, Morgan and Billy). All four have been raised on the tough streets of South Boston. They have a fierce loyalty to each other. The stories and myths that form their tool kit are constructed from the blue-collar existence of their uncles and cousins, which they now share. Their main strategy of action in conflict with the five sectors is to fight, and if there are no takers, then to get drunk. To maintain their own place in the collective unit, each must follow this code. This can be seen clearly in the circumstances that brought about Will's latest arrest.

While drinking beer at a Little League game, Will spotted Bobby Champa, who used to beat Will up in kindergarten. Seeing Bobby again shook Will's four dimensions; all the feelings of neglect and abuse came rushing to the surface. The void began to howl; his self was reminded that it was bruised; his lived world screamed for retribution; and the holy demanded justice. Drawing on the tool kit of his collective unit, Will moved into action. Waiting for just the right time, he and his friends saw Bobby and others walking through the neighborhood. Will asked Chucky to stop the car. Jumping out he confronted Bobby with a strategy of action born from his collective unit: a right hook to the face. Chucky and Billy (Will's friends) didn't think twice, they jumped out of the car to join in the brawl.

The tool kit had set their actions: when one brother fights, all brothers fight. This is seen clearly in the response of Morgan; not all that keen on fighting (now that he held a double burger in his hand) he proclaimed as the car stopped, "I am not going; we've got snacks now." As Will jumped out of the car, Chucky turned to Morgan with a finger in his face, stating, "Listen, if you're not out there in two seconds, when I am done with them you're next!" In the next scene we see Morgan punching someone in the face. To be part of the collective unit is to share the same actions and practices within culture and in conflict with the ideologies of the five sectors.

I have laid out a complicated understanding of the person as he or she stands within the multiple sectors and forces of culture. We have seen that culture is made up of five sectors. And when a person confronts the ideologies of these five sectors in his or her unique location, they give direct data to the person, which becomes the person's history. This history must be assimilated into the person's four dimensions.

But things are even more complicated. Persons exist within collective units (tribes, neighborhoods, families, congregations). These collective units have their own shared tool kits that are formed from important stories and myths that make sense of culture and its five sectors. These collective units provide further information about one's history, giving a lens to see the data from the five sectors, but they also offer strategies of action which are used to engage the ideologies of the five sectors.

A relational youth ministry of place-sharing is practiced with an understanding of the complicated person (in four dimensions) and culture (in its multiple layers). In so doing the youth worker is corresponding to reality (as Bonhoeffer would desire). Such an understanding helps us see that the adolescent is more than just a free will, choosing or not choosing a faith commitment or healthy behavior. Rather the adolescent exists as a complicated four-dimensional person within a complex of multiple cultural forces. A meaningful ministry must be cognizant of all these factors.[22]

---

[22]I have argued throughout this book that relational youth ministry has too often been about influence. Through Bonhoeffer's theology we saw that influence is the driving force of our (so-called) relationships, and therefore transcendence (of both God and the human other) is lost. From this perspective Jesus is seen as only a pattern ("Jesus did it this way, so we do too") and not as a living person. The pattern of Jesus becomes a story or myth that forms the strategy of action, and nothing more. The

This is all fine and good, but we need to address the adolescent's transformation into the new humanity, which is, as we have seen through Bonhoeffer's theology, the objective of the gospel. So I will flesh out our picture further by turning to the transcendent otherness of God in chapter eight. Then Bonhoeffer's theology of relationship will come to life as one person meets another in the transcendent otherness of God.

---

youth worker often places him- or herself on the dashed line between the adolescent's subjective history and the collective unit. Here the youth worker tries to provide the adolescent with different stories and myths (a new tool kit) with which to understand him- or herself and from which to engage culture. Of course this is not all bad; many adolescents need a new collective community. But the question remains, can such a community be transformative at the level of the new humanity if it takes no account of the otherness of God's transcendence? And can a practice that avoids the otherness of God's transcendence be faithful to the transcendent otherness of our human neighbor? Or will we instead demand that the other look and act a certain way to find a place in our collective units?

8

Picturing Relational Transformation

The other day my mother-in-law was in town. She was here to visit my wife and me, but more importantly, to see our two-year-old son. It had been a while since she had seen him, and, as all parents know, a lot changes from week to week with infants and toddlers. After playing with him for a while she crossed my path in the kitchen; looking back at his wispy blond hair and pale skin she asked me, "Do you feel like he is your clone, like when you look at him you're looking in a mirror?" I knew what she meant, we do look alike (which right now serves him well but he may need prayer in the future). Yet as she said it, all I could think about was his eyes, the utter mystery that encounters me when I look into them. He isn't my clone, but is as different from me as can be. My mind flashed back to the many times I rocked him, stared into his eyes and felt struck by his otherness. I thought about the many funny and wonderful things he has said and noticed, about the rich thoughts his two-year-old mind clung to and constructed. No, he is not my clone, a copy of my own being, but is radically different from me. Sure, we share a great deal of DNA, and I will inevitably nurture in him a worldview similar to my own (even if I desire not to). But the more I love him, the more I experience his transcendence, the more I realize he is a mystery, that he is too beautiful to be possessed—

the depths of his person are too deep for my mind to comprehend and my heart to capture. His otherness is his transcendence, and his otherness can only be experienced through our relationship of transcendent person to transcendent person. Encountering his transcendence has radically transformed me. This chapter seeks to understand and illustrate theologically why encountering another's transcendence is transformational.

TRANSCENDENCE/REVELATION

Transcendence is that which is other or beyond us, that which has no direct correlation with our own being. In 1919 Reformed pastor Karl Barth shocked European theology with his "new beginning." Having been trained in Europe's top theological faculties, Barth realized that the theology he had been taught gave him nothing to preach to his working-class congregation in the Swiss city of Safenwil. Barth resolved to start his theology all over again. Beginning by rereading the book of Romans, he discovered on page after page, as though seeing it for the first time, the all-encompassing biblical claim that God is wholly Other—transcendent. Barth's new theology asserted, according to Bromiley, that

> God is God, not man writ large; and he cannot be spoken of simply by speaking of ourselves in a loud voice. He cannot be taken for granted as simply "there" in our religious sense, our spiritual depth, or our moral awareness, for he transcends, he stands over against all of these. . . . There is absolutely no continuity, similarity or resemblance between God and man . . . or between God and anything else at all.[1]

Before the Barthian revolution, theology had largely given up on transcendence. In a post-Kantian world it was believed that all we could know for sure is what we could experience with our five senses. Since God could not be known beyond doubt through our sensory experience, theology stopped discussing the unique action and character of God and spoke instead of the subjective experience of God by humans. Therefore, German liberal theology focused on religious experience; American Social Gospel theology focused on governmental action for the betterment of an industrial society.

---

[1]Geoffrey Bromiley, *Introduction to the Theology of Karl Barth* (Edinburgh: T &T Clark, 1991).

More recently, following this perspective, certain forms of liberation and feminist theologies have focused on economic and societal opposition to oppression, and even conservative groups like Focus on the Family have fallen into this trap by giving attention to a particular form of family as a sign of God's will. All of these perspectives have eliminated the transcendence of God, shifting theology from a discipline that reflects on God's transcendent revelation to a discipline that can say nothing of God's otherness and therefore attends only to the five sectors of what I have called the cultural field.

All of these theological perspectives (with some exceptions) have reduced revelation to the cultural field, which is to concede our ultimate eschatological hope to the five sectors, none of which (being sinful systems) have the power (otherness) to break the hegemonic ideologies. In the end, theology sacrificed to the ideologies of the five sectors will finally become only a subpoint of one of the five sectors. Eliminating transcendence by transposing revelation into the cultural field negates the power for transformation in relation to the person of God.

Therefore, in developing our picture of relational transformation we must have two fields: cultural totality and transcendent otherness. These two fields must not be confused but must remain differentiated. This does not mean that theology is somehow outside of culture; rather theology is locked within its particular location, which is always bound culturally. However, even culturally bound theology reflects on that which is outside of culture, and in doing so it breaks into culture, working for its transformation.

Dietrich Bonhoeffer followed Barth in seeing the need for theology to focus on the otherness of God. Bonhoeffer's perspective adhered to Barth's in maintaining a distinction between the otherness of God's revelation and the movements of the five sectors of culture. Yet, unlike Barth, Bonhoeffer was working from a Lutheran perspective. Luther claimed that all of our knowledge of God must come solely from God's action and person as seen on the cross (Luther's theology of the cross, *theologia crucis*). Nevertheless, especially in Germany in the 1930s and 1940s, this perspective was not appreciated in Lutheran theology. Rather, Lutheran theology kept the otherness of God and the operations of culture separate, maintaining that culture operated freely through the orders of creation. It was believed that

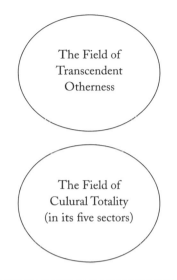

Figure 8.1. Two fields of relational transformation

certain orders, almost matching the five sectors of culture, were forms God used to govern creation without direct connection to God. Therefore, these orders of creation were distinct and separate from the revelation of God in Christ. There were two separate spheres (two kingdoms) demanding two kinds of obedience and responsibility: the kingdom of the world and the kingdom of God.

Bonhoeffer found this perspective troubling. Following Luther's theology of the cross Bonhoeffer maintained that "in Jesus Christ the reality of God entered into the reality of this world. The place where the answer is given, both to the question concerning the reality of God [the transcendent field] and to the question concerning the reality of the world [the cultural field], is designated solely and alone by the name Jesus Christ."[2] For Bonhoeffer the five sectors of culture are not distinct orders of creation but rather orders of preservation.[3] Green explains, "All orders of our fallen

---

[2]Dietrich Bonhoeffer, *Ethics* (Minneapolis: Fortress Press, 2005), p. 58.
[3]"In *Creation and Fall* Bonhoeffer published a major revision of the Lutheran theological tradition. He set a concept of 'orders of preservation' in place of the traditional Lutheran doctrine of 'orders of creation' " (Clifford Green, *Bonhoeffer: A Theology of Sociality* [Grand Rapids: Eerdmans, 1999], p. 203). The major difference between the orders of creation and the orders of preservation rests in

world are God's orders of preservation that uphold us and preserve us for Christ. . . . They have no value in themselves; instead they find their end and meaning only through Christ."[4] Therefore, the five sectors remain under God's control; they are gifts of God used to preserve human life. But in themselves the five sectors can provide no direct knowledge of who God is. They are given to humanity as gifts; there is freedom to use the gifts for wholeness and peace or for violence and abuse. In themselves the five sectors (the orders of preservation) cannot lead to an encounter with the living God; rather the living God must break in and make Godself known (revelation) from outside the sectors, within human existence and history.

Therefore, when the field of cultural totality stands alone and works to determine who the person is through the ideologies of each of its sectors, it has failed to take account of Jesus Christ. Bonhoeffer states clearly, "The world has no reality of its own, independently of the revelation of God in Christ."[5] Because Jesus is incarnate, both fully God and fully human, and has lived in culture and been crucified by it, and has overcome it through the resurrection, his very person mediates person to person, person to creation, and person to God through his own living person. Jesus Christ is the *who* that encounters others through his own person, standing *pro me* for all humanity. This then means that there remains two distinct fields, but these distinct fields cannot be considered reality for humanity. The field of cultural totality cannot be reality, for it takes no account of the revelation and otherness of God in its ideological structures. The field of transcendent otherness cannot be human reality, for it is outside and beyond the person; to remain transcendent it must remain other. But these fields, according to Bonhoeffer, have been melded into one reality constituted by the person of Jesus Christ. This is Bonhoeffer's unique understanding of transcendence. God is wholly Other, but we experience the otherness of God in the nearness of our human neighbor—but only as we understand our neighbor as

---

the understanding of God's action or agency within them. The orders of creation are bestowed by God and operate free from the agency of God. This then leads to a clear separation between the world (and its orders) and God's activity. By giving attention to the orders of preservation Bonhoeffer hoped to overcome the separation by providing a way to think of God's activity within the orders of the created world.

[4]Ibid., p. 205.

[5]Bonhoeffer, *Ethics*, p. 58

a transcendent mystery that can never be seen as tool or object. Therefore, for Bonhoeffer, the fields are different in kind but bound in the very humanity of Jesus, who encounters persons as a person.

In continuing to develop our picture of relational transformation, we must maintain two fields, for without two fields the otherness of God is lost in the human operations of culture, and humanity is left to its own devices. But these two fields must not be left separate, for to do so is to fall into the trap of the "two kingdoms theology" that Bonhoeffer opposes. Leaving the fields separate would allow us to compartmentalize our lives, living one way, with certain commitments and responsibilities in the cultural field, and then another way, when we imagine ourselves in the transcendent field. There is an overlap where the field of transcendent otherness breaks into the field of cultural totality. For Bonhoeffer this overlap is mediated by the person of Jesus Christ, who is the very revelation of God and who has moved and continues (through his Spirit) to move within the many cultures of the world. The place of the overlap I have labeled "reality" because Bonhoeffer asserts that the person of Jesus Christ is reality, for in his person he stands with and for all persons in the *pro me* structure mediating all person-to-person relationships with each other, creation and God.

We partake in and taste the reality of Jesus Christ through person-to-

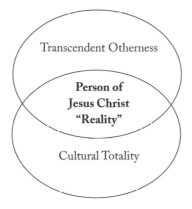

Figure 8.2. The transcendent and culture: the overlap in the two fields of relational transformation

person social relationships of place-sharing. What happens when person meets person in relationships of place-sharing? When we act as place-sharers (1) we experience the concrete presence of Jesus Christ as transcendent in our relational bonds with the other, (2) we discover that the other person is transcendent to our own being and as such is beyond or more than cultural definition, (3) our actions for and with the other, who is transcendent, are governed by Jesus' own actions of place-sharing, and (4) we experience the transformation of our very person in encountering the transcendent other. Let's explore these phenomena.

Experiencing the presence of Jesus Christ as transcendent in relational bonds. Reality is constituted by social relationships because person-to-person encounter is the pattern of Jesus' ministry, for he is ontologically *pro me.* The place of Jesus' concrete presence calls persons to encounter persons in actions of vicarious love, and in so doing partake in the eschatological mission of God, which is to return humanity to humanity in the new humanity of Jesus Christ. Therefore, to be in the new humanity is to join in bonds of relationship (constituted solely by the person of Christ) which meet the other (my neighbor) as a transcendent mystery. According to Bonhoeffer, transcendence is no longer beyond us in an other-worldly manner but is close at hand—in the neighbor, who we meet as other than us in relational connection.[6] Transcendence is still wholly other than our being, but it is no longer far off. It is close at hand in our human neighbor, whom the transcendent God has become near to as the incarnate, crucified and resurrected One. Ray Anderson, building on Bonhoeffer, explains it this way: "Instead of transcendence defined as that which lies beyond or at the furthest reach of finite reason, and thus a limit which man 'places' at the boundary of his existence, I chose to think of transcendence in terms of the act by which a personal agent moves beyond his own self-existence

---

[6]"Transcendence is not God's otherness beyond humanity and above the world; the holy, creating, sustaining, and reconciling love of God which is revealed in Christ is God's lordship in the world among human beings. . . . God is present in the encounter of individuals and their communities as *Kollektivpersonen.* The 'other,' as individual person and corporate person, is the 'form' in which God is really present as the divine 'Other' in the world. Transcendence in Bonhoeffer's theology of sociality, then, is socia-ethical transcendence. Its form is the social form of human personal life, and its content and goal is to create and redeem community between human beings and Christ and among human beings themselves" (Green, *Bonhoeffer,* p. 64).

to confront and inter-act with an 'Other.' "[7] In the construct of person meeting person, or social relationships, the revelation of God breaks into human existence. Because Jesus Christ is person, there is no way into reality but through person-to-person encounter.

The other as transcendent to cultural definition. Persons are more than their place in culture; they are more than how the five sectors define them. Emmanuel Levinas has built his philosophy on a critique of Heidegger's *Dasein* ("being there"), which he believes is dangerously open to totalizing persons, defining who they are by their place in the five sectors of culture. Levinas has asserted that the human person is more than just being, for being can be totalized. Someone might say, "Oh, I know you fully, you're a single mother with a large inheritance, living in big house in an all-white neighborhood and belonging to a large Christian church." But most would agree persons are more than just their being; they are more than their location in the five sectors. There is something mysterious about persons that spills over or transcends the definitions of being. Levinas asserts that persons are being, but they are also metaphysical; therefore the other person confronts me with more than his or her cultural locale but also with a transcendent infinity. Confrontation with this infinity happens when I am moved beyond my own conceptions of the person, when I confront the uniqueness of the other's face. Persons, when we meet them as persons, always escape totalization. Persons are transcendent. We discover who someone truly is not through the lens of culture but through relational bonds with another.[8] I discover my gifts, shortcomings, sufferings, joys and loves within my relational bonds to another. In his or her otherness I am drawn from the self-determination of cultural sectors into the revelation of my unique own person, a person established by the nearness of my neighbor who loves from the nearness of Christ.

A mother is a mother not because culture has determined her as such but because she has given herself to her child. Culture may determine that

---

[7]Ray Anderson, *Historical Transcendence and the Reality of God* (Grand Rapids: Eerdmans, 1975), p. 190.

[8]Of course if relational bonds fail me, I am left with only culture to help me. Relationships are made more complicated by the impact of culture, but culture is never finally determinative of who one is. In deep relationship culture's determinative power is overthrown in loving embrace.

her child is worthless and unlovable, but the mother has looked into her child's eyes and seen an ocean of wonder and beauty. She swears she can see God in her child's smile; she is prepared to die for her little one. What is real to her is not her baby's deformity but her baby's person as it encounters her. In person-to-person interaction we are freed from the totalizing definitions of the five sectors of culture and partake in the transcendent through the otherness of the neighbor. I realize that the other is more than his or her family status, financial position, benefit to society or religious commitments; Jesus Christ is for and stands beside this other.

Therefore, by being in relationship, by my acting with and for another, he or she is defined first and foremost as friend. The other's experience of the cultural sectors become only his or her history, not reality, for our reality is determined already by Jesus Christ. In seeing another's infinity (the mystery in his or her eyes) I am drawn into relational bonds; my I is connected to the other's you, and so I experience the transcendence of God in Jesus Christ who stands for this other I encounter. Therefore, in relationship with the other I partake in the transcendence of God by partaking in the concrete mystery of the other. By acting responsibly for the other I enter into reality—Jesus Christ—where the transcendent and cultural fields are arranged in a cohesive whole.

This social connection is what Ray Anderson has called "closing the circle of transcendence." He explains, "The Christian closes the circle of transcendence by living 'as Christ' in the world."

> Thus, instead of pointing away from himself, from his own humanity, to Christ, the Christian must say: to become involved with me is to come up against Jesus Christ who is "present" to our humanity through the divine communion. . . . One should live and speak incarnationally so that Christ again has hands to reach out into the world to give, feet to walk the roads of life with men, and arms to embrace the lonely and hold close the estranged.[9]

Our actions for the transcendent other are governed by Jesus' actions of place-sharing. When we close the circle of transcendence, we are conformed to Christ, who is place-sharer to all humanity. Therefore, the circle of transcendence is molded around the person of Jesus Christ. My actions

---

[9]Anderson, *Historical Transcendence and Reality of God*, pp. 274, 263-64.

to the other, if they are bound in the relationship of I and you, of person meeting person, must be governed by Jesus himself. Therefore, my relationship with the other must be open and closed, be responsible, be mutual, provide honest judgment, and in all correspond to reality (both the reality of Christ and the reality of the other's history). In these actions I move beyond seeing the other as a totalized product of culture and see him or her as a transcendent mystery for whom I am called to be responsible. These actions are the action of Jesus Christ, who in his person is open and closed to humanity as fully God and fully human; is responsible by being incarnate, crucified and resurrected; shares in our humanity, gives honest judgment by opposing all dehumanizing actions; and corresponds to reality by confronting the true suffering and death of humanity, taking it upon himself and forging a new reality in his person. In this action to and for the other we together partake in the person of Jesus Christ, who leads to the transformation of persons into the new humanity.

We experience the transformation of our very person in encountering the transcendent other. In person-to-person encounter, where one is place-sharer to the other, the adolescent's (and our own) four dimensions are transformed. In encountering us the adolescent is given new data that is taken directly into his or her four dimensions. Therefore, there is more than one stream that leads into the inner dimensions of the person and his or her personal history. In encountering us the adolescent is given new data about him- or herself and about his or her history. The adolescent (as well as the youth worker) is given a new look (a true look) at reality in connection to an other.[10] In words and actions of place-sharing we say to the youth, "You may think you're unlovable, but look at me, I love you." "You may think you're no good, but you have helped me." "You may think that no one cares, but here I am." We can also shed new light on the adolescent's history. "It must have been hard to live like that; that should have never happened to you." In relational bonds with us the adolescent is trans-

---

[10]Anderson says, "It dawns upon us that we are loved freely and intelligently by another; where the inner logic of that love is undeniably present, not in our own needs, but in the other's actions, not even in our own spirit, but in the other's body. And thus it is here that we come up against the transcendence, not the beyond, the infinite, which extends out from us, but the 'nearest to hand,' the flesh which carries in it the logic of spirit" (ibid., p. 104).

formed (changed, converted), because he or she is opened to reality, to
Jesus Christ. In relational bonds new data confronts historical data, altering the historical in light of the relational, the cultural in light of the theological. Both the adolescent and the youth worker are given a new perspective, a perspective from the vantage point of relationship, to see our shared
or distinct collective units and the tool kits they have provided.

Through encounter with the other, the stories and myths of our tool kits
must come under judgment. I recognize that people are poor not because
they are lazy but for complicated reasons. The adolescent discovers that
racism is not a thing of the past but remains a troubling issue. This new
perspective may cause the adolescent to leave his or her collective unit in
search of a new one, or he or she may remain within it, integrating the new
perspective into the life of the collective. Regardless of whether the adolescent departs or remains, he or she is given a new collective unit to belong
to, the church community, which calls the adolescent to give of him- or
herself in continued relational bonds to persons in the church and world.
From within this collective, and its theological stories and biblical myths
that are continually crucified and resurrected in relationships of place-
sharing with others, we are given the actions and practices to engage the
five ideological sectors of culture, confronting their dehumanizing ideologies because they have sought violence against the neighbor whom we have
loved in relationship. We engage culture to transform it into a place where
our neighbor can live freely as a human being, as God intended. I confront
the ideologies of the five sectors because they are no longer able to preserve
the humanity of my neighbor, but in their sinfulness are used to destroy
him or her.

Now furthering our picture of relational transformation (fig. 8.3) we
must place persons (including the four dimensions) to the right and the
left of the overlapping circles. Accompanying each person is his or her history and collective tool kit. This overall structure represents a relational
bond. The arrows on each side of the small circle (oval) formed by the
larger overlapping circles represent the many actions of place-sharing by
one person to the other. These actions are open and closed, are responsible, are mutual, provide judgment, and correspond with reality. They are
molded around the person of Christ, who stands between each person,

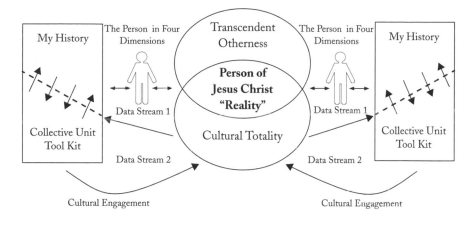

Figure 8.3. Paradigm of relational transformation: person meeting person

showing that all actions are done unto Christ for the other.

The small circle formed by the overlap defines the actions of relationship and is the circle of transcendence, for it is the place where we concretely encounter the mystery of Christ in the mystery of the other. The set of arrows pointing from the overlap to the persons point in two directions because each person interacts with and for the other from his or her four dimensions, but in so doing is also acted upon, which provides new data to be assimilated into the person's own four dimensions. These arrows are called "Data Stream 1" because the relationship can provide primary data, which overrides the message of the persons' histories.[11] Therefore, person-to-person interaction can help us redefine our unique I, understand our perceived world differently, silence the void in the care of the other, and increase hope of the holy in mutual support.

The arrows on the other side of each person lead to his or her history. This arrow shows that when our four dimensions are transformed in relational bonds, our history in the five sectors is also transformed. This does

---

[11]John Macmurray explains, "The 'I' and the 'You', we have said, are constituted by their relation. Consequently, I know myself only as I reveal myself to you; and you know yourself only in revealing yourself to me. Thus, self-revelation is at the same time self-discovery" (*Persons in Relation* [London: Faber & Faber, 1961], p. 170).

not mean that our abusive past is forgotten, but that now, having been provided with new data to know ourselves, we are free from the determinative power of our history. Therefore, we become more than our suffering and hurt. While still part of us, suffering and hurt are no longer our prison.

The four arrows between the dashed line separating "My History" from "Collective Unit" remain, but now following the path of transformation from data stream 1, our reconceived history leads to a reconceived collective community, which provides new stories and myths, leading to new actions and practices of cultural engagement.

An arrow points from the sphere of "Cultural Totality" to each person's history. This represents the fact that ideologies continue to press in on us, as though to define our existence. This can never be escaped. Therefore, there remains a data stream from the five sectors to each person's unique history. This is labeled "Data Stream 2" because it continues to be a force in our lives, but it is relegated to secondary position in light of the connection of I and you in the person of Jesus Christ.

Now is the time to take what I hope is a very rich theoretical conversation and place it back into the lives of Kelly and Will. We will see that in meeting each other in the transcendent reality of relationship their own person is transformed in the actions of place-sharing.

KELLY AND MANDI, WILL AND SEAN

Kelly's life was quickly spiraling out of control, and Mandi knew it. Mandi often heard yelling and screaming followed by slammed doors in Kelly's home. She would look out her window to see Kelly running to the car of one of her ever-changing boyfriends. Mandi was worried about Kelly. To make matters worse, Kelly was not coming around as much. And when Mandi reached out to Kelly, her care was returned with sarcastic comebacks and nasty stares. Mandi reminded Kelly that she could talk with Mandi if she ever needed anything, and Mandi continued to pray for Kelly.

One day Mandi gave it another try. Seeing Kelly and three of her friends (an older girl and two guys), Mandi approached them. "Hi, Kelly," Mandi said in an upbeat way, as she crossed the lawn to meet them. Kelly gave a half smile that quickly turned into a sneer as she turned back to her friends. Mandi thought she heard Kelly say under her breath, "Oh great, here comes that fat b***h." Her friends laughed. Not sure of what Kelly said and past the point of no-return, Mandi asked, "Who are your friends?" Mandi had met the girl, but not the boys. Kelly said, "You know Jana, and this is Jorge and Mark." And then with a vicious look on her face that said get ready to hurt, Kelly looked into Mandi's eyes and said, "And guys, this is Mandi. She lives across the street; she's thirty-two and has no husband. And I have never seen a guy come to her house, but that might be because her house smells like onions, and is filled with lame s**t like beanie babies, not to mention she dresses like old Mrs. Hunter" (their sixty-year-old English teacher).

Trying not to cry and matching sarcasm for sarcasm, Mandi responded, "Thanks for the nice introduction, Kelly." After staying just long enough for it to appear that Kelly's comments didn't crush her, Mandi left, returning home in tears. She watched from her window as Kelly's friends left. After Kelly waved goodbye from the driveway, Mandi opened her door and asked Kelly to come over.

Sitting at Mandi's kitchen table as they had done many times, Mandi looked intensely into Kelly's eyes and asked, "Kelly, is that really who you think that I am? An overweight, single woman with no family, who dresses poorly? Is that all I have been to you?" Kelly looked down half angry that the question was asked and half ashamed.

Mandi continued, "Kelly, when I look at you, I don't see a girl who is too skinny, who can't read well and is the daughter of a drug addict. No, I see Kelly, my friend, who I laugh with and talk about movies with; I see someone I have let know me. Today, Kelly, you have hurt me, and I want you to know; I want you to look at me, and see that I am a person who deserves better than that. I won't allow you to treat me like that again."

Kelly looked back up, now totally ashamed, and said in a whisper, "Sorry." But something had changed for the better; Mandi had become a barrier to Kelly. Mandi had asserted her own closedness (while affirming her own openness). Kelly would have to respect the mystery of her otherness or choose to no longer be in relationship with her.

It is Will's first appointment with Sean. Will has a knack of chasing away potential counselors and plans to do the same with the Sean. Will's strategy is to find something personal and to exploit it to get the upper hand. He did this successfully with his first two counselors, questioning one's sexuality and mocking the legitimacy of the other's therapeutic techniques. He enters Sean's office and begins probing for Sean's weak spots. Will asks, "Did you buy all these books retail, or do you send away for like a 'shrink kit' that comes with all these volumes included?" Sean entertains Will's musing, not threatened by Will's disdain.

Will needs another angle. When he smokes a cigarette, Sean states, "Hey, you would be better off shoving that cigarette up your ---, it would be better for you!" Will shoots back sarcastically, "You're right. It really gets in the way of my yoga." Will spots a possible new strategy; he probes, "Do you lift?" "Yes, I do," Sean responds. "Nautilus?" Will asks skeptically. Sean shoots back, "Free weights." Finding a possible point of attack, Will asks, as if challenging him, "Oh yeah? Me too. What do you bench?" Sean smiles and states confidently, "285."

Will has no response; another failed probe. Will realizes that he'll need to swing from his proverbial heels to shake Sean. Standing up, Will walks to the corner of Sean's office, to a picture of a man rowing a boat that Sean painted. Will begins deconstructing it, critiquing the colors, but Sean is not bothered. Then Will presses for what the picture means, still looking for an upper hand with Sean. Will asks Sean, "You ever heard the saying, 'any port in a storm?'—Well, maybe that means you. Maybe you were in the middle of a storm, a big . . . storm—the waves were crashing over the bow, the . . . mast was about to snap, and you were crying for the harbor. So you did what you had to do to get out. Maybe you became a psychologist."

Sean is still not bothered, but Will senses that he is closer; he takes one more shot, "Maybe you married the wrong woman." Sean turns and states intensely, "Watch your mouth." Will has him now; he has found Sean's soft spot. Sean's broken humanity is at the surface. Will goes for the kill. "That's it, isn't it? You married the wrong woman. She leave you? Was she [seeing] someone else?"

Like a volcano Sean shoots across the room, grabs Will by the throat and growls through clenched teeth, "If you ever disrespect my wife again . . . I will end you." The barrier has been set; Sean's action states, "No further. This is closed to you. You will not use my suffering as tool for your own games. I am a person and you will respect my boundary." With Sean's hands around his neck, Will musters a breathy, "Time's up." The game is over. Will found Sean's weak spot, but unlike his other counselors Sean doesn't run or quit on Will. Instead, Sean opens his humanity and in word and action states, *This is me. No further!*

The next week Sean takes Will out of the office to a park; he needs to talk with him, express to him that Will cannot cross his boundary, that Sean is not Will's property, that he is a person more than the simple definitions culture provides. Sean explains this to him and invites Will to know him, but only if he will respect Sean's closedness and is willing to open up and share his own person with Sean. Sitting in the park, Will starts, "So what's with this place? You have a swan fetish? Is this something you'd like to talk about?" But Sean has no time for his strategies. Turning to Will, Sean says confidently and calmly, "I was thinking about what you said to me the other day, about my painting. I stayed up half the night thinking about it, and then something occurred to me and I fell into a deep peaceful sleep and haven't thought about you since. You know what occurred to me?" Sean continues:

> You're just a boy. You don't have the faintest idea what you're talking about. You've never been out of Boston. So if I asked you about art you could give me the skinny on every art book ever written . . . Michelangelo? You know a lot about him I bet. Life's work, criticisms, political aspirations. But you couldn't tell me what it smells like in the Sistine Chapel. You've never stood there and looked up at that beautiful ceiling.
>
> And if I asked you about women I'm sure you could give me a syllabus of your personal favorites, and maybe you've been laid a few times too. But you couldn't tell me how it feels to wake up next to a woman and be truly happy. If I asked you about war you could refer me to a bevy of fictional and non-fictional material, but you've never been in one. You've never held your best friend's head in your lap and watched him draw his last breath, looking to you for help.
>
> And if I asked you about love I'd get a sonnet, but you've never looked at a woman and been truly vulnerable. Known that someone could kill you with a look. That someone could rescue you from grief. That God had put an angel on Earth just for you. And you wouldn't know how it felt to be her angel. To have the love be there for her forever. Through anything, through

cancer. You wouldn't know about sleeping sitting up in a hospital room for two months holding her hand and not leaving because the doctors could see in your eyes that the term "visiting hours" didn't apply to you. And you wouldn't know about real loss, because that only occurs when you lose something you love more than yourself, and you've never dared to love anything that much.

I look at you and I don't see an intelligent, confident man. . . . I see a boy. Nobody could possibly understand you, right Will? Yet you presume to know so much about me because of a painting you saw. You must know everything about me. You're an orphan, right?

Will nods, and Sean continues, "Do you think I would presume to know the first thing about who you are because I read *Oliver Twist?* Personally, I don't care. There's nothing you can tell me that I can't read somewhere else. Unless we talk about you. And if you do then I am in, I'm hooked. But you won't do that." Sean stands, looks back at Will and states, "Your move, Chief."

Sean frees Will from being a sick, deviant prodigy and invites him into a friendship of persons. He invites Will to reveal his transcendence, which escapes all the cultural definitions that have been strangling Will's humanity. Sean's words contrast totality and infinity; they are the texture of an open and closed relationship. We can assume that this is the first time that Will has come up against someone completely for him and yet other than him. Sean's assertion of his own humanity calls Will back to his humanity. As unpleasant as the encounter may have been, it nevertheless draws in Will and captivates him. From this moment Will and Sean's association is changed into a relationship.

Confronting Kelly in the open-and-closed dynamic deepened Mandi's relationship with her. Mandi was a youth pastor and had a number of connections with teenage girls, but somehow now things felt different with Kelly. Kelly came over more regularly; they picked up where they left off talking about school, movies and a little about music (though Mandi hated all of Kelly's favorite songs). One evening, Kelly noticed a picture in Mandi's living room. It was a picture of a husband, wife, three small children and a yellow Labrador retriever. "Who are these people?" Kelly asked. Mandi looked at Kelly as if being caught with something she'd been hiding. "Oh, that's my sister, her husband and their kids," she responded. "They seem nice. Do you see them often?" Kelly questioned. "Um, yeah, no, I mean yeah." Mandi stumbled. Taking a deep breath she explained, "My sister's husband is Paul. I set them up, we went to college together. Well, I guess a year and half ago now, Paul and their oldest son, Stevey, were coming home from one of Stevey's T-ball games and a truck swerved over the line." Trying to keep her composure, Mandi continued, "and they were both killed."

As Kelly looked at the picture Paul and Stevey seemed to be smiling at her. She was shocked, sad for Mandi and her sister, but also paradoxically warmed by Mandi's willingness to share it with her. Though sounding trite, Kelly's heartfelt response was, "Man, that totally sucks!" Mandi just nodded and took a deep breath. Mandi said more, "The hardest thing is that they had like the perfect marriage and family, and to be honest I was totally envious of them. Now I am stuck wishing that I had someone to share my life with and that my sister had her husband back. Both of us are alone."

Feeling she was sharing too much, Mandi tried to break the emotional tension by stating more jokingly than seriously, "I just wish I had a man to do all the yard work." Kelly, not picking up the hint that Mandi wanted to steer the conversation in a different direction, looked directly at Mandi and in a completely genuine offer stated, "Mandi, I am good at picking weeds. I'll help you anytime." Mandi laughed; somehow it was the perfect thing to say.

Kelly left Mandi's place feeling closer to Mandi than ever, feeling like she saw Mandi for who she really was, a beautiful person. As Mandi closed the door, she too felt things had changed; her honest sharing had connected them even deeper. By sharing from the pain of her own broken humanity, she had allowed Kelly to truly meet her as a person. As Mandi walked back into her living room she thought, *That was a holy moment.*

Will has been back to see Sean. In their next session after the discussion in the park Will remained silent; Sean refused to talk first, trying to uphold both his barrier as well as Will's freedom. Finally, the following week, Will breaks the silence. He does so by telling an off-color joke; Sean entertains it and laughs. Will then continues, "I *have* been laid, you know," responding to Sean's comments in the park. Will continues, "Yeah, I went on a date last week." Sean is interested: "How'd it go? Are you going out again?" Will shrugs his shoulders and responds, "I don't know. Haven't called her."

Sean, acting more as a friend than a therapist, responds, "You are an amateur." Will assures Sean, "I know what I'm doing. She's different from the other girls I met. We have a really good time. She's smart, beautiful, fun . . ."

"So call her up," Sean interrupts.

"Why? So I can realize she's not so smart. That she's boring. You don't get it. Right now she's perfect, I don't want to ruin that," Will reasons.

Sean responds in firm but loving judgment, "Well, I think that's a great philosophy, Will; that way you can go through your entire life without ever having to really know anybody." Will looks away, respecting the judgment but uncomfortable with the truth it proclaims.

Sean turns the topic on himself, opening himself up in mutuality. "My wife used to fart when she was nervous. She had all these little idiosyncrasies, she used to fart in her sleep." Now both laughing heavily, Sean continues, "One night it was so loud it woke the dog up. Yeah, but, Will, she's been dead two years and that's the stuff I remember."[12]

Composing himself, but still smiling ear to ear, Sean continues:

That's wonderful stuff, that's what I miss the most, those little idiosyncrasies that only I knew about. Those made her my wife. And she had the goods on me too. Little things I do out of habit. People call these things imperfections, Will. It's just who we are. And we get to choose who we're going to let into our weird little worlds. You're not perfect. And let me save you the suspense, this girl you met isn't either. The question is whether or not you're perfect for each other. You can know everything in the world, but the only way you're findin' that one out is by giving it a shot. You sure won't get the answer from an old [codger] like me. And even if I did know, I wouldn't tell you.

Laughing, Will responds, "Why not? You told me every other . . . thing.

---

[12]Will and Sean's unique relationship should not be constituted as a model for client-therapist boundaries. The screenplay is presenting two broken people who in their meeting are mutually transformed. I am using this narrative to look at this occurrence. We could assume that Sean may maintain more traditional boundaries with other patients. To maintain the open-and-closed dynamic, there may be good reason for a therapist to uphold the patient-client distinction.

You talk more than any shrink I ever met."

Sean has transcended his role as constituted by culture and become Will's place-sharer. Sean can respond only by poking fun at himself, "I teach this [stuff], I didn't say I knew how to do it." Will smiles, taking in Sean's advice and judgment.

After a few seconds of silence, Will respectfully asks, in direct contrast to their first session, "You ever think about gettin' remarried?" Sean responds quickly, "My wife's dead." Will vollies quickly, "Hence, the word *remarried*." "My wife's dead," Sean repeats. Will then looks at Sean in mutuality, sharing his own judgment using Sean's very words, "Well, I think that's a wonderful philosophy, Sean. That way you can go through the rest of your life without having to really know anyone."

They have entered into a depth of relationship engendered from mutuality and judgment that respects the open-and-closed dynamic; they have encountered the other's transcendence, the mystery that culture cannot define.

There had been conflict at Kelly's house; Mandi had witnessed Kelly and her mom fighting. Kelly also seemed to be walking through life with something on her mind, but she was reluctant to share what it was. Mandi asked a number of times, but every time it seemed like Kelly was going to say something, she stopped herself. Mandi had decided not to pry; respecting Kelly's closedness, Mandi reminded Kelly that she was available to talk. A week later Mandi noticed something very strange. Kelly was at home in the middle of the day. Mandi thought little of this, just noticed it. However, the next day she was home again, and again the next. Mandi knew something was up.

That evening Mandi got a knock on the door. She imagined that it was Kelly. As she ran to the door she thought, *Good, finally I can find out what's going on with this kid.* But when she opened the door, it wasn't Kelly, but Kelly's mother, in tears. Mandi, shocked to see her and even more shocked that she was crying, quickly invited her in.

As they sat down Kelly's mom gained her composure enough to talk through the tears. "I am sorry to come over like this, but I don't know what to do. I know Kelly thinks highly of you, so I thought I would talk with you." "What is it?" asked Mandi. "Kelly is refusing to go to school and told me last week that she is going to drop out!" Kelly's mom blurted out as the tears began streaming down her checks. "She says that she is so far behind that it is pointless, and that she is not smart enough to get caught up even if she wanted to. I don't know what to do. I don't want to see her drop out of school and get pregnant or in trouble and have no future." Mandi was shocked but not surprised; she assured Kelly's mom that she would talk with Kelly.

Later that day she explained to Kelly that dropping out was a bad idea, but Kelly assured her that she had no choice, that she was too far behind to continue. Kelly justified that she could just take the GED later, but Mandi knew it was doubtful that Kelly would ever do so and that taking such a road would be detrimental to her. Mandi asked Kelly, "What if I help you? What if I help you get the tutoring you need and go with you and your mom to talk with your principal and teachers?" Mandi knew a handful of the teachers from her interactions at the school as a youth pastor, and a couple of the teachers attended her church. Kelly shrugged her shoulders as she bit her lip to keep a smile from appearing. "OK," she said, but as if needing to qualify it so as not to get her own hopes up, she continued, "But it probably wont help."

Mandi visited a number of Kelly's teachers, asking them if there was anything that Kelly could do. A few were skeptical, but all were willing to work with Kelly and her mom to get Kelly back on track. Using retired people and others from her congregation, Mandi set up tutoring sessions for Kelly and helped Kelly get to and from her appointments. Kelly rejoined her class at school, and within two months she was caught up.

Mandi had set up tutoring meetings for Kelly every weeknight but Friday (for Kelly's sake) and Wednesday, for her own. Wednesday night was Mandi's confirmation night. Kelly knew that Mandi was at church that night and that she couldn't stop by for homework help or to talk. Kelly wondered what happened at confirmation; she had been to a number of concert nights and lock-ins with her friends at Mandi's invitation, but wondered how confirmation was different. She knew that it was very important to Mandi and wanted to experience it for herself. Mandi was shocked when Kelly asked if she could participate. "Confirmation is for those students who want to take their faith seriously and become part of the church. You understand that, right?" Kelly did, and she still wanted to go.

Kelly participated every week, anticipating the opportunity to discuss her own views and hear those of others. For two years Kelly contributed weekly at confirmation class. In the spring of her junior year, Kelly was confirmed and became a member of Mandi's congregation.

Through her tutoring sessions and confirmation small group, Kelly began to spend more time with other adults in the congregation and less time with Mandi. Mandi was overjoyed as she watched Kelly become a mature, beautiful woman who was growing as a disciple of Jesus Christ. Mandi witnessed an amazing transformation in Kelly's life; her old friends stopped coming by and Kelly developed new friendships. Kelly's family life was still chaotic at times, and she still had fears and pains about her past and worries about her future, but she no longer felt alone. Her very humanity was secure in relationship with Mandi and the congregation she now belonged to.

On graduation Sunday the pastor of the church asked Kelly if she would give a five-minute testimony to the congregation. She stood before them, shaking in her low-cut jeans, her belly-button ring reflecting off the lights in the sanctuary. She began, "I am lucky because my life was crazy and, like, totally out of control, but I was lucky because Mandi was my neighbor. She, like, became my friend and helped me through a lot of bad times and introduced me to so many people in this church. It's meant so much to me. Right before I came to this church I almost quit school, but Mandi took responsibility for getting me back on track, and now next week I am going to graduate. And in the fall I am going to community college so someday I can be a teacher like my mom and help kids like Mandi helped me. I am going to Crescent Valley so I can still come to church and keep worshiping and praying and following Jesus with all of you. Thanks."

Will is pushing everyone away from him. His relationship with his girlfriend Skylar has deepened and a number of opportunities have been presented to him to leave low-income poverty behind. Skylar has asked Will to commit to her; she has revealed to him that she loves him deeply and wants him to be with her as she moves to California. Fearing that her offer of love and commitment is not genuine, Will has (metaphorically) hit Skylar before she could hit him, telling her that he doesn't love her, though he does. Will has decided it is better to hurt her than to be hurt himself.

Gerry Lambeau, the mathematics professor who advocated to keep Will out of jail and set up his meetings with Sean, has set up a number of job interviews for him with some of the top organizations and think tanks in the world. Will has the possibility of doing what he was born to do, of grasping with two hands an opportunity to work from his giftedness and live into his destiny. But Will has sabotaged his interviews, deciding that he would rather stay in South Boston, waking up in his run-down apartment and working construction than take the risk of being who he was created and gifted to be.

Will's fear of relational intimacy and his inability to accept his vocation are linked, and Sean knows it. After Will explains to Sean how he passed on another job offer, Sean asks bluntly, "Do you think you're alone?" Will, confused by the question, can only return, "What?"

"Do you have a soul-mate?" asks Sean. "Someone who challenges you in every way? Who takes you places, opens things up for you? A soul-mate." Will responds, "Yeah." Sean waits, knowing that Will is lying and interested to see where he goes in his answer. "Shakespeare, Nietzsche, Frost, O'Connor, Chaucer, Pope, Kant . . ."

"They're all dead." Sean interrupts. Will fires back, "Not to me, they're not." "But you can't give back to them, Will." Will tries to avoid the truth of Sean's comments with humor, "Not without a heater and some serious smelling salts . . ." But Sean pushes forward, "That's what I'm saying, Will. You'll never have that kind of relationship in a world where you're afraid to take the first step because all you're seeing are the negative things that might happen ten miles down the road."

"Oh, what? You're going to take the professor's side on this?" Will says with anger. Sean bounces back, "Don't give me your line of s**t. It's not about that job. I'm not saying you should work for the government. But you could do anything you want. And there are people who work their whole lives layin' brick so their kids have a chance at the kind of opportunity you have. What do you want to do?" Sean has entrenched himself as Will's barrier and he is not leaving. Sean has made it clear that Will will have to confront his demons, but not alone, through Sean's otherness.

Will has continued to meet with Sean and they have continued to grow close, but Will now stands between Sean and Gerry, both trying to help

Will but having distinctly different ideas of what that looks like. Sean and Gerry have conflicting ideas on what is best for Will and at what pace he should be encouraged to move forward. The conflict comes to a head in Sean's office as both men wait for Will to arrive for another appointment with Sean.

Gerry is angry with Sean. "This is a disaster! I brought you in here to help me with this boy, not to run him out . . ." Sean rebuts, "Hold on! I know what I'm doing and I know why I'm here!" Gerry continues his tirade, "Look Sean, I don't care if you have a rapport with the boy—I don't care if you have a few laughs—even at my expense! But don't you dare undermine what I'm trying to do here. He has a gift and with that gift comes responsibility. And you don't understand that he's at a fragile point . . ."

Sean tries to free Gerry from his own personal ambitions and to return the conversation to Will's concrete humanity, "He *is* at a fragile point. He's got problems." Gerry is having none of Sean's compassion: "What problems does he have, Sean, that he is better off as a janitor or in jail or hanging around with a bunch of retarded gorillas?"

Sean's temper is rising as he fires back, "Why do you think he does that, Gerry? Why is he hiding? Why doesn't he trust anybody? Because the first thing that happened to him was that he was abandoned by the people who were supposed to love him the most! And why does he hang out with those 'retarded gorillas' as you call them? Because any one of those kids would come in here and take a bat to your head if he asked them to. It's called loyalty! And who do you think he's handling? He pushes people away before they have a chance to leave him. And for twenty years he's been alone because of that. And if you try to push him into this, it's going to be the same thing all over again. And I'm not going to let that happen to him!"

As Sean is yelling this, Will walks to Sean's office door and stops outside it, listening as Sean fights in complete responsibility for the fullness of Will's humanity over and against the ambitions of the professor. But Gerry isn't convinced. "Now don't do that. Don't you do that! Don't infect him with the idea that it's okay to quit. That it's okay to be a failure, because it's not okay! I am a success because I was pushed."

Sean, visibly angry, shoots back, "It's not about you, you mathematical [jerk]! It's about the boy! He's a good kid! And I won't see this happen to him—I won't see you try and [mess] him up like you're trying to [mess] me up right now!"

Gerry refuses to see Sean's point. "You're wrong, Sean. I'm where I am today because I was pushed. And because I learned to push myself!" Sean responds with arms waving, "He's not you!"

Upon hearing the responsibility of Sean being his place-sharer Will enters Sean's office interrupting the argument. Gerry, a little embarrassed, grabs his coat and leaves the room. "I was just leaving," he says as he walks out. The office is now dramatically calm, like a prairie right after a thunderstorm has blown through.

Sean breaks the silence, "That wasn't about you, it's between us, stuff that goes a long way back." But Will knows better; he has witnessed Sean being his place-sharer.

"What's that?" Will asks pointing to a file on Sean's desk. Sean explains that it is Will's file that Sean needs to sign and send back to the judge. "What does it say?" asks Will.

Sean offers Will an opportunity to read his file; Will passes, but then asks further, "Do you have any experience with that?" probing for further mutuality. Sean explains that he has seen quite a bit of abuse in his days as counselor, but that is not what Will is asking. He wants to know if Sean has personally been hit by someone who was supposed to love and care for him. Sean has. He tells his story, which prompts Will to do the same. It is the first time Will has ever discussed these experiences.

Referring back to his file Will asks, "What does it say, like 'Will has a detachment disorder and fear of abandonment'?" Sean pauses and takes a step toward Will, positioning himself so he is looking right into his eyes and states, "Hey, Will, I don't know a lot, but I do know that this is not your fault."

Will looks away trying to keep his pain at arm's length as he has managed to do for his whole life, "I know," he says as he looks away and gives a half smile.

Sean walks closer, bringing his own broken humanity nearer to Will's, and states again, "Look at me, son; it's not your fault!" Will tries to brush it off again, "I know."

Sean walks closer, providing the barrier Will desperately needs in order to know his true person, and through his otherness Sean speaks the truth of God that demands a response from the core of Will's humanity. "No, no, look at me. It is not your fault!"

Will pulls himself upright from his leaning position and tries to avoid Sean's barrier of truth by moving, but Sean will not let him, continuing to repeat, "It's not your fault." Will cannot avoid the truth; it is breaking in upon him. His broken humanity is rushing to the surface; he shoves Sean, "Don't [mess] with me, Sean, not you, not you!" he asserts through deep emotion.

Sean pushes in closer bringing the barrier, his mutually broken humanity closer to Will's, stating with his presence, *You are not alone. You are not worthless. You are more than an abused child. You are my friend whom I love. You are not at fault. You are God's beloved. You are free.* Sean comes in even closer and repeats again, "It not your fault."

The hard kid is broken; Will crumples and Sean embraces him. As he does, Will begins to sob and throws his arms around Sean. They stand embracing, having met one to another, experiencing each other's transcendence, and both have been transformed. Their transformation is a sign of God's inbreaking through relationship.

WHEN SOCIAL CONNECTION IS NOT RELATIONAL TRANSFORMATION

At this late point you may have an objection, asserting that not all relationships are transformative in the manner we have explored. Therefore not all relationships can be the place of God's inbreaking. Yet I would pose a question to you: are connections and relationships the same thing? We need to recognize the distinction between connections and relationships. When Will was a child, he found himself in a social connection with his foster father, but in this social connection he was abused and treated like an object, therefore eliminating the possibility of it being a relationship. Will found himself in a relationship when he encountered Sean. This is because a relationship occurs only when an I meets a you as other and transcendent.

Whenever a person demands that another person assimilate to his or her perspectives or use the other as a tool or punching bag (either physically or emotionally), a relationship is no longer present, for the other has been stripped of his or her transcendence and made into an object. Therefore, the other person is either accepted or rejected because of his or her correlation with another individual's ideological understandings. Abusive, hurtful persons may claim to have friendships; two neo-Nazi's may claim to be loyal friends. But the friendship is not based on the otherness of the friend but on a shared commitment to a cultural ideology. If one of the so-called friends, for whatever reason, decides that racism is evil and no longer holds to the shared ideology, the connection is severed, for it was built on an ideology and not on transcendent otherness. Therefore there was never a meeting of I and you, only a sharing of the same cultural ideologies, which allowed for a mutual connection.

Being in a relationship binds one to another beyond (and at times against) the strictures of ideology. Not all true relationships lead to radical transformation (though they always lead to some transformation) nor should all persons look to make all encounters into relationships. Rather we must also live with many connections. Will's connection with his collective unit (his friends) originated and was based on a shared ideology, on a blue-collar hit-or-be-hit mentality. Will's friend Chucky lacked the otherness to be the barrier Will needed to find transformation for his four-dimensional person. But Chucky was willing and hoping for Will's transformation, and when Will decided to seek his distinct otherness, Chucky agreed to remain committed to Will even as he changed, taking on new perspectives that challenged their shared ideology. Thus it can be said that Chucky and Will are in a relationship, for they have respected their unique otherness, committing themselves to each other's humanity, recognizing that each is more than their shared ideological history.

This is an important qualification for those practicing a relational ministry of place-sharing. There are many relationships we have with adolescents that lack radical transformation. This does not disqualify these relationships or eliminate the possibility of God's concrete presence in them. The goal of ministry is not to bring about (healthy or holy) transformation, for this is solely the work of God. The goal of ministry is to be faithful to the humanity of the adolescent, seeing him or her as other and transcendent, and committing to be place-sharer to his or her person. And when transformation is witnessed, ministry is lived out in doxology. If Kelly would have dropped out of school, gotten pregnant and never made her way to Mandi's church, they would have still shared in a relationship of deep meaning, a relationship within which Mandi could have claimed that God was mysteriously and paradoxically present.

We cross paths with many different people who must remain only connections to us (e.g., the grocery store clerk, the telemarketer, the fellow employee in another division, a neighbor, or even a brother or sister we rarely see). There is no evil in having connections. A potential evil, though, is moving within our connections without being open to having them turn into a relationship. That is, someone I am connected to may call out for me to meet him or her in a relationship. I cannot reach out in relationship with every person in my world; I can only recognize that the video store clerk is a human being created by God, nod and move on. But when this same clerk runs up to me in the parking lot, grabs my elbow and says, "Are you the youth pastor at Holy Lord Lutheran Church? Um, I'm in big trouble, I need some help," he or she has reached out beyond the connection into relationship and the demand of Christ is now presented to me.

One of Bonhoeffer's most perplexing (and interesting) comments in *Ethics* is that "it is better for the truthful person to tell a lie then for a liar to tell the truth."[13] Such a statement needs more unpacking than we have space for here. Nevertheless, there is something relevant in Bonhoeffer's comment for this discussion on the difference between connections and relationships. What is most dangerous in relational ministry is to promise relationships and provide only connections. Again, while there is no evil in being connected to people, there is great evil in promising a relationship and encouraging others to open their humanity when no true relationship is there. And when they can no longer hold to the accepted ideology the connection is severed, leaving them battered. Some have rightly spoken against relational ministry, for they were spiritually abused by those who promised place-sharing but snatched it away when the individual could no longer accept or live up to the ideology. It must be stated again, these situations were never relationships of transcendent otherness but only con-

---

[13]Bonhoeffer, *Ethics*, p. 77.

nections of shared ideology.

To bring this in more direct conversation with our picture of relational transformation, such connections cannot lead to healthy or holy transformation because they lead with their ideologies and have refused to be in relationships of transcendent otherness. Therefore such connections are shut out from the transformative data stream of relationship. Bonhoeffer explains, "Those who act on the basis of ideology consider themselves justified by their idea. Those who act responsibly place their action into the hands of God and live by God's grace and judgment."[14] When connections demand a rigid commitment to an ideology, they operate only from data stream 2 (the data stream coming from the cultural totality) and are transformative not in relational otherness that is bound by the reality of Jesus Christ but only by convincing the person to assimilate to the other's ideology. This, I fear, is what has happened in most relational youth ministries of influence. The youth worker has met the adolescent with the (perhaps unacknowledged) agenda of getting him or her to conform to the ideology of conservative Protestantism, and by so doing has eliminated the possibility of meeting the adolescent's true otherness and vice versa.

In figure 8.4 the transcendent field of otherness is deleted and in its place are two boxes labeled "Ideology" which are connected by two arrows going in both directions. These arrows represent a connection. This connection can support each individual's personal ideology or it can oppose it. Therefore a connection can lead to either fortifying an ideology or directly opposing two entrenched ideologies, which often results in violence. When the two arrows meet in a shared ideology, the person is fortified in his or her commitments. This embeds the person more deeply in his or her four dimensions and gives further perspective to the person's subjective history, and therefore provides more ammunition to engage the ideologies of culture with his or her own ideological perspective.

When the arrows are two persons meeting with different and oppositional ideologies there is a clash in which each person's humanity is lost in their ideological commitments, making it easier (and at times necessary) to hurt (or even kill) the other person. It may be helpful to return to my

---

[14]Ibid., p. 269.

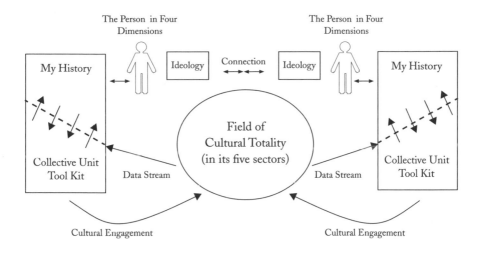

Figure 8.4. Paradigm of anti-relational transformation idcology meeting ideology

neo-Nazi example. Two neo-Nazis meet in ideological agreement, thus fortifying each other's own person in the four dimensions. Seeing the unique I as oppressed by non-Aryans, and constructing a lived world around a fight for white power, the holy and void point to the person's subjective history, which is filled with abuse and loneliness in a working-class family where poverty was blamed because "all good jobs were going to blacks." Each individual then engages culture with practices and actions that need to force culture to support his or her ideology.

Or the point where the two arrows meet in connection may be a conflict. A Crip (a Los Angeles-based gang member) and a skinhead may encounter one another in the kitchen of a fast food restaurant where they both work. Each sees the other's symbols of cultural engagement. The Crip is dressed in all blue, sporting a backward cap which is angled to the side, covering his cornrows. The skinhead is in all black, wearing heavy Doc Martin boots; he has a tattoo of a swastika on his neck, which is very visible because of his completely shaved head. Their committed ideologies are plain to see. The Crip and the skinhead are connected through their mutual work, but their entrenched ideologies will not allow them to meet. They must either ignore each other or, worse, kill each other to maintain the integrity of their ideologies. These two have a strong connection, but no relationship. They see each other only as the ideology that has been produced from their history and place in culture.

Perhaps a less dramatic example would help. A male youth worker with a theological and political ideology of conservatism encounters an adolescent. He connects with the adolescent with the hope that he may convince the adolescent to change or convert to the youth worker's own ideological commitments. The adolescent may hope he will experience intimacy through a relationship. After years in the youth ministry and what the adolescent believed was a relationship, the adolescent begins to question some of the ideological perspectives of the youth worker. The youth worker accuses the adolescent of apostasy and the connection is broken. The adolescent is hurt because he thought the youth worker was his friend; he thought they had a relationship. But they never did; they had a connection built on ideology; there never was a meeting of transcendent otherness where one becomes committed to the other's humanity beyond any ideology.

CONCLUSION

In chapters seven and eight we have built on the theology of Bonhoeffer to present a picture of relational transformation for a incarnational youth ministry of place-sharing. This picture presented us with three major components to examine: the person, culture and transcendence. I have traced the multiple paths of transformation and have asserted that when person meets person in relationship, they encounter one another in the reality of Jesus Christ. Thus they are given direct data which can transform them, their histories and their interaction with culture and its ideologies.

Now, taking this picture of the inner reality of relationship, in chapter nine we must ask how youth ministries and congregations should live into this reality.

9

Rules of Art for Place-Sharing in Community

I was finishing the question-and-answer time following my lecture when a hand shot up. I was a finalist for a faculty job and had just made a public presentation to the seminary community. The audience had my résumé in their hands and were deciding whether I was someone they wanted to invite into their community as a teacher. Looking intensely over my résumé, the student waving his hand said, "I can see from your résumé that you are relatively young and have a number of diverse experiences, but many of us are training to go to congregations and stay in those congregation for a long time; if you haven't had that experience, how can you help us?"

Pausing out of respect for the importance of the question, I thought, *Should I take the advice of late Secretary of Defense Robert McNamara and move around the inquiry by answering the question I wish he had asked, or should I take on this question directly?* I decided to take the heat. I said something like:

> I truly believe that all ministry is contextual; it is different in every place because we confront distinctly different people and different systems. I don't think it would matter if I had been in one ministry for fifty years; while that qualifies me to know some things, it does not qualify me to know *your* ministry context. You can only know a context from the inside. I see my job as inviting students to articulate their own unique experiences, and then to help us all, as a class, reflect on these unique experiences. What I will do is provide theories and perspectives that may help us interpret all of our unique

situations. The truth is, ministry is different in every context, and assuming students will not be in one job their whole careers, it is essential to teach them how to interpret contexts and think theologically about those contexts.

I got the job!

I can imagine that as you have read this book you have been thinking, *What would this look like?* In this chapter I will address your question, but I must admit that I'm not qualified to tell you exactly what a relational youth ministry of place-sharing will look like in your ministry context. I simply don't know your context! Therefore, what I will provide in this chapter is *not* a model of how *everyone* should do incarnational ministry but rather some "rules of art" for a relational ministry of place-sharing.

Rules of art are "descriptions of how to perform certain actions and practices in light of both the actual empirical condition of the church and a vision of what it might become in the emerging context."[1] It is my hope that these rules of art can be used by congregations like those presented in chapter three to have a faithful relational ministry with adolescents like Kelly and Will.[2] I have organized these rules of art under three broad

---

[1]Richard Osmer, "Rhetoric and Practical Theology" (Princeton University, 2003), p. 8. The term "rules of art" is taken from Friedrich Schleiermacher's book *A Brief Outline of Theology.*

[2]The rules of art that follow will be organized by the shared characteristics of exemplary youth ministries as discovered in a study funded by the Eli Lilly Foundation in 2004-2005. The study, called *Exemplary Youth Ministry,* sought to discover the common practices and characteristics of empirical communities (the rules of art) that were doing commendable work with adolescents. The congregations that qualified to be studied were those consistently helping their young people own and live out their faith. This study defined mature faith by identifying seven key characteristics: seeks spiritual growth, both alone and with others; believes God is present and active in the world; acts out of a commitment of faith; is active with God's people; possesses a positive, hopeful spirit; lives out a life of service; and lives a Christian moral life. The study discovered nine themes and characteristics shared by such youth ministries and their congregations; their practices are guided by and constructed from a commitment to these nine characteristics. These practices are (1) a sense of the presence and activity of a living God; (2) emphasis on spiritual growth, discipleship and vocation; (3) promotion of outreach and mission; (4) congregational support for youth ministry; (5) development of a committed competent leadership; (6) focus on families; (7) development of effective practices; (8) an integrative, context-sensitive approach to youth ministry; and (9) fostering significant relationships and a sense of community (from www.exemplarym.com, accessed October 15, 2005). The study was both a quantitative and qualitative project. After surveying hundreds of congregational youth ministries the study returned to twenty-one for qualitative research. The study was quite diverse, encompassing seven denominations. Exemplary youth ministries were those that had been consistently involved in supporting youth with vital faith. For further background of methodology, goals and findings of this study see www.exemplarym.com. The study's findings were presented at The Spirit of Youth Ministry National Conference on August 4-6, 2005, at the Marriott Farmington Hotel in Hartford, Conn. The project director was Roland Martinson of Luther Seminary.

headings: "Rethinking the Youth Pastor and Adult Leader," "Rethinking the Youth Ministry" and "Rethinking the Congregation." The place where a rule of art is listed and examined is only its starting point; some rules of art could be placed in more than one section for further construction. What is presented here is not conclusive but only a start. Nor are these rules of art applicable to all contexts; rather it is my hope that they might provide fodder for further reflection on one's ministry context and the use of the practice of a relational ministry of place-sharing. (The rules of art are set in italics. They are also listed in a text box at the end of each section.)

RETHINKING THE YOUTH PASTOR AND ADULT LEADER

Meaningful relationships as the presence of God. For most youth pastors (and adult leaders), relationships with young people can be both a great joy and a great burden. It is a great joy and honor being invited into relationship with an adolescent, for in relationship we are invited into the very center of his or her existence. But walking into another's existence is never easy; it comes with frustrations, fears and exhaustion. Therefore, if relational ministry is to be practiced from within the theological reality of relationships, it must be stated that it is impossible for the youth pastor or an adult leader to be in relationship with all the adolescents in his or her congregation or local community. As I have sought to show, relationships are too complicated and meaningful to allow us to encounter many other persons, sharing in their sufferings and joys at the level demanded for relational transformation. Yet, this is not an excuse for a youth pastor to ignore many (or even a few) of the adolescents in his or her congregation. Rather, all adolescents have a right to feel a *connection* with the youth pastor—that the youth pastor knows their name, a little about their background and cares about them. Therefore, the youth pastor *should have a connection to all adolescents in the congregation but be in a relationship with a few.*

This rule of art is the same for the adult leader. For instance, an adult leader, Mary, who has formed a strong relational bond with three girls in the youth ministry, should not feel as though this isn't enough, that she should have this same kind of deep relational bond with most adolescents in the youth ministry. Rather, Mary should be released to continue these relationships even if they lead her (upon the girls' graduation) out of the junior high ministry and into the high school ministry.

Nevertheless, to avoid the danger of creating exclusive cliques within the youth ministry, Mary should be encouraged (held responsible) to make further connections with other adolescents in the congregation, knowing their names, leading them in activities and sharing her story of faith. By allowing Mary to be in relationship with only a few, it is more likely that she will be a place-sharer to them, making their relational interactions the place of God's activity. But by encouraging her to remain connected to all of the adolescents in the congregation, her relationships with a few are protected from being exclusive and becoming closed to others, destroying their theological and relational validity.

The assertion that a youth pastor or adult leader cannot be in relationship with all adolescents in his or her congregation is neither new nor profound. It as been stated by a number of popular youth ministry writers discussing incarnational ministry.[3] However, I find this perspective problematic, as it allows some adolescents to be overlooked. It encourages us to focus on only a handful and leaves many youth without any possibility of developing a deep relationship with an adult in their congregation. Others counter that such students will be included more deeply in the relational life of the youth pastor (or adult leader) once these youth have developed in their faith, moving "down the funnel" or "toward the center of the bull's eye" (i.e., the adolescent progresses from being merely a part of the regular crowd to a committed student). But such a perspective ignores the dynamic reality of relationships, which asserts that all transformation, starting from whatever level, is brought forth through relational action. Therefore, *though the youth pastor can only be in relationship with a few, all adolescents should be invited into relationships of place-sharing.*

This means that it is not the youth pastor's job to be a super-relational juggernaut, as though this were possible. Rather it is his or her job to facilitate encounters between each adolescent and a possible place-sharer,

---

[3]One has put forth the 5-3-1 model, where the youth pastor or adult leader focuses his or her relational energy on five, goes deep with three, and maybe even deeper with one. See Doug Fields, *My First Two Years in Youth Ministry* (Grand Rapids: Zondervan, 2002).

making spaces for each to meet the other's humanity. Therefore, the youth pastor can be shy and introverted and still move the congregation toward relational ministry of place-sharing. Relational action is never solely the youth pastor's, or any other person's for that matter. Bonhoeffer pointed us toward a relational ministry of place-sharing that is a *community activity*, a congregationwide ministry. Of course, for educational training purposes it will be helpful (and theologically necessary) for the youth pastor to have relational bonds with adolescents, but it is not his or her job to carry the burden of relational initiative. Instead, the youth pastor's job is to go to adults within the congregation and invite them to become a place-sharer to an adolescent. The youth pastor is not just inviting adult leaders to help out with the youth ministry (though some individuals and parents may choose this role) and support the youth pastor's work; rather, these adults are invited to open their own person to the person of the adolescent.

This may seem overwhelming to both the youth pastor and the adult leader, but it doesn't need to be. The youth pastor is the coordinator (or matchmaker) of adult and adolescent bonds. He or she provides open spaces and organizes activities and programs where organic relationships can develop. This means youth pastors should have a deep knowledge of both the adult and the adolescent population, inviting adults to see, hear and act for the adolescent in their congregation or local community. They do this in both planned and informal settings, introducing adolescents and adults, hoping that in their meeting, each will see the other and begin to share in one another's existence.

We can't be rigid about bonding adult to adolescent, for relationships cannot be coerced. But like a good matchmaker we can say to an adult who has expressed interest in ministry to adolescents, "Hey, Paul, do you still have the NFL Ticket on DirectTV? Are you and your family still watching the Steelers? Well, Eric, who is a tenth grader, loves the Steelers. If it's cool, you should invite him over after church." If Paul agrees, we can provide Paul helpful information: "Just so you know, the reason he is a big Steelers fan is because he was living in Pittsburgh with his dad last year. I am not sure of all the issues, but I think things got a little crazy for him." We don't need to place any obligation on the adult; we only provide an opportunity for both to meet.

Later, we may check back with Paul, "Hey, how were things with Eric?" Paul may respond, "Good, he stayed for dinner with my family." We may answer, "Well, Friday I'm going to his JV football game; would you like to join me?" At the football game, we may discuss further how Paul might become involved with Eric and how the thing Paul is doing with Eric is central to the vision for ministry. Later that fall, when the youth go on their annual retreat, we could make sure that Eric's cabin has Paul as its leader. *The youth pastor is to support, encourage and assist adult and adolescent relationships of place-sharing so these relationships will develop as organically as possible.* Subsequently, *for adult leaders, relationships should be built around shared interests or a common task.*

A youth pastor doesn't need to provide willing adults like Paul with a meticulous how-to manual (though direction is always helpful). Rather, he or she prompts adults to reflect on their own lives, asking them to recall the people in their own adolescence, or thereafter, who stood with and for them as place-sharers. A youth pastor then asks the adults to see, listen and act in the same manner for the young people surrounding them. No long training period is needed to mold willing adults into model youth leaders, for there is no such thing. Rather, what is needed is for the adult leader to be an authentic human being with and for the adolescent, opening his or her unique person to the adolescent, inviting the adolescent to share in his or her life.

No doubt this will take our support, encouragement and responsible coaching. What is most needed in a coach is helping adult leaders understand how to live with and for adolescents in an open and closed manner. We can do this by helping adult leaders articulate their boundaries and express these to the adolescents with whom they are in relationship. Expressing these boundaries can be the substance of a number of their first few meetings, because it is in articulating what is open and closed to adolescents that we invite them to share in our very person.

An adult leader might say, "I want you to know that if you ever need to talk, you can call me any time; but please don't just stop by, our children go to bed early and our dogs bark, not to mention that my husband and I like to spend the evenings catching up." Such a statement communicates that the adult is open to talk and wants to help, but that she is also mother and wife, and that for the adolescent to know her is to know her in such a way. This is welcoming to relational bonds, for it sets up a barrier that reveals who she is in relation to the other and herself. In the acknowledgment of mutual barriers, the adolescent sees her and is drawn into relationship, where God is present. *Relationships should develop as organically as possible, in which adults are authentically human (in an open-and-closed manner) alongside adolescents.*

Outreach and mission. If we are to follow Bonhoeffer's theology and push the relevance of the paradigm of relational transformation, we must be willing to widen our perspective, imagining rules of art for a relational ministry of place-sharing that can be used for outreach and mission. Of course, it was for outreach and mission that an incarnational approach to youth ministry was born in the first place. Yet this desire for outreach and mission was misunderstood as a fight for cultural legitimacy. What then does a relational ministry of outreach and mission look like from the vision of place-sharing? Is there still "contact work," going to adolescents in their own milieu?

If contact work is thought of as going to adolescents to stand with and for them, then contact work is essential to missional place-sharing. Yet contact work can be exhausting for youth pastors and adult leaders when it is viewed in terms of influence—seeking to strike up conversations with adolescents we don't know, trying to show them that we are relevant, cool, hip and worthy of sharing their company. Yet, when contact work is viewed as *place-sharing* rather than *influence*, things can be quite different. The obsessive dance of influence is broken as we are called into the common humanity of the other.

The objective of going to adolescents is not to find the golden ticket of influence, believing that in influencing the right students we will be able to influence many others (like a business pyramid scheme). Rather in contact work based on place-sharing we enter the school campus or adolescent gathering place not to influence the influencers but to stand for those in need (e.g., lonely students in the corner, the friend of a girl in the youth group whose mother just died or students who have experienced racial prejudice). Place-sharing contact work is about participation in suffering, not success. We enter into the suffering of all, offering the solidarity of the church to all those in high school or junior high. Faithful contact work aims not to draw new adolescents into the church's youth ministry but to bring adults from the congregation alongside adolescents, saying to them in words and actions, "I see your suffering. I feel your suffering. You are not alone in your suffering." *Contact work does not wield influence but shares the place of adolescents, participating in their suffering.*

It is important for adults who want to minister to adolescents to understand the difference between influence and place-sharing. There has been a lot of discussion in popular youth ministry books about the need for adult leaders to understand themselves as servants. This of course is important, but the question must be asked, Servants to whom? In much youth ministry there is a kind of passive-aggressive strategy of adolescent influence. By showing that we are "servants," we hope that adolescents will be drawn to us to be influenced by us. But to be a servant is to follow Jesus Christ, who is the human being for others. To be a servant of Christ is to serve as Christ, who was the suffering Servant because he took responsibility for humanity, giving his own person so all could be human persons.

Therefore, mission is about being responsible for the unique person of the adolescent, standing with and for him or her in the midst of suffering. An adult may choose to join the youth pastor as he or she weekly visits a school campus, imagining that he or she will be welcomed or, at least after a short period of awkwardness, appreciated. Yet when contact work is understood as standing with those who suffer, offering our own person in solidarity, we will be called into suffering. We will have to suffer as we look deeply into the abandonment and abuse of another, as we witness the other's beautiful humanity dehumanized. But we will also need to suffer *from* the adolescent. From his or her own dehumanized core the adolescent will lash out at those of us who offer support and love, for such people have failed him or her before. The adult leader should not say, "I didn't sign up for this," but must be informed that *missional place-sharing is about suffering, not receiving adolescent adoration.*

If incarnational youth ministry is to be missional place-sharing, then it must be practiced by the whole congregation not just the youth pastor and his or her team. Going out to youth must include returning; the adult place-sharer comes back to the congregation and may bring the adolescent he or she has encountered. When they return, the congregation must be welcoming, providing legitimate spaces for adolescents to enter the congregational community and be known. The youth pastor, with the help of the other pastoral staff, must take the opportunity and have the ability to teach the congregation a theology of incarnation, which will lead them to recognize the need to suffer with and for others. The congregation must be kept abreast of the missional actions of the youth pastor and adult leaders, with some asked to join them in going and all called to pray and offer their resources for those children who suffer in their community. The congregation should commission these individuals like all other missionaries, pledging to support them as they follow Christ, who is present suffering with and for adolescents. *Outreach and mission is not just youth pastors going to adolescents but church communities receiving adolescents; it is the invitation (maybe represented by one person) to participate in the life of a multigenerational community of persons meeting persons in the new humanity of Jesus Christ.*

Spiritual growth, discipleship and vocation. It is often believed, whether explicitly stated or not, that the youth pastor and his or her team of adult leaders are solely liable for reaching nonbelieving, doubting or uninterested students, moving them into discipleship and helping them sense the presence of a living God. It is assumed by some in the congregation that now that they have a youth pastor, it is his or her job (and not their own responsibility) to pass on the faith. In Christian Smith's expansive study of American adolescent religiosity, he discovered two overarching traits; his first discovery, which is well documented, is that most adolescents (with notable exceptions) have little-to-no understanding of the tenets of their faith. Therefore, Smith believes there is an epidemic of missing catechetical instruction within congregations. Second, congregations with a youth ministry or with someone who focused on or welcomed adolescents did a much better job than those without such things of assisting adolescents to see the significance of their faith commitments and tradition.[4]

We may extrapolate from Smith's findings that those congregations

---

[4]See Christian Smith, *Soul Searching* (New York: Oxford University Press, 2005), chapters five and seven.

which provide adolescents with relational bonds fare better (or at least are more prepared to provide meaningful catechesis to young people). We may assume that this is so because discipleship is always lived out within a concrete context. When an adolescent has deep relationships with others in the faith community, he or she is given a concrete location in which to live and practice the faith that he or she is learning. But the context is not only the place to live out the faith with others, it also provides the very learning itself. By being in relational bonds with another, the adolescent is invited to witness the discipleship of another, to watch and listen as he or she practices baptism, prayer, communion and worship from the location of his or her own personal faith journey within the life of the community. Therefore, *relationships of place-sharing can provide the context for understanding and participating in discipleship in the faith community, for discipleship is born of uniting with one another as together we follow Christ.*

This does *not* mean that the adolescent is simply catechized by osmosis; rather deliberate training and encouragement must be given to a place-sharer so that he or she is prepared, from within the context of his or her own life, to share the meaning of the faith and his or her experience of it. No doubt the adult leader will need some information and resources to do this.[5] Having specific tasks and desires for your relational bond does not destroy relationship, as long as the desired steps do not become more important than the other. Therefore, the place-sharer can take deliberate steps to move the relationship into catechesis. For instance, the adolescent and the place-sharer could read Luther's Small Catechism together. They could stop at points along the way for the adult to share his or her own experience of what Luther is discussing. This perspective may actually be most honest to Luther's desire for the catechism, which was designed to be shared in the relational bonds of father and child or of pastor and congregation in the small German villages. There also may be reasons and times for all young people to come together for more directed instructional teaching.

---

[5]Richard Osmer explains the term *catechesis*, "I have borrowed it from late Christian tradition, where it was used to refer to the instruction offered new converts in preparation for baptism. Etymologically, the core image laying behind catechesis is 'to echo' or 'answer back.' When adult Christians were baptized, they were asked several questions based on the baptismal creed and 'answered back' to affirm their acceptance of the pattern of teaching to which they had been entrusted in their baptismal catechesis" (*The Teaching Ministry of Congregations* [Louisville: Westminster John Knox, 2005], p. 27).

RETHINKING THE YOUTH PASTOR AND ADULT LEADER

Rules of Art for Meaningful Relationships as the Presence of God

- The youth pastor should have a connection to all adolescents in the congregation but be in a relationship with a few.
- All adolescents should be invited into relationships of place-sharing. ·
- The youth pastor is to support, encourage and assist adult and adolescent relationships of place-sharing.
- Relationships should be built around shared interests or a common task.
- Relationships should develop as organically as possible, in which adults are authentically human (in an open-and-closed manner) alongside adolescents.

Rules of Art for Outreach and Mission

- Contact work does not wield influence but shares the place of adolescents, participating in their suffering.
- Missional place-sharing is about suffering, not receiving adolescent adoration.
- Outreach and mission is not just youth pastors going to adolescents but also church communities receiving adolescents. It is the invitation to participate in the life of a multigenerational community of persons meeting persons.

Rules of Art for Spiritual Growth, Discipleship and Vocation

- Relationships of place-sharing can provide the context for understanding and participating in discipleship in the faith community.
- Catechesis can be done within social relationships between adult and adolescent.

Relational approaches to ministry often are opposed to all forms of instruction. But this doesn't have to be the case. Those adults who choose to be place-sharers to adolescents need to be given the training, resources and forums to pass on the tenets of the Christian faith. This could happen in a one-on-one meeting, or a class could be offered where adolescents and adults are mutually given instruction and then provided time to reflect on it together. This approach might be integrated into a confirmation curriculum.

In many of our congregations catechetical instruction is a problem not only for adolescents but for adults as well, who may also lack significant knowledge of their faith tradition. Therefore, a congregationwide education initiative could be implemented in which adolescents (especially older ones) share the classroom with adults. In creative and thoughtful ways, *catechesis can be done within social relationships between adults and adolescents.*

The youth pastor must not see catechetical instruction as coming only from the church classroom or individual place-sharer, but also from parents who participate in such instruction at home through prayer and conversation. Therefore, the youth pastor is not only a practical theologian who is a relational coordinator but also a catechetical facilitator. What is of ultimate importance is that catechesis be taken into relationships, where the biblical stories and theological tradition are made alive through the concrete life of the other.

RETHINKING THE YOUTH MINISTRY

Often, youth ministry has been either the center of wholesome adolescent entertainment or an exclusive enclave (i.e., separate from the larger congregation and not particularly open to other adolescents in the local community). Yet, if we are to confess, as Bonhoeffer has led us, that meaningful relationships are the concrete location of Christ's presence, then the youth ministry must take the form of place-sharing. Therefore, the youth ministry as "youth group" may not need to exist. Surely there are good reasons to give adolescents periods of time exclusively within their age cohort, but too often this has been more the rule than the exception.

For youth ministry to be a relational ministry of place-sharing the focus must move away from the group and toward the congregation. The objective must not be to construct a large and exciting youth *group*; rather the youth ministry should work to provide all adolescents with meaningful relationships of place-sharing with adults in the congregation. This may be a change in perspective more than a change in organization. The youth ministry may still have a weekly meeting, retreats and mission activities, but all these activities would be viewed as spaces where adults and adolescents can encounter one another and have meaningful interactions.

Focus on households and families. If relational ministry is to truly be about relational bonds where one can discover and come to know him- or herself, then it must give direct attention to the adolescent's most primary (and for some, troubling) social environment. For some adolescents the family is a vital place where they are upheld as a distinct person and where they share in deep relationships with their father and mother. Yet for other adolescents the family rests on a tragic foundation; though it is set up to be a place of meaningful relational interaction, it provides no relationships but only connections of individuals who have neither the power nor the resources to be open to one another. And there are families that are violently open, raiding the humanity of each member to sustain itself. Hence, another rule of art: *A relational youth ministry should not only connect an adolescent with a place-sharer but also help the place-sharer be a resource to the adolescent's family.*

The adult place-sharer reaches out to the humanity of the adolescent *and* to the adolescent's family. The place-sharer can provide this support by encouraging adolescents to communicate with their parents, and by helping them frame situations to see their parents' perspective. The place-sharer can also invite parents to call him or her any time there is trouble or concern about the child, assuring the parent that he or she is a friend—not vying for loyalty or competing with the parent—and is committed to supporting the family.

Place-sharer and parent interaction not only helps the family but also helps the youth pastor understand the multiple relationships taking place in the adolescent's life. When parents discuss the deep bonds their children share with neighbors, Sunday schools teachers and relatives, the youth pastor can be confident that the adolescent is being drawn into the relational otherness needed for transformation. With this information, the youth pastor can continue to provide the adolescent with further opportunities to connect with adults through mutual service and worship, but he or she doesn't need to call specific adults to take extra initiative to reach out to this adolescent.

Yet, for any of this to occur, parents must be presented with a vision of the youth ministry's relational desires. It may be quite worrisome for parents when a strange or little-known adult begins hanging around their child. At the same time it can be quite intimidating for an adult leader to be questioned by a skeptical parent. Therefore, there is a great need for constant communication between the adult place-sharer and parents, and the youth ministry leadership and families. If the adolescent's family does not attend the church, then there is even greater need for the youth pastor (or a trusted associate) to inform the family of the youth ministry's philosophy and vision, which ultimately must be shared by families. Therefore, our next rule of art is that *the youth ministry must maintain a shared vision and open lines of communication with families.*

One of the important benefits of rethinking youth ministry along the lines of an incarnational ministry of place-sharing is that it is moved from a satellite ministry back into the life of the congregation. Rather than being its own isolated ministry, where adolescents are ushered to the youth room never to associate with the rest of the congregation, adolescents are integrated into the church community. This happens as adults become partners in ministry. Those who prefer isolating youth with their peers will undoubtedly resist moving youth ministry into the center of the church's congregational life. Thus it is vital that parents and families demand that their children be included in ministries, and work to open up the power structures (such as committees and groups) to their own children and other adolescents. Therefore our next rule of art is *parents are the essential agents of integrating the youth into congregational life and ministry.*

Participating in common youth ministry practices. Though we have discussed some ways to reimagine youth ministry, not all of the long-established practices are unneeded or unhelpful. There are many common youth ministry practices that have been beneficial and may, in and of themselves, be applicable in a relational ministry of place-sharing. Yet each of these needs to come under practical theological scrutiny. What do these practices teach adolescents about themselves, the church and Jesus Christ? How are these practices affecting adolescents? Do they take into account adolescents' unique environments and address their unique pressures and issues? Many of the established practices will simply be tweaked to more fully reveal theological truth or deal with psychological or social issues. Therefore, another rule of art is *use established youth ministry practices, but center them around relational place-sharing encounters.*

Here are two examples: (1) The youth ministry may continue to offer an annual mission trip to Mexico, but this year a major objective will be for adolescents to connect with adults as they share together in service and worship. This might mean opening more spots on the trip for adults from the congregation. (2) The annual ninth-grade retreat now has more adults participating. The retreat may look very similar to years past—playing paintball or capture the flag, sitting around listening to music and drinking hot chocolate—but there are more opportunities for adolescents and adults to connect as the adults share stories of their faith journeys and listen to adolescents tell theirs.

The youth ministry should also be looking for other ministry opportunities in the congregation, identifying overlap with its own ministry and possible places adolescents could participate. For instance, the youth ministry may want to include high school girls in the women's Bible study and allow students to participate in the quilting club. Why not open the adult education seminar on the global AIDS pandemic and the denomination's response to high school students?[6] And singing in the choir and serving as an usher could be opened to all ages. The youth ministry then should not only be in a continued process of rethinking its own practices but should *include adolescents in as many churchwide practices as possible.* This will draw adolescents into congregational life and give them opportunities to encounter adults who can either take the initiative or be encouraged to be an adolescent's place-sharer.

Yet our vision for youth ministry must not stop with ministry action but go on to analyze the very *telos* of this action. In other words, what is the goal of each youth ministry practice? Why do we want adolescents to participate in the youth ministry and be drawn into relationships of place-sharing? No doubt we desire their transformation as they encounter the living Jesus Christ within the living persons of the church com-

---

[6]This approach is common for ethnic churches, especially African American churches, as well as small rural churches.

munity. But our telos stretches deeper. Ministry is transformational only when those being transformed become incarnational agents themselves; that is, they too go into the world as place-sharers. Therefore, our final rule of art is that *the telos of relational ministry is the transformation of persons such that they too become responsible place-sharers for others and the world.*

Custom-designed youth ministry. When reimagining youth ministry we must always be sensitive to the multiple contexts we confront. It is important to understand the youth ministry's history, the congregational system and the outside cultural forces confronting individuals. When rethinking anything we must ask, How will this affect persons? Therefore, relational youth ministry of place-sharing, whatever the shape, must be custom designed around the cultural context and unique locale of the adolescents and their families.

We cannot be a place-sharer to another if we refuse to see the forces that confront the other's humanity. We must start with their location; helping adolescents and adults encounter each other will look very different in different places. The youth ministry practices you use will depend on the common youth ministry practices already in place. But the particular youth ministry must be shaped not only by the traditional activities of the church and youth ministry but also by its location in culture. For instance, a church may be in a community where most parents work long hours and the school system and other social agencies are unable to provide childcare and after-school tutoring. Recognizing this situation, the youth ministry may decide that it has the resources to provide after-school tutoring in a safe and pleasant environment. In planning such an initiative the youth ministry will have to be sensitive to its location. Therefore, the youth pastor must help all those willing to be place-sharers to understand the social and political issues affecting the adolescents they encounter.

This leads us to two closely associated rules of art: *the youth ministry must be custom-designed around the multiple forces affecting adolescents and families,* and *the youth ministry should speak (both to adult leaders and adolescents) of sociopolitical issues and the call to responsible action.*

RETHINKING YOUTH MINISTRY

Rules of Art for Focusing on Households and Families

- Youth ministry should not only connect an adolescent with a place-sharer but also help the place-sharer to be a resource to the adolescent's family.
- Youth ministry must maintain a shared vision and open lines of communication with families.
- Parents are the essential agents of integrating the youth into congregational life.

Rules of Art for Participating in Common Youth Ministry Practices

- Use common youth ministry practices, but center them around a focus on relational encounters.
- Include adolescents in as many churchwide practices as possible.
- The telos of relational ministry is the transformation of persons such that they too become responsible as place-sharers for others and the world.

Rules of Art for Custom-Designed Youth Ministry

- Youth ministry must be custom-designed around the multiple forces affecting adolescents and families.
- Youth ministry should speak (to both adult leaders and adolescents) of sociopolitical issues and the call to responsible action.

RETHINKING THE CONGREGATION

Throughout this chapter I have made a plea that we see the youth ministry and adolescents as having a vital part of the overall life of the congregation. I have argued against youth ministry as a satellite ministry that is attached to but autonomous from the rest of congregational life. Yet, if adolescents are to be included more fully in the life of the congregation, then we must also begin to rethink how youth ministry relates to the congregation. If we follow Bonhoeffer and assert that Christ is concretely present in relationships within the church, then it is essential that we consider how to invite our children into the center of the church's life, opening it up as a context in which they can know themselves as they encounter the transcendence of God in the lives of others. Because we want our young people to hold onto their faith, we must provide them with opportunities to participate in the multigenerational life of the whole congregation.

For many adults, the thought of moving adolescents into the center of congregational life is troubling, to say the least. I understand this, and therefore I provide only a few suggestions, artistic moves that you might take in your situation.

The need for congregationwide support. In many churches, congregational support will not come easily but must be earned. This sad reality speaks to widespread division between youth and adults in our culture. It must be stated, however, that earning this support will not come from growing the youth group or having the most exciting youth ministry in town, for such accomplishments only perpetuate the youth ministry's satellite perspective. Rather, to bridge the gap support must be earned by the youth pastor and others working on both sides of the adolescent-congregation divide. Therefore, in order to build congregationwide support for adolescents *the job of the youth pastor is to work at bridging the congregation and its adolescents.* To do so, he or she must possess enough capital of trust and respect in both groups to facilitate opportunities for mutual interaction between them. Hopefully the gap separating adolescents and adults in the congregation is not a wide chasm (though it may be perceived as such) and the youth pastor may function as a helping hand as adolescents and adults reach out to form social transformational relationships. It is unfortunate that there is a divide at all, but when the youth pastor makes it a ministry priority to connect adolescents and adults in relationships of place-sharing, the gap separating adults and adolescents can be bridged.

For this to be accomplished with any long-term validity it must become the concern of the whole congregation; an incarnational ministry of place-sharing is the operation of the whole community. It will help this process for the youth pastor to see him- or herself (as well as being seen by the senior pastor and others) not as the pastor to youth at the church but as the pastor to the congregation who gives special attention to adolescents. The youth pastor then stands in the gap. Of course, simply having a changed perspective, though important, is not enough. The youth pastor must also do the hard work of communication and motivation.

The youth pastor calls parishioners to see, listen to and act for the adolescents in the congregation and local community. The paid youth pastor is not a solo relational juggernaut, but facilitates and encourages relational connections between adults and adolescents. The job of the youth pastor is not to be crazy, wild and maniacally outgoing. Rather, his or her job is to sensitively encourage adults, prodding them to see, listen to and act with and for adolescents in their community. Churches (and adolescents) do not need youth pastors who look and talk like fifteen-year-olds, or youth ministries that are adolescent daycares. Rather, the church desperately needs youth pastors who can go before the congregation and through education, worship and prayer prompt the congregation to see the humanity of its children and to reach out to them in faithfulness to the humanity of God. Therefore, it is not enough for the youth pastor to be liked by adolescents; he or she must also have the gifts and skills to communicate, motivate and assist others in relational connections of place-sharing.

Committed, competent leadership. When a congregation's leadership is adamant about keeping adolescents locked within the youth ministry, little can be done to bridge the gap. But in most congregations the leadership is either welcoming or at least open to the possibility of including adolescents more fully in congregational life. Of course you may find much more resistance (among adults and the youth) to the idea of having adolescents read Scripture in worship than to inviting them to participate in Bible studies on Wednesday night or Sunday morning. Therefore, it is best to start where there is least resistance, taking small steps toward bridging the gap.

Yet with leadership that is willing (at whatever level), a number of things can be done to communicate that young people are a vital and equal part of congregational life and must be cared for and called on in relationships of mutuality. Therefore, another rule of art is *regularly schedule preaching on a theology of the incarnation that encourages the congregation to reach out as place-sharers to all adolescents.* It would be best if most of this preaching is done by the senior pastor, giving legitimacy to the need to bridge the gap. But if this is not possible, it can be done by another pastor or even the youth pastor. If the youth pastor preaches, it must be seen as an opportunity to proclaim God's Word and not merely as a fifteen- to thirty-minute youth talk or promotional time. If the youth pastor can preach a relevant

RETHINKING THE CONGREGATION

Rules of Art for Congregationwide Support
- The job of the youth pastor is to work at bridging the gap between the congregation and its adolescents.
- The youth pastor calls parishioners to see, listen to and act for the adolescents in the congregation and local community.

Rule of Art for Committed, Competent Leadership
- Regularly schedule preaching on a theology of the incarnation that encourages the congregation to reach out as place-sharers to all adolescents.
- Include an annual "Commissioning and Calling" Sunday specifically designed for youth ministry adult leaders who act as place-sharers.
- Churchwide, regularly and frequently honor adolescents and their leadership.

and exegetically meaningful sermon, he or she can make powerful inroads toward bridging the gap.

Congregations should *include an annual "Commissioning and Calling" Sunday specifically designed for youth ministry adult leaders who act as place-sharers.* While this could be a simple standing and prayer time, I recommend including a discussion of calling and place-sharing as an essential ministry of the church, a short liturgy, and laying on of hands. Another commissioning-and-calling service could include those adolescents who are participating in the ministry of the congregation, from stocking the food shelf or running the sound system to singing in the choir or helping in the nursery.

The church should *regularly and frequently honor adolescents and their leadership.* The congregation should allow time and space for the celebration of graduations and community honors as well as thanks and appreciation for the adolescent ministry within the congregation. This is a common practice for many African American churches; adolescents and children are often honored for their accomplishments and thanked for their service to the community as junior ushers and Sunday school teachers. Often, these congregations have had very strong adolescent involvement even without a specific youth ministry. They seek to include their adolescents in their common life, expecting their participation and celebrating their accomplishments.[7]

CONCLUSION

In this chapter I have presented a few artistic moves, or rules of art, that can be used in constructing a relational ministry of place-sharing. It is up to you, then, to build in your context an incarnational youth ministry that moves beyond influence and into the theological reality of the incarnate, crucified and resurrected person of Christ, who is place-sharer to the world. With hope and anticipation I pray that you might participate in relational transformation with adolescents in your community, made possible by the power of the human God, Jesus Christ.

---

[7]This can be seen clearly in the life of Witherspoon Street Presbyterian Church in Princeton, N.J. In their long history, without ever having a formal youth minister, they have had adults who have served as place-sharers and thus their adolescents have been deeply involved in their congregation, with many young people returning to raise families in the same church.

Appendix

While Dietrich Bonhoeffer's theology never addresses issues of adolescence directly, we can argue on good grounds that adolescents have a solid place in his work. Bonhoeffer was just nineteen when he wrote *Sanctorum Communio* (his dissertation and first book), and he originally imagined that his *Habilitationsschrift* (a kind of second dissertation that qualified scholars to lecture in the German university system) would be directed toward issues affecting children (due to ministry experiences as a vicar in Barcelona). Though he settled for a more philosophical piece, the end of *Act and Being* nevertheless picks up his original inspiration.

In 1932-1933 he was ministering as the new confirmation teacher to an unruly group of blue-collar, poverty-stricken urban youth in the Wedding district of Northern Berlin. This was the same year he was crafting his lectures, which would become *Christ the Center* and *Creation and Sin* (published as *Creation and Fall*), two texts that draw out the incarnational life of Christ and the necessity of human relationships. Bonhoeffer took the boys to the country for weekends at his parents' cottage and brought them to evenings at the orchestra, paid for out of his own pocket. John Godsey details Bonhoeffer's ministerial interactions with these boys:

[Bonhoeffer] moved into the district on New Year's Day of 1932 and lived among his young "parishioners," inviting groups of them to his room in the evenings to eat and to play games, and finally to read the Bible and to receive catechetical instruction. Moreover, he resolutely visited the home of each boy, an eye-opening experience. . . . In March the members of the class were confirmed in the church, and although his official relationship was now at an end, Bonhoeffer remained in fellowship with many of the boys for years.[1]

Around this same time, and leading into the war years, Bonhoeffer was the secretary of youth in the ecumenical movement.[2] So while Bonhoeffer's theology never specifically addresses adolescence, we may logically assert that issues of adolescence made their way into his theology.[3]

---

[1]John Godsey, *The Theology of Dietrich Bonhoeffer* (Philadelphia: Westminster Press, 1958), p. 82. Right after this period Bonhoeffer was also a major part of a youth center created to help out-of-work blue-collar adolescents find employment and gain skills. The youth center was shut down because of suspicions that it was a breeding ground for communist thought.

[2]For a broader historical explanation of Bonhoeffer's interactions within the ecumenical movement, I quote Eberhard Bethge: "During the summer between his return from America and the beginning of his career was his participation in the ecumenical conference in Cambridge. His interest in the ecumenical movement was at first incidental, but it took such a hold on him that it became an integral part of his being. He was soon furiously involved in the internal battles about its orientation, and he defended it enthusiastically in public. The emerging world of the Protestant ecumenical movement became a vital part of his theology, his role in the church struggle, and ultimately his political commitments. The Berlin ecumenists, primarily Superintendent Max Diestel, made [Bonhoeffer] a member of the German youth delegation to the annual conference of the World Alliance of Promoting International Friendship through the Churches. . . . There the executive committee appointed him as one of the three European youth secretaries. At the same time, the world political crisis was converging with the ecumenical movement's own impulses to force new ideas upon the movement" (*Dietrich Bonhoeffer: A Biography* [Minneapolis: Fortress Press, 2000], pp. 189-90).

[3]It is often forgotten that Bonhoeffer's first direct run-in with the National Socialists came when a radio address he was giving was cut off. The title of that address is "The Idea of the Fuhrer for the Younger Generation."

Index